MEASURING PROGRAMMER PRODUCTIVITY AND SOFTWARE QUALITY

MEASURING PROGRAMMER PRODUCTIVITY AND SOFTWARE QUALITY

LOWELL JAY ARTHUR

A Wiley-Interscience Publication

JOHN WILEY & SONS

New York Chichester Brisbane Toronto Singapore

Library of Congress Cataloging in Publication Data:

Arthur, Lowell Jay, 1951–
    Measuring programmer productivity and software
quality.

    "A Wiley-Interscience publication."
    Includes index.
    1. Computer programming management. 2. Electronic
digital computers—Programming—Quality control.
I. Title.

QA76.6.A766   1984   001.64'2'068   84-13176
ISBN 0-471-88713-7

Printed in the United States of America

10 9 8 7 6 5 4 3 2 1

to my parents

PREFACE

No one likes being measured. This seems to hold true even in the avant-garde society of information systems (IS). The very word *measurement* seems to carry a negative connotation: to control with cautious restraint, or a basis or standard for comparison *(Webster)*.

But software measurement can provide all programmers and analysts with feedback to improve their abilities. It can reduce the amount of maintenance they perform, leaving room for new development, something each company sorely needs. Measurement can improve reliability and reduce operational costs. It can help improve the quality and productivity of new development. How can a tool that has such a potential to help the programmer, analyst, and manager be conceived as such a threat?

Simple. Every tool is a two-edged sword; a person can use the tool for constructive or destructive purposes. A programmer can use software metrics to enhance the reliability and maintainability of a computer program. A manager, on the other hand, can misuse metrics as an unfair and incorrect measurement of the programmer or analyst. If you are looking for a tool to bring that lazy pack of programmers in line, then I hope you will set this book back on the shelf, because you will do more harm to your company than you can imagine. If you are looking for ways to improve your software quality and productivity, however, read on; this is the book for you. With the application of the techniques in this book, you will help all of your personnel achieve moderate to excellent analysis and programming skills. As their skills improve, they will cut the cost of development and maintenance efforts, thereby giving your company the time and resources to pursue the new projects that will ultimately affect its ability to meet the competitive challenges of the future.

I have organized this book with you in mind. It need not be read in any specific order. My intent is to show how measurement, especially software measurement, can benefit productivity and quality improvement plans. The first chapter examines how measurement has influenced and improved our lives. It provides a historical perspective on measurement. Chapter 2 examines ways of measuring productivity in the software environment. It examines traditional productivity theory and its application to software measurement. Chapter 2 also discusses the most widely applied productivity metrics. Since no clear champion has arisen from the productivity metrics, I recommend collecting all data possible. It will provide information you do not currently have, and it will help influence the selection of representative productivity metrics that apply to your existing programming environment.

One of the purposes of metrics is to select qualities that you would like in your software and then find some way to measure the presence or absence of those qualities in the code and documentation. Chapters 3 through 16 examine quality and the most commonly desired qualities of software. Complexity has been studied most thoroughly, so I recommend reading this chapter if none of the others. The other qualities such as flexibility, maintainability, and reliability have a strong impact on the cost of software. They are also worthy of your consideration. Some of the chapters are fairly light. Little or no research or study has been done in these areas. But I do suggest avenues for collecting and studying qualities like integrity and interoperability.

Next, it seems likely that different people wearing different hats in the organization will require different metrics reported in different ways. Toward this end, Chapter 17 focuses on managers, analysts, and programmers and how they can use software measurement.

Chapter 18 discusses programming style. Style can affect readability and complexity to a great degree; one style can be five times more productive and maintainable than another. Doesn't it make sense to identify the best styles and train all programmers to meet these superprogrammer criteria?

Code is the one thing that influences productivity and quality beyond all others. There are best ways to code virtually everything. Measurement can help identify the best style for any given language, function, module, or program. Chapters 19 through 21 examine how programming style affects IBM assembler language, COBOL, and PL/I code. If you use FORTRAN, ADA, or even fourth-generation languages, and you are familiar with COBOL or PL/I, you can apply the concepts and examples in Chapters 2 through 21 to define your own metrics for quality, productivity, and programming style. The application of software metrics varies little among languages. Only the verbs and data-naming conventions vary.

Finally, how should you go about implementing software productivity and quality measurement? Chapter 22 discusses the tools you should build, buy, and install in your environment. Hopefully, my experience will serve you well in this endeavor.

This book should also serve as a textbook for courses in software metrics, software quality, quality assurance, and programming style. Programmer productivity payoffs come from the application of the best knowledge available to produce the best, most economical software possible.

I believe that measurement can elevate system developers from common village craftsmen to sophisticated engineers. It can identify weaknesses that are counterproductive. It can also verify that new techniques, methodology, and technology are paying back management's investment. Put measurement to work in your IS organization and watch it reap great rewards. With measurement comes information, and with information, knowledge to constantly improve quality and productivity. Measurement is not something to be feared, but a tool to build strong, flexible software that supports the information needs of your company.

LOWELL JAY ARTHUR

Denver, Colorado
December 1984

CONTENTS

MEASURING PROGRAMMER PRODUCTIVITY AND SOFTWARE QUALITY

CHAPTER ONE

MEASUREMENT

The ability to measure has fueled virtually all of the past technological advances. Each new measurement has given us ways to extend our crude natural abilities to better measure height, width, depth, weight, texture, smell, temperature, and a myriad of other things in the realm of our senses. This is the major advantage of measurement—it enhances our ability to sense things not accessible to our native abilities and intelligence.

Humans seek to understand, know, and control everything within the realm of their environment. As they explore, testing and measuring the phenomenon surrounding them, new vistas of knowledge often appear and more pieces of the puzzle fit into place. Every item of information is then compared to what is already known, enhancing the total knowledge about whatever has been measured. For example, small differences in the path of the planet Neptune led to the discovery of Pluto; comparing the predicted path of Neptune to the actual led to the assumption that another planet was pulling it out of orbit. Mathematically, it was then comparatively easy to identify the location of this phantom planet. Finding Pluto would have been impossible without the accuracy of modern astronomical telescopes and other measuring instruments. Unaided, our brain takes in all of the data from the senses—sight, sound, touch, smell, and taste—transforming these crude impulses into measurements, estimating distances; dimensions; the clarity, bouquet, and flavor of wine. In the search for tools to control and understand the world, people turn to measurement devices that closely resemble natural abilities. Chemistry has provided the means to measure the properties of wine that correlate with the human senses. Spectrophotometers enable us to

1

measure the full range of light, not just the narrow band of visible light, but every wavelength. Telescopes extend our ability to see visible light that is too faint for unaided detection, giving astronomers a view of Hailey's comet 60 billion miles in space. Radar enables us to detect ships and airplanes through fog, clouds, and over great distances. Sonar helps ships and submarines *see* through water. Computer-enhanced photographs from orbiting satellites help pinpoint military secrets, crop and forest infestations, weather formations and provide countless other pieces of information not readily detectable from the planet's surface. Space probes have relayed information about the rings of Saturn and the atmosphere on Venus. Simple instruments such as the yardstick, tape measure, plumb line, and level aid in the construction of buildings. Geiger counters detect radiation undetectable by humans. Extremely complicated measurement systems combine to help predict the weather.

There are instruments to measure almost every principle and practice in most fields, but not in software development and maintenance. Nearly all of these tools extend, refine, and improve human capabilities by increasing sensitivity, range, speed, accuracy, precision, and consistency. Each tool may be used as a convenience. A spelling checker for this book could have found all of the misspelled words without human intervention.

1. WHY MEASURE?

Count what is countable, measure what is measurable, and what is not measurable, make measurable.

Galileo Galilei (1564–1642)

In physical science a first essential step in the direction of learning any subject is to find principles of numerical reckoning and methods for practicably measuring some quality connected with it.

Lord Kelvin

Productivity, quality, and software measurement are inextricably bound together. Looking back, one of the major leaps in productivity and quality came with the introduction of structured programming. Structured programming caused a significant improvement in design quality that was then reflected in the quality of the code and resulting system. The quality improvements, made possible by structured programming, also increased productivity.

Quality improvements reduced the number of errors passed from the design process into the coding and testing process. Correcting an error in code costs four times as much as the same error corrected in design. Correcting the same error in test costs 15 times more than it would have in design. Correcting the same error once the program is in production costs 30 times as much. Structured, GO TO-less programming also reduced the errors passed from coding into testing and production. Each of these quality improvements depended heavily on methodology borrowed from manufacturing: design and product inspections, both of which are forms of measurement.

Structured programming used walk-throughs to formalize the measurement process. Manual inspection, however, is laborious, costly, less than exact, and consumes productive work time. Software metrics can automate much of the analysis normally performed in code walk-throughs, freeing programmers to identify quality problems quickly and take corrective action. Software quality measurement encourages quality improvement, which ultimately affects the productivity of maintenance programmers and end users.

High-quality programs are easier to enhance or maintain. They incur fewer costs for reruns. They rarely leave the user waiting for an on-line response or batch report. Quality measurement tools give the programmer, analyst, and manager immediate feedback about the quality of existing or emerging code. Measurement is the foundation of code quality. And code quality helps reduce future maintenance and operational costs. Information Systems is primarily concerned with the productivity of their development and maintenance programmers. But the larger impact of quality measurement comes from the production environment. Reruns of failed systems consume much of the resources, in terms of both hardware and people's time, of an operations center. And what of the end user? Hundreds or thousands of users may be incapacitated by the failure of an on-line system. A single hour of down time means hundreds of hours of productive time lost forever. Often, these productive hours are wasted and replaced with overtime at higher salary rates. Quality problems are the basis of most productivity problems.

Quality improvements are a gold mine, not a hole in the ground down which to pour the resources of information systems. And the only way to ensure high quality and productivity is to measure products as they are produced. To measure quality and productivity effectively, the measurement process should be mechanized wherever possible.

Before you can take a measurement, however, you have to know what it is you intend to measure. How do you define the quantity, quality, or other characteristic to be measured? In the case of software metrics, the measurements should provide information about software quality and productivity. Software quality should be broken down even further into maintainability, reliability, and the other quality attributes discussed in later chapters. These measurements are all conceptual. They must be converted to physical properties before they can be measured. Few, if any, are directly measurable, but quality measurements can be inferred from combining a number of other separate measurements. Software metrics have to be broken down into simple steps that extract the needed data and combine it to produce the required measure. From these steps, a measuring instrument can be designed and built. Unfortunately, translating physical quantities into conceptual metrics is rarely exact. Software metrics tools can measure precisely the content of a program or document, but have only begun their refinement into completely accurate predictors of quality and productivity.

The main reason for this lack of refinement is the next property of measurement: The metric sought is always a comparison of the measurand with a reference quantity of the *same kind*. Because of software metrics' comparative infancy, few reference quantities—other than subjective ones—exist, and by definition, a subjective reference is not the same as a quantitative reference. But in many cases, a subjective reference will have to do.

2. TECHNIQUES

There are a variety of ways to collect measurement data; each has been used in numerous industrial applications. Some will help software measurement; others will not. The measurement techniques include: amplification, negative feedback, conversion, magnification, and analysis. Measurement methods involve three basic entities: units, standards of those units, and scales that suit the units. There must be some means of taking a measurement, converting it to a number of units and converting the units into the knowledge sought. Some phenomena are so slight that to make them perceptible to humans, the measuring instrument must *amplify* the signal carrying the measurement information. Electrical measurement applications use amplification because of the rapid response that can be achieved. This technique is rarely useful in software measurement.

Negative feedback and *conversion* of the measurement into digital form are also used to maintain the measurement signal. Software metrics will use digitalization to extract, summarize, and store the measurements in computer readable form.

Magnification enlarges a measurement to bring it to your attention, waving the red flag over potential problems. Software metrics should identify error-prone code in several ways to help the programmer or analyst improve reliability and quality.

Analysis is another useful technique. Most systems have a characteristic period variation or resonance. To know these is to understand how your systems are built and maintained. For example, a system will experience alternating design, code, test, and operation phases. A system under release control should display rhythmic fluctuations in each of these measurement areas. Systems with no control should fluctuate sporadically. Understanding these cycles will help management identify variations from the norm when developing systems and provoke quick action to resume course.

Many measurement systems use computers for high-speed collection of measurement data and rapid analysis. Software metrics will use the computer extensively to collect, summarize, and report measurements taken. The purpose of metrics is not to burden the programmer or analyst with more work, but to reduce the painstaking work of manual review. Only the computer can provide the resources to analyze all of the definitions, designs, code, and tests produced in a common data processing shop, and it will at least be impartial and accurate. Not only will it aid in processing all of this data, but it also provides a variety of ways to display the data.

Displays help the metrics user read, understand, and act on measurement data. Typical displays include pointers to a scale, printed reports, graphic screens, and even television.

3. MEASUREMENT ERROR

Errors in measurement can result from: an imperfect definition of what you are measuring, an imperfect understanding of how to convert what you are measuring into the measurement signal, failure to establish the correct conditions for taking the measurement, human errors, and defective or deficient measurement instruments.

Considering the comparative youth of software metrics, you should expect imperfect definitions of productivity and quality measurements. They will improve with time and experience, however. The metrics presented in this book vary from proposed to widely validated measurements.

Software measurement tools rarely suffer, as other measurement tools do, from conversion of the measurand into a measurement signal. Software metrics are all some form of numeric sum. They rarely experience problems caused by noise, interference, drift, slow response, hysteresis, resolution, precision, or accuracy. These terms are useful for describing problems involved in measuring physical characteristics. For example, a voltmeter may experience drift between times that it is calibrated, but a design analyzer should produce a consistent measurement each time.

Software measurements do not depend on a constant temperature or humidity, so conditions should not play a part in proper measurement. Two remaining potential problems will have the most impact on software metrics: The human may misinterpret the results produced, or the metric tool may be deficient. In fact, it probably will be deficient for many years, until time and experience fine-tune the current measures and add new ones derived from constant usage. Variations in measurement and interpretation will occur within the operator, between operators, and among programs.

Because of the potential for measurement errors, no measurement tool—especially software metrics—should be viewed as a perfect tool. But programmers and managers alike will tend to view each measurement as an absolute. Using inexact measurements leads to misuse.

Bang, bang, Maxwell's silver hammer came down upon her head.

The Beatles

The problem of people misusing an otherwise useful tool cannot be underrated. Atomic reactions can be a great tool to provide energy independence; they are also used in the most terrible weapons ever invented. Improperly used, software metrics can destroy the quality, productivity, morale, and strength of a data processing department. Use the tool, forget the weapon.

4. METRICS DEVELOPMENT

Development of a measurement tool consists of five major phases:

1. Definition phase.
2. Research and development phase.
3. Production design phase.
4. Production phase.
5. Application phase.

During the definition phase, you select what to measure: productivity, quality, or any of their submetrics. Then choose measurables that will combine into the required metrics. Next, you should research and develop prototypes of instruments to measure the required metrics. Concurrently, identify when, where, and why to take the measurement. Design how humans will interact with the metrics. This is the production design phase. Finally, produce or install the measurement device and begin its application.

These phases tend to overlap, as you will see. Never remain satisfied with the measurement instrument; revise, refine, evolve, and improve it constantly. Each bit of knowledge will direct further development and new metrics.

5. HISTORY

To imagine how software measurement can impact the world of software development and maintenance, let's review the evolution of other measuring instruments and their contribution to technological growth.

Measurement began in ancient times; the word *measure* has its roots in Latin. Measurement was a method of comparing an unknown item against some standard unit to determine its size or weight. The shadow clock of the Egyptian civilization demonstrates the use of a standard unit to measure time. The use of length, mass, and volume measures facilitated what we today call "fair trade." How could we know that we have received fair value for our money if there were no standard units for the pound or kilogram?

The earliest significant developments in measuring revolved around astronomy and navigation. The invention of the telescope in the early 1600s led to an explosion in astronomical knowledge and measurement. The astrolabe originated with the ancient Greeks, allowing the determination of time, length of day or night, and the rising or setting of a star. The compass, originally a small magnetized bar of iron floated on a reed or stick in a bowl of water provided the first directional device that did not depend on the stars. It is doubtful that world trade and the empires built from it would have been possible without these two devices. Another important navigational development revolved around accurate time keeping.

John Harrison, a carpenter from Yorkshire, spent most of his life developing chronometers. To reduce navigational errors, loss of life and ships, the British government offered an award of 10,000 pounds sterling to the inventor of a method for determining a ship's longitude to within one degree, requiring a measurement accuracy of two minutes gained or lost in six weeks. Harrison's chronometer garnered the next higher award, £20,000, for an accuracy of 54 seconds in five months, allowing calculations of longitude to an accuracy of less than ½ degree of arc.

Industrial needs stimulated the development of mechanical gauges used in the manufacture of interchangeable parts and temperature control. Inventive people developed measuring devices that controlled furnace temperatures by thermostatic devices connected to dampers on the furnace, contributing to the quality of the metals produced. In 1865, the invention of the centrifugal governor to control steam engines aided the development and use of trains, which opened up vast portions of America to ranching and agriculture, supporting the markets on both coasts.

Four major historical movements stimulated the continued development of measuring instruments.

1. The industrial revolution from 1700−1900.

2. Twentieth-century expansion of industry.
3. The development of computers.
4. Space—the last frontier.

5.1.   The Industrial Revolution

This period initiated the development of many crucial measurement tools. Among them, the most important ones assisted in the measurement of dimensions, electricity, and the analysis of materials in ways not previously possible.

Dimension Measurement

Prior to the industrial revolution, all goods were handcrafted, each piece meticulously formed and fitted to its neighbors. This type of production prohibited exchanging defective parts for new ones thus causing extended delays for repair. It was also too slow a way to create new products. The manufacture of industrial equipment required precise ways to measure the dimensions of the machines and their products. Enter the screw micrometer, first developed in 1638 to assist in astronomical measurements. Refinements in its design led to models that could accurately measure to 0.00001 inch. The precision achieved by the screw micrometer paved the way for mass production techniques. Each part could be manufactured to close tolerances in large quantities and later assembled into the required product. It made product repair a simple act of replacing a defective part with a new and equivalent one.

Interestingly enough, many of the techniques for mass production evolved during the Civil War. The demand for firearms caused Remington and other manufacturers to seek better and faster ways to provide the military with weapons. Many of the techniques developed and used to supply the war effort were used later to increase production of all manufactured goods.

Electrical Measurement

During the 1800s, many of the properties of electricity were discovered, leading to the growth of electrical industries, their demand for accurate measurement instruments, and the demand for products. Where would we be without Edison's light bulb or the television or the computer? In 1820, Hans Christian Orsted discovered that current in a wire could cause deflection in a pivoted magnet. Seventeen years later, the tangent galvanometer evolved to provide precision measurement of electrical current. The spring ammeter was developed in 1879 to provide portable measurement of current. In 1843, the Wheatstone bridge provided a means to measure resistance by comparing an unknown resistance to a standard one. It is still a common circuit in many electrical instruments.

Without these measurement devices, radios, televisions, and computers probably would not exist.

Analysis

Analytical instrumentation evolved mainly in the areas of chemistry, medicine, and astronomy. The improvements in the microscope allowed advances in medicine and metallurgy. The development of the spectroscope provided the ability to determine the elements in a chemical sample by the light it emits during combustion. It also allowed the evaluation of elements in the sun and distant stars.

5.2. Twentieth-Century Industry

Continuous industrial growth created new requirements for measuring instruments. Technology demanded the measurement of more variables to control the manufacturing of better quality products. As better methods evolved, older measuring instruments became too slow or insensitive. And as process control could be shifted from humans to automatic controls, measuring instruments took over the routine, boring operations.

Many of the advances in the twentieth century are due to the increasing use of electronic circuitry. Once upon a time, a measuring device could only produce a readable output; now, the measuring device merely changes the measurement into an electrical signal that can be converted into the variable under study. For example, the thermocouple converts temperature into electrical signals and the photocell transforms light. These measurements can now be displayed, recorded, or used to control the process at hand.

World War II stimulated improvements in measuring and control devices. The manufacturing demands were enormous. Any defect in materials or manufacture could put "our boys" in peril. Postwar improvements mounted, reducing the time involved in measuring and analyzing the collected data. An integral part of these instruments was the vacuum tube, soon to be replaced by the transistor. Both of these allowed the development of the ultimate measuring device—the computer.

5.3. The Computer

First-generation computers made their debut in the early 1950s, causing a revolution in instrumentation. Here, finally, was a tool that could easily process, display, and store the output of measuring instruments while performing an endless variety of analyses on the resulting data. It could also provide instantaneous control of the measured system.

Each generation of computers allowed the exploration of new and expanded horizons in instrumentation and control. With the birth of the computer chip, a small inexpensive control device was put in the hands of every engineer. Now, computer chips are an integral part of systems as simple as your car, identifying potential problems, increasing fuel efficiency, you name it. Imagine the future, with microprocessor-controlled solar devices that track the sun for maximum energy transfer, or the automated home.

5.4. Space—The Last Frontier

To some extent, the chip was born out of the space age. The less weight shot into space, the smaller the rocket required to boost the payload into orbit. So, rather than build larger rockets, NASA opted for smaller components. This led to a need for miniaturized parts—one of them was the chip.

Satellites required small cameras to photograph weather, enemy targets, and military installations. This need for espionage information led to advances in forestry and agriculture from satellite mapping of the earth. These orbiting measurement platforms could only carry small antennas, hence the need for large dish antenna on earth. But now, with the space shuttle, it is possible to put enormous transmitter/receivers in space; the Dick Tracy two-way wrist-radio or telephone will now be a reality.

And then again, Big Brother, George Orwell's 1984 fantasy, is with us as well. Telescopes orbited by the space shuttle could be much larger than existing ones and provide a detailed report of number of weeds growing in your front yard, classified by type, and your nation-wide rating for yard care, not to mention the exact time you leave the house, arrive at work, go out for lunch, or sneak out for coffee—the ultimate invasion of privacy.

Whether these are instruments for good or evil, depends on how they are used. It is up to us to control our instruments and not let them control us.

6. SUMMARY

Productivity, quality, and software measurement are intimately connected. Software measurement fosters an environment for the routine production of high-quality programs and systems. High-quality systems, in turn, reduce the costs for maintaining, operating, and using the system over its expected life span.

The development of measurement instruments has always led the development of new and improved technology. Software metrics will serve to refine software development and maintenance into a controllable, productive task. Without measurements, management, programmers, and analysts will never experience the breakthroughs that other sciences have enjoyed from refined measurement tools.

The development of measurement tools requires a definition of what to measure, selection of what can be measured, development and testing of the measurement device, and production and application of the measuring tool. Measurement errors can creep in from any of these steps plus the variations in the humans using the metrics. Metric tools must be evaluated constantly and upgraded to provide clearer, more meaningful data. There is no magic solution, no ruler you can buy at the corner market that will provide this information. You must design and build instruments to collect the data you need and then to refine it into the measurements necessary to support improved project control, productivity, and quality.

Each step to a scientific awakening begins with a small step, many of which have already been taken. This book summarizes those steps and, hopefully, will lead you to some new ideas about the science of software development. The next giant step is up to you.

CHAPTER TWO

PRODUCTIVITY

Reprinted by permission of Tribune Company Syndicate, Inc.

Progress is what happens when impossibility yields to necessity.

Arnold Glasow

"It's impossible to measure programmer productivity!" Or so I've been told. With the IS personnel costs escalating as they are, necessity demands that we learn how to measure programmer, analyst, manager, and department productivity.

What is software productivity, and how can we measure it? Data processing managers have been grappling with this problem for many years with limited success. James Martin predicts that without significant productivity improvements, we will need 27 million programmers by the year 1990 to fill the demand for information systems. The U.S. Department of Labor estimates that 50% of the U.S. work force will depend on some form of information processing by 1990 (International Computer Programs (ICP), 1982). It also predicts that 20% of the work force will be employed by the information processing industry. In 1955, people and software accounted for only 15% of the IS budget; by 1985, it will be more than 60% for an expected cost of $77.88 billion. In 1955, it took only six months, on the average, to produce an

12

application system; now it takes more than a year. One IBM study (Walston, 1977) found that development of new batch or on-line systems takes from 12 to 18 months.

Maintenance costs are increasing dramatically in line with system complexity. Often 70−80% of the budget is consumed by the maintenance of existing systems. This figure is a fact of IS life, but it fails to anticipate the increasing demand for new systems, which grows at 30% per year, while programmer productivity increases at only 5%.

Traditionally, information systems managers have measured productivity by means of subjective performance evaluations. Performance evaluation aims at understanding the physical, technical, and economic phenomena that contribute to changes in productivity, costs, and profits. These measures can only indicate what an information systems department has done, not what it is capable of doing. How much is enough, when looking at productivity? How is productivity measured?

Productivity most often refers to the relationship between inputs and outputs, typically a ratio of outputs to a single input such as output per person/day, or in the DP case, lines of code per person/day. These ratios tend to lead to misinterpretations; increases in output per person/day may or may not be desirable. Elementary productivity theory indicates that productivity changes occur through substitution of inputs or the development of new technology. For example, reducing response time to two seconds may optimize a programmer's productivity at the terminal, while the use of nonprocedural languages or the implementation of a word processor for system design may increase productivity by the substitution of new technology. From these simple examples, it should be apparent that the analysis of productivity has to recognize the interaction of all inputs, integrating them into a set of meaningful measurements.

Productivity is affected by changes in each of the inputs, changes in the proportions of each input, differences between full capacity and underutilization of the available capacity, and changes in managerial decisions and external factors. Little measurement work has been done in this area, but the time has come to begin. Similarly, little effort has been applied to measuring the quality and cost of the outputs from system development and the correlations among the inputs and outputs.

1. MANAGEMENT SPEAKS NUMBERS AND DOLLARS

Changes in productivity have a major influence on a wide range of managerial problems: wage levels, cost-price relationships, capital investment, labor utilization, and competitive standing. Underlying these problems is the widespread misunderstanding of the nature and effects of productivity adjustments. There are four basic rules to adhere to when measuring productivity:

1. Productivity analysis serves a variety of purposes, so it requires a corresponding variety of carefully designed metrics.
2. The productivity of any system should not refer to a single input/output ratio, but rather an integrated network of such measures.
3. Productivity adjustments depend on their sources, the nature of changes in the input/output relationships, the managerial choices for harnessing the benefits, and not just on the magnitude of the change.
4. Evaluating the effects of productivity changes requires that the network of input/output ratios be supplemented with cost measures and then still broader criteria until they accurately reflect the true objectives of the study.

Productivity adjustments assume many forms—installation of new technology, methodology, or improved management style. A manager may seek to improve productivity by decreasing the quantity of each input per unit output, by altering the quality of the inputs, by adjusting proportions of inputs, or by reducing input costs. In the information systems department, the two major inputs are human resources and machine resources. Productivity improvements demand that fewer of each be consumed to produce programs, systems, and maintenance changes. You can reduce the number of managers, analysts, or programmers, but will that really help? The use of programming assistants and coders are two examples of adjustments to the proportions of inputs and possibly the quality of those inputs. Machine resources can also be adjusted: 10-second response time can be reduced to two seconds. On-line software packages can be substituted for batch ones. Software packages can also be substituted for programmer and analyst manual processes. Fourth-generation and report-writer packages can be substituted for conventional COBOL development where appropriate. Microcomputers can easily replace many trivial programs that currently exist and meet the individualized needs of the corporation without IS intervention. Structured programming substituted a better quality methodology for the existing haphazard one. Quality circles have often been employed as an improved management style. Productivity improvements are obtained through a continuous commitment to adjusting these inputs and the process that forges them into programs and systems. But as much as IS management may be concerned with cutting costs in relationship to their output, is it really important to the corporation?

Reducing costs relative to output is less important than raising income relative to costs; increasing profit relative to total investment is often more important than either. Although not necessarily intuitive, increases in productivity levels may not be beneficial, nor will the same pattern of productivity enhancements prove equally successful in varying environments. Productivity increases are merely a means to achieve more important goals such as reduced costs, maximized return, and increased competitiveness. To maximize all of these at once, a manager needs the following information:

Managerial control ratios	Rate of profit to fixed investment
	Product prices
	Total unit costs
	Capacity utilization
	Productivity of fixed investment
Unit costs	Unit material costs
	Unit wage costs
	Unit fixed costs
Cost proportions	Materials to total costs
	Wages to total costs
	Fixed costs to total costs
Input prices	Material prices
	Wage rates
Output productivity	Output per worker hour
	Output per materials
	Capacity per fixed investment
Input proportions	Materials per worker hour
	Materials per utilized fixed investment
	Worker hours per utilized fixed investment

Perhaps the toughest job faced by information systems managers is the development, evaluation, and measurement of their department's contribution to the company. Management has approached this problem in numerous ways, most notably, and most unsuccessfully, the study of lines of code per person per day. IS management has used a variety of performance measures to conquer this problem. They fall into two categories: work units and cost units. One involves human resources and levels of service; the other, revenues and expenses. The key to a successful program of software measurement is the analysis and feedback of these metrics to all personnel involved, especially management. Let's take a look at each of the possible measurements.

1. *Global Cost Measures*. Information systems managers attempt to identify performance as a ratio of expense to some other quantity. For example, the ratio of IS expense to total company expense, IS staff as a percentage

of the total company staff, or IS capital investment to total company assets. This information then forms the basis for nice graphs and trend analysis that can be compared to other similar industries. "Look, we're comfortably ahead of Company XYZ in capital investments in computer technology." But does this really mean that the IS department is more productive and fully utilizing all of this additional technology? Perhaps not.

2. *Budget Measures.* Information systems managers also attempt to quantify their increased productivity by increases in the budget. "We must be getting more value for the increased expense." But the increase may only reflect salary increases or additional hardware and not the benefit derived from either. Just like the global measures, the budget measures tell where you are and where you are going, but they require other data to support their validity as a productivity measure. A department's budget may be increasing while its productivity is declining due to underinvestment in new technology.

3. *System Measures.* Lines of code (LOC) has been proposed as an effective measure of programmer output. The major problem with this metric is the method of counting it. Some zealots count every line, some exclude comments, some exclude data definitions, and others count only the executable verbs. Differences in counting techniques results in a difference of more than two to one (Jones, 1978). Even when these metrics were carefully controlled and counted, most researchers failed to find a good correlation between LOC and development productivity.

Other problems with LOC include: its ineffectiveness for measuring noncoding tasks, its tendency to represent assembler language coders as more productive than COBOL or other high-level language programmers, and its ability to incorrectly motivate programmers to produce more and poorer quality code. LOC measures also exclude the quality of the code, which bears heavily on the future productivity of the maintenance staff.

Lines of code metrics represent only 10–20% of the actual development process. What about the proposal, feasibility, definition, and design stages? What about the management and nonmanagement resources used? Oddly enough, the IBM study (Walston 1977) showed that LOC could describe the productivity of the entire development process. But they also found that productivity rates per project could vary widely, from 150 to 440 LOC per month. The difference may not be due to programmer productivity, but may reflect the vagaries of these other development stages.

Lines of code metrics tend to reward assembler language programmers and punish those who program in high-level languages. Consider the example of two programmers writing the same program, one in assembler, the other in COBOL. The assembler language takes one month and produces 1000 lines of code, while the COBOL programmer takes two weeks and 250 lines of code. The COBOL programmer's productivity will be 500 LOC/month and the assembler language programmer's, 1000. The COBOL programmer was clearly more productive, creating the new program in just two weeks instead of four, but the LOC metrics incorrectly indicate the reverse. Similarly, another COBOL programmer might have coded the same routine in two weeks and 200 lines of code, resulting in a productivity of 400 LOC/month. The two COBOL programmers are equally productive, creating the same program in the same amount of time. But you will rarely have an opportunity to allow two programmers to code the same program, nor will you be able to consider that the smaller routine may be more maintainable and therefore less costly than the larger one.

Lines of code metrics may incorrectly motivate programmers to produce more code than is necessary. This padding increases the complexity of the program and reduces its quality—exactly the opposite of the desired effect. In the previous example, the 500 LOC per month programmer may have padded the program to show an apparent increase in productivity. Compared to the 400 LOC per month programmer, however, the first programmer was producing poorer quality code. This is the inherent danger in using LOC metrics as the only metric of productivity—it will incorrectly motivate the programming staff to code LOC-ladden programs that will consume the IS maintenance budget. Management must introduce LOC metrics as an information gathering tool that will tell them more about the development process than they already know or suffer the consequences.

This evidence brings forth two rules: only compare LOC metrics within the same language; never compare two programmers on LOC metrics unless they have coded the same program and the quality of the resulting code is known. LOC metrics of productivity are representative only when taken for a large project. Lines of code can be used to successfully track the growth of a project and compare it to similar projects using identical technology. The Walston and Felix study (Walston 1977) showed that over a wide variety of projects of varying size, that effort per man-month could be adequately compared to lines of code and documentation metrics.

4. *Return on Investment (ROI).*   Are the benefits of this project worth the costs? What's the bottom line? ROI is perhaps the final measure of the success or failure of a software project, indicating the effectiveness with which IS management used the available resources, staff, and computer power. It allows IS management to choose among different projects and to compare the results of completed ones. They will be motivated to invest in new technology and innovation only when the ROI appears beneficial. Return on investment, however, may be difficult to calculate before initiating a new project and its ultimate merits may bury themselves in the overall operation of the company: Consider a management support system that aids in timely decision making. Where would the company be if decisions are delayed or made incorrectly?

Quantifying these kinds of intangible benefits in real dollars is often impossible, so ROI may not serve as a good productivity measure in all cases.

5. *Operational Measures.* Every operations center maintains statistics of the number of jobs run, lines printed, terminals and transactions served, and so on. Charting this information may serve to dictate when new equipment is required, but it still fails to tell anything about productivity, unless IS can show that the unit cost for each item decreases.

Running an older computer system at capacity may cost more than leasing newer systems. The newer systems also support productivity enhancing tools not available with older technology. Older systems are also less reliable, incurring greater user costs for down time. Existing computers may have cost hundreds of thousands of dollars, but could be replaced with less expensive microcomputers that are more productive.

Another group of productivity measures involves operational data. Number of compiles, tests, and so on are often useful as rudimentary productivity measures. Connect hours and CPU hours per programmer month have also been collected and studied. They vary widely, however, from programmer to programmer. CPU or connect hours per 1000 LOC is a better metric and will have more meaning when applied over an entire project or group.

6. *User Service Measures.* What do users want? Can IS provide the services required in a reasonable time frame? Is the user satisfied? IS can determine each of these metrics with client surveys, but only good communication can demonstrate IS concern and a desire to help.

More often than not, the user measures IS productivity by four factors: responsiveness, timeliness, quality, and image. The client measures response time as the mean time to repair (MTTR) production and program problems. Timeliness is a function of meeting due dates. Quality may include metrics such as mean time between failures (MTBF), accuracy, user friendliness, and cost/benefits. Image can be measured as the amount of repeat customers.

7. *Top Management Measures.* One of the ways to measure productivity depends on subjective metrics employed by the user and IS top management. Establishing IS credibility often serves as stronger support for good productivity than all the numbers and reports that can be compiled. But top management is also measured by dates kept and missed, employee turnover, absenteeism, and their ability to work with resource constraints. Top management has the ultimate responsibility for assuring quality. Toward this end, top management needs a quality assurance organization to provide evidence that the quality function is being performed by all members of IS.

Many of the limitations of classic productivity measurement are traceable to the effects of early developments in agriculture and manufacturing processes. Agriculture developed the "input creativity" theory of productivity; relative fertility of equal plots of land was measured in output per acre. Because the differences were attributed to the unequal fertilities of the different plots, fertility was considered the "creative" input. The later meaning comes from manufacturing and the engineering concept of efficiency, which reflects the relationship between actual and the potential output for any process. For example, the automobile industry operating at 60% of capacity would be a "conversion efficiency" metric of productivity.

The conversion efficiency theory shifts the scope of measurement from comparing total output with one input to comparing total output with total input, also shifting the explanation of productivity changes from the creativity of inputs to the effectiveness of the conversion process. The effectiveness involves not only engineering, but also managerial contributions to system performance. The problem with both of these theories is that they fail to account for changes in the nature and composition of output (i.e., the change from assembler to COBOL code); the volume, quality, and utilization of other inputs (computer usage); and the nature of production processes (batch versus on-line testing). Further, the general conclusion that increases in output/ input ratios are economically beneficial rests on the assumption that the costs of the inputs and the prices of the outputs remain unchanged. Note that neither the quality of the inputs nor the outputs have been measured in a typical software factory.

As a manager, you are probably less interested in output per unit input and more concerned with the cost of each input in relation to unit output. Furthermore, you should be concerned with the total cost per unit output. This will allow some creative decision making in terms of substituting technology, methodology, and managerial skills for labor.

2. PROGRAMMERS FEAR MEASUREMENT

Everyone seems to fear productivity measurements. The major reason for the fear involves the absence of an acceptable standard. Since software measurement is relatively new, there are few validated, useful productivity metrics.

People don't really mind being measured, as long as they are compared to a mutually agreed-upon scale for productivity. And there's the rub. None have been found that will work for the *entire industry*. Once you have used them to collect your own data, however, you can then formulate an acceptable scale for your organization.

3. PRODUCTIVITY MEASURES

There are four main theories about measuring programmer productivity: measure the number of functions provided, the number of lines of code, the code complexity, or the quantity of object code generated. Each has their appeal and problems. The measurement of object code is the easiest to strike down; an optimizing compiler produces 25% fewer statements than a normal one. This alone invalidates any comparisons. It is more difficult still to compare the object code generated from assembler language with COBOL, FORTRAN, or PL/I. Ratios of object lines per source instruction vary from 1.6:1 to 6:1 (Jones 1978). This leaves only functions, lines of code, and code complexity as potential productivity measures. Let's look at each, their benefits and drawbacks.

4. FUNCTION METRICS

Functions are those pieces of code that perform some specific activity for the system or the user. They edit transaction records, update files, select report data, or write reports. They process run control and audit files.

Measuring productivity by function is intuitively reasonable. Each function should be something the user wants, whether it is coded in 200 lines of code or 2000. Some functions may be common; their inclusion in multiple programs should show a higher productivity for that system.

Where lines of code are the physical output of the development process, functions are the logical output of the development process. They represent a box on a hierarchy chart or a bubble on a data-flow diagram. Functions are a tangible output of the system life cycle and therefore can and should be measured as such. There are two existing methods for counting functions. The first depends on the existence of functions (like PERFORM and CALL) in the code. The other dwells on the external aspects of the system: user inputs, user inquiries, user outputs, master files, and external system interfaces. The second system of measurement also takes into account the complexity of these various system requirements. Let's take a look at both and see how they provide further data about productivity measurement.

4.1. Function Productivity

One study of interest (Crossman, 1979), showed promise for defining productivity from the measurement of functions. This study collected not only lines of code, LOC per person/day, number of compilations to a "clean" compile, and the number and types of errors found during coding inspections, but also focused on counting the number of functions in each program.

For the purposes of the study, a function was defined as a part of the program that performs only one activity, has a single entry and exit point, conforms to the logic of structured programming (i.e., no GO TOs), and has between five and 50 executable lines of code. Since the experimenters coded in COBOL, they chose the number of paragraph names as a suitable measure of the number of functions in each module.

Using six developed systems, they then divided the hours worked by the number of functions; hours worked included all development time except system testing. The results? They found that development times, per function, were either two or four hours for the varying systems. The common denominator of the systems requiring four hours per function was the introduction of advanced technology—new languages, new operating systems, or new data-base software. Any new technology employed for the first time was then referred to as "breakthrough" technology.

Through additional research, the team found that it was possible to ignore all productivity variables other than the number of functions and the technology employed. The time to develop a function remained between 1.7 and 2.1 hours, implying that once a design has been taken to the function level, the time to develop the program could be calculated easily.

They found that identifying program functions and verifying the interfaces among modules took the most time. The time to develop the function did not depend on the number of executable statements. Using time-per-function as a metric of productivity tended to reduce the analytical complexity normally involved in calculating cost per function. Changing costs and inflation, however, made productivity comparisons difficult.

Using the data collected, they then attempted to determine the linearity of their data. To be linear, the data had to provide them with an equation of the form:

$$t = mf + c$$

where t = calculated time for completion (in hours)
f = the number of functions in the program
m and c are constants

The data, when fitted to this equation gave the following:

$$t = 1.06f + 14.9$$

This equation gave a coefficient of correlation of 0.93—a strong indicator of the validity of this metric. Based on your own usage of new technology and methodology, this equation may not predict productivity adequately. It may be low or high. Collecting your own data, developing this formula, and examining the results is the only way to determine the validity of this metric in your own environment. It does have certain advantages.

First, it should be easy to calculate the number of functions in a program. In IBM ALC, the number of BAL (branch and link) instructions gives a basic metric of the number of functions. Only BAL instructions to unique labels should be counted, however. In COBOL, the number of paragraphs or PERFORMs of unique paragraphs should provide a reasonable function metric. In PL/I, it is the number of PROCEDURE, DO WHILE, and DO UNTIL statements.

A second advantage to function point productivity measurement is that it does not depend on the measurement of program complexity, LOC or programmer ability, which are hard to determine before the program has been coded.

Third, it could help solidify project estimates following the design stage; no more waiting until the beginning of the coding phase to get an estimate of development time—the design should establish the schedule. A simple measurement of the number of functions in the design should provide an estimate of the resources needed to develop the whole program.

Finally, it provides a continuous feedback mechanism to identify problems, successes, and hopefully ways to avoid problems, while implementing successful methodology and technology into the system development process.

The only drawback to this method of productivity measurement is the absence of a way to analyze maintenance work. Intuitively, however, it would seem easier to maintain a program with one function than one with 50. Little research has been done in this area. It does, however, provide additional information to help a developing project establish control and objective, rather than subjective, metrics of project completion.

4.2. Function Points

The second function-oriented measure of productivity comes from Allan Albrecht of IBM. The basic approach concentrates on the number of user inputs, inquiries, outputs, master files, and external system interfaces to deal with in the system development process. These five measurements are then weighted, adjusted according to varying environments and user requirements, and then summed to provide a measure of "function points."

Element 1 = Number of user inputs
             Simple $* 3$
             Average $* 4$
             Complex $* 6$

Element 2 = Number of user outputs
            Simple   * 4
            Average * 5
            Complex * 7

Element 3 = Number of user inquiries
            Simple   * 3
            Average * 4
            Complex * 6

Element 4 = Number of files
            Simple   * 7
            Average * 10
            Complex * 15

Element 5 = Number of external interfaces
            Simple   * 5
            Average * 7
            Complex * 10

The values 3–15 are the weights determined by trial and error that represent the function value provided to the user. The sum of these function points is then adjusted for the complexity of the project by use of a worksheet. The degree of complexity could increase or decrease the function points by 35%.

There are 14 factors that affect complexity:

1. Does the system require reliable backup and recovery?
2. Are data communications required?
3. Are there distributed processing functions?
4. Is performance critical?
5. Will the system run in an existing, heavily utilized operational environment?
6. Does the system require on-line data entry?
7. Does the on-line data entry require the input transaction to be built over multiple screens or operations?
8. Are the master files updated on-line?
9. Are the inputs, outputs, files, or inquiries complex?
10. Is the internal processing complex?
11. Is the code designed to be reusable?
12. Are conversion and installation included in the design?

13.   Is the system designed for multiple installations in different organizations?

14.   Is the application designed to facilitate change and ease of use by the user?

The degree of influence of these factors is then rated from 0 to 5, ranging from no influence (0), incidental (1), moderate (2), average (3), significant (4), to essential (5). The sum of these factors gives the total degree of influence, from which the complexity adjustment is calculated and the function points delivered:

total degree of influence (N)

complexity adjustment $= (0.65 + 0.01 * N)$

function points = unadjusted function points $*$ complexity

Function points are the measurable output of the development process. To obtain a productivity measurement, the unit output has to be compared to the unit cost. Cost was calculated as the work hours spent by IBM and the customer through all phases of development. System design, project management, and system architecture all contribute to the final productivity, so to ignore them would exclude costs from the productivity metric.

productivity = function points/total work hours

Albrecht's analysis of 22 projects over a four-year period showed a 3:1 increase in productivity between 1974 and 1978. The study included 16 COBOL, 4 PL/I, and 2 DMS/VS systems. The factors associated with the higher productivity included a disciplined development process, use of PL/I and DMS/VS, on-line development, and the use of improved programming technologies such as structured design and code.

Albrecht also found that PL/I was 25% more productive than COBOL and that DMS/VS was at least 30% more productive than COBOL. Lines of code were also measured as a secondary metric. DMS/VS averaged 25 LOC per function point; PL/1, 65 LOC; and COBOL, 110 LOC.

The function point metrics provide a way of comparing productivity between projects that are coded in different languages or that use differing technologies. Prior to the development of function points, project comparisons were only possible between projects using the same language and the same development technology. Productivity was based primarily on lines of code metrics.

5. LINES OF CODE METRICS

Lines of code have always been intriguing as a way to measure productivity. Each line of code is a nut or a bolt in a vehicle that will transform the company's data into information. In manufacturing, productivity can be calculated as the number of bolts tightened per hour; why not the same with programs? The key to using LOC as a productivity metric is to state the counting method and never to compare different languages, varying technologies, or whatever. You might compare IMS COBOL development systems of roughly the same size. You would not compare ALC to COBOL, IMS on-line to batch sequential, or a 10,000 LOC project with one million LOC projects. Lines of code will not provide a reliable metric of productivity in this varying environment. You should further anticipate that productivity will vary according to the type of system under construction. Fred Brooks (1975) identified four different levels of product complexity that impact productivity.

Type of Product	Cost Factor
Program	1
Programming system	3×
Programming product	6×
Programming system product	9×

Producing a programming system product like IMS would take three times as long as producing an application programming system in COBOL. Similarly, turning an existing application system into a programming product will take as long as the original development.

The studies of Crossman (1979) and Johnson (1977) found that productivity, measured in function points or LOC, would decrease with the application of new technology or any large-scale innovation.

Thus, anytime that new technology, whether it is a new language or a new data-base management system, is introduced into the development of software, productivity will be reduced by as much as one-half.

Variations in software products and the technology used have contributed to the problem of using lines of code to measure productivity. Factoring these variables into LOC metrics, however, can give reasonable measurements of production.

There are three methods of counting LOC: count total lines of code (TLOC), executable lines of code (ELOC), or the number of lines changed during maintenance (MLOC).

5.1. Total Lines of Code

First, look at total lines of code (TLOC). This metric includes every line in the program or module. Consider the examples shown in Figure 2.1. The first statement is written in one line; the second in four. Was the programmer who coded the second example more productive? No. But what is apparent? The second example is more readable. TLOC, when considered without other metrics, tells little about productivity. It does, however, indicate the number of pages it will take to print the program listing. This in itself may tell something about the overall size of the code and how long it will take to type the program into the machine. The difference is obvious between two programs of size 100 TLOC and 8000 TLOC. The first is a short story; the second, a novel. The plot of the former is more easily understood, enhanced, and maintained. The latter will take longer to type into the machine, let alone compile and test. TLOC, based on these examples, is still a crude metric of productivity. The next logical refinement of TLOC are ELOC.

5.2. Executable Lines of Code (ELOC)

ELOC include every occurrence of a programming language verb. For example, in IBM assembler language: MVC, CLC, BE, etc. would be executable verbs; in COBOL: PERFORM, MOVE, etc.; in FORTRAN: DO, IF, and READ; and in PL/I: "=", COS, SIN, DO WHILE, etc. Each of these verbs actively works toward implementing a desired function for the corporation. ELOC is a better metric of productivity than TLOC, but it has its drawbacks. Work by Thomas McCabe (1976) and others has shown that productivity may be a function of the number of decision elements in a program. It is far easier to understand a MOVE statement than a PERFORM . . . VARYING . . . UNTIL loop. ELOC counts the MOVE and PERFORM equally. This effect can be seen in the work done by Walston and Felix at IBM (Walston, 1977). Averaging the ELOC per staff month, over projects ranging in size from 4000 to 476,000 ELOC, led to the following equation as a way to calculate effort.

$$\text{effort (in staff months)} = 5.2 * (\text{number of 1000 ELOC})^{0.91}$$

The productivity data collected in their study converged to this equation, but variations from program to program were caused by the complexity of the routine implemented, the source language used, and the experience of the programming staff. A complex routine might be programmed at 150 LOC per month, while a less complex report routine might be coded at 500 LOC per month. Is the latter programmer better than the former, or providing more value to the company? Probably not. They might be equal, or the coder of the

```
IF A ≠ B THEN B = C; ELSE C = D;


IF A = B THEN
    B = C;
ELSE
    C = D;
```

FIGURE 2.1. Total lines of code comparison.

more complex routine might be more beneficial, coding the routine in fewer statements by using the better features of the language.

ELOC also breaks down as a metric when used for maintenance programming. A new development programmer may be highly productive compared to a maintenance programmer who takes two weeks to put a five-line fix into an existing module. The complexity and size of the maintained module makes it difficult, if not impossible, to properly maintain and enhance the code. ELOC has been found to be a crude predictor of how long it will take to fix or enhance a given program (Curtis, 1981). It will be a factor in the overall productivity metrics, but it is only useful as a broad measure of productivity and breaks down when applied at the program or programmer level.

5.3. Maintenance Productivity

The maintenance task still defies measurement. Or does it? Maintenance causes the programmer to add, change, and delete code from existing programs. Perhaps that is the way to measure not only change but also productivity in existing systems. This method was validated in actual studies (Sheppard, 1980). For example, consider Figure 2.2: A programmer adds 100 TLOC to a program while deleting 90 TLOC from another part of the same code. The increase in TLOC is only 10; the increase in ELOC, possibly less. In reality, the programmer affected 190 lines in the program. Further, imagine that the program is 1000 TLOC to begin with; the programmer has affected 19% of the total program. Additional testing effort will be required. Compared to the increase in TLOC of 10, or 1% of the total code, which metric has more validity? Alternatively, should the maintenance programmer get credit for 1010 LOC—the total for the revised program?

Intuitively, the total change has more validity. Furthermore, why not quantify this addition, change, and deletion by type of lines? Perhaps the programmer only added 100 comments and deleted 90 others. The program has not changed; it need not be tested. What about the alternate situation where the programmer adds 10 decisions, changes 10 loops, and deletes 10 MOVE statements, when the program only had 4 decisions and 10 loops to

Program XYZ
Maintenance Statistics

Total Lines of Code

Original		1000
Added	100	
Changed	0	
Deleted	90	
Total		
Change	190	
New TLOC		1010
Percent		
Change	19%	1%

FIGURE 2.2.   Maintenance lines of code
metrics.

begin with? The programmer has increased the decision complexity and
affected all of the loops, demanding more coding and testing effort than the
previous example. The additional effort required to test the modified program
should decrease the productivity of the maintenance programmer. Another
interesting approach to measuring maintenance productivity involves cost
units.

5.4. Maintenance Costs

The costs of changing a program or system and the cumulative costs for the
same code may have meaning as productivity metrics. Both metrics have the
unit: cost/1000 LOC, which provides a scale for comparison of different
programs. For example, if the maintenance costs of one system are $100/1000
LOC and $200/1000 LOC for another, which group of programmers is more
productive? The latter group may be as productive as possible, considering
that they are working with an unstructured system. The former group may
be more productive because they are maintaining a documented, well-
structured system. These metrics tell more about the benefits of advanced
technology, methodology, and management style, than about the programming staffs involved.

Cumulative system costs provide another productivity measure that accounts for the quality of the original system. The cumulative system costs start
with the cost of the basic system, in cost per 1000 LOC, and then add the costs
of all maintenance activities. For example, one system may be built for
$10,000/1000 LOC, while another may cost $20,000 per 1000 LOC. Following
conversion, the less expensive may cost $1000 per 1000 LOC to maintain,
while the more expensive system costs only $100/1000 LOC. The cumulative
costs for the cheaper system will quickly eclipse the more expensive one.

The research community has done little work in the area of studying change and costs as possible metrics of maintenance productivity. But they are intriguing and bear further investigation.

6. DOCUMENTATION

The study by Walston and Felix (Walston, 1977) also found a relationship between the number of pages of documentation and the number of thousand lines of code. This could provide a means to measure not only programmers, but also systems analysts. Walston and Felix's data indicated that this metric ran between 30 and 180 pages per 1000 LOC, with the median at 69. This metric included all documentation: proposals, definitions, designs, test plans, and so on. Divided into their separate categories, these documentation metrics might more reasonably measure the contributions of each participant in the development. For example, if the user develops the definition document, then this figure should be compared with the final lines of code. System and program designs could be compared separately as well.

When the number of pages of documentation was compared with actual productivity, in LOC per person month, the study found that typically they were inversely related: the greater the number of pages of documentation, the lower the productivity. Some systems analysts can state the program design concisely, and some cannot. Cryptic documentation can be harmful as well, but the findings indicated that once pages per 1000 LOC exceeded 30, productivity declined sharply—from 320 down to 195 LOC/month. Of course, many other variables affected the productivity rates. Their observed ratio of pages to LOC is

$$D = 49L^{1.01}$$

where D = number of pages of documentation
          L = number of 1000 lines of code

7. HALSTEAD'S SOFTWARE SCIENCE

Two additional metrics have shown promise for measuring coding productivity: McCabe's Cyclomatic Complexity and Halstead's Software Science. These two metrics have been widely validated in industry and the laboratory as excellent predictors of how long it will take to construct, maintain, or enhance a given program or module. Let's examine both and the research results that verify their validity.

Maurice Halstead (1977) began the study of what he called software science. Researchers throughout the world have continued that work and found, in virtually all cases, that the software science metrics are extremely good predictors of development and maintenance productivity. The idea itself is simple and intuititve: Determine productivity from the numbers and types of words used in the program. This is the same method that is used to study the complexity of the English language.

7.1.　Length and Volume

Halstead began by counting the number of unique operands (data names and literals) and unique operators (executable verbs). He said that these two metrics comprised the total vocabulary of the program. You could, for example, count all of the unique words in this book and have its total vocabulary. He then counted every occurrence of the operands and operators, summing these two metrics to provide a length. This would be similar to counting all of the words in this book to obtain the length. Vocabulary and length then formed the basis from which Halstead went on to calculate the effort necessary to understand, create, and maintain a piece of code. To this point I have covered six basic metrics:

$$n_1 = \text{the number of unique operators}$$
$$n_2 = \text{the number of unique operands}$$
$$N_1 = \text{the total number of operators}$$
$$N_2 = \text{the total number of operands}$$
$$n = \text{vocabulary} = n_1 + n_2$$
$$N = \text{length} = N_1 + N_2$$

The next step was to transform these metrics into some sort of area or volume. We already have the length, and if we think of the vocabulary as a depth or width, we could derive the volume as Halstead did:

$$\text{volume} = \text{length} * \log_2(\text{vocabulary})$$

Researchers at IBM (Christensen, 1981) found strong correlations among the executable lines of code, length, and volume metrics, leading them to conclude that the three are relatively equal measures of program size. Length and volume are more universal metrics, however, since they are both language independent, whereas lines of code are not.

7.2. Difficulty

The next metric is difficulty (Christensen, 1981), which is actually the inverse of Halstead's *level* metric. An increasing difficulty metric seems more logical than a decreasing fractional level metric.

$$\text{difficulty} = n_1/2 * N_2/n_2$$

Since each program must have at least two operands, an entry and an exit, Halstead chose to divide the unique operators by 2, giving a starting point of 1. Compare how this part of the metric will vary with the coding language: IBM ALC has 255 operators; while COBOL has 56; and PL/I has over 150. Because of the variety of operands, an ALC difficulty metric could be as much as five times greater than the COBOL metric for the same program. PL/I has the same basic operators as COBOL, but also an extensive subroutine library. The use of these operator/subroutines is the same as PERFORMing or CALLing a subroutine in COBOL, so the PL/I difficulty metric should not be three times as great as the equivalent COBOL program. Because programmers have fewer operators to deal with in a high-level language, the programs produced will have a lower difficulty and that is why most IS shops have moved away from assembler language code. This is also why more users are turning toward nonprocedural, or fourth-generation languages—the number of operators is reduced even further, causing a decrease in difficulty and a corresponding increase in productivity.

The IBM study also found that the number of unique operators increased with the use of the GO TO, causing further increases in the difficulty metric. This was in part due to their counting method; they counted every GO TO to a different label or paragraph name as a unique operator. If you only count the GO TO as a single unique operator, you will find an increase of not only one for the GO TO, but also one for the use of EXIT statements in COBOL. You will also find the use of GO TOs and EXITs increases the total number of operators, with a corresponding increase in the length and volume metrics. This case against the GO TO was also verified by another IBM study (Fitsos, 1980).

The second part of the difficulty metric is the average occurrence of each of the operands. So the difficulty metric is just the product of the number of unique operators (adjusted to start at one) and the average number of occurrences of each operand.

Difficulty reflects the effort required to understand, code, and maintain a given program or chunk of code. Thus it is reasonable to assume that it also has a bearing on productivity. With some historical knowledge, a ratio such as person-days/difficulty seems a likely candidate for the study of development and maintenance productivity.

7.3. Programming Effort

The next metric is Halstead's calculation of actual programming effort (E).

$$effort = difficulty * volume$$

This number gives a rather esoteric number that equates to the number of elementary mental discriminations required to understand, code, and maintain the module or program. "What is an elementary mental discrimination?" you might ask. Halstead theorized that the mind makes decisions and grasps information at a rate of between 5 and 18 mental discriminations per second. I assume that 5/second accounts for unintelligent programmers while 18/second is Harlan Mills. If the major gurus are right, however, the difference is more like 1:10, so the range might be 2–20 or 5–50 for all we know.

Regardless of the meaning of the number, researchers have found a strong correlation (Sheppard, 1980) between effort and the actual productivity in person days or months. Another study found effort to be a better productivity metric than ELOC (Curtis, 1979).

Software science metrics show great potential for use as a productivity measurement. There is no known way of comparing across the whole industry; the application work varies from writing compilers to business applications to microcomputer software. With your own productivity data, however, you can derive a relationship between hours worked and the software science metrics: length, volume, difficulty, and effort. Use these to enhance your understanding of productivity and its measurement.

8. McCABE'S CYCLOMATIC COMPLEXITY

Thomas McCabe proposed a complexity metric (further described in the chapter on complexity) called cyclomatic complexity. It is mentioned here because researchers have found it to be the next best thing to the software science effort metric as an indicator of productivity in both the development and maintenance environments. It is based strictly on the number of decision elements—IF-THEN-ELSE, DO WHILE, DO UNTIL, CASE verbs—in the language and the number of AND, OR, and NOT phrases in each decision. Cyclomatic Complexity is calculated from these counts and represents the total number of structural test paths in the program. It also represents the sum of the logic in the program, a major factor in how long it takes to design, code, and test a new program. It looks like this:

$$cyclomatic\ complexity = number\ of\ decisions +$$
$$number\ of\ conditions + 1$$

It also reflects the effort required to understand, maintain, and enhance a program. Studies have found that a cyclomatic complexity of ten or less yields the greatest productivity, least errors, and most comprehensible code. So, when you analyze your programs looking for potential candidates for rewrites or rework, cyclomatic complexities over 10, 100, or 1000 should be your primary candidates. These modules are where you spend your precious maintenance resource. New programs that exceed the limit of 10 should be closely examined for functionality and modularity. Rework of the errant module is called for to reduce the cost of testing, maintaining, and enhancing the code.

9. HOW TO MEASURE PRODUCTIVITY

In decision making in large organizations, the factors that bear upon a decision tend to be weighted in direct proportion to the ease with which they can be quantified.

The most critical factors may be difficult, if not impossible to quantify.

William F. Zachmann

The previous sections have presented the major productivity metrics now under study. None are ideal in and of themselves. Therefore, you should begin to collect and understand what they mean to your organization, not what they mean to someone else. Which have the most validity? Which are easiest to collect? Which most accurately reflect your organization? The only way to answer these questions is to begin collecting and studying each of the proposed metrics. Critical factors like morale, motivation, experience level, skills, design quality, and so on, which affect productivity, may be impossible to quantify.

Remember that:

1. Productivity analysis serves a variety of masters, requiring a corresponding variety of carefully designed metrics.
2. The productivity of any system should refer to an integrated network of input/output ratios. No single measure can depict accurately all of the vagaries of productivity.
3. Productivity adjustments depend on changes in the input/output ratios and managerial choices for harnessing the increased productivity.

4. The network of input/output ratios must be supplemented with cost measures and other criteria until they correctly reflect objectives of productivity measurement.

How to go about mechanizing these metrics is presented in the last chapter. Collect this data, study the information, and your intuition will begin to suggest other metrics and ways to combine the existing ones to give a true picture of productivity.

CHAPTER THREE

QUALITY

Reprinted by permission of Tribune Company Syndicate, Inc.

One of the keys to improving productivity is to improve quality. A better designed, more maintainable system will accrue fewer lifetime costs; higher productivity, measured in cost per unit output, will be possible. More reliable programs will have a greater mean time between failures (MTBF), a shorter MTTR, and so on. As mentioned in the previous chapter, productivity measurements are worthless unless they are substantiated by quality measurements.

Quality can be built in, or added on later at considerable expense. Software metrics provides a way to quantify the presence or absence of quality in your programs and systems. In the sixties, the phrase "made in Japan" had a negative connotation due to the relative quality of their goods; now the reverse is true—it implies excellent quality and value. Unfortunately, much of our software is "made in America," and that is not good.

1. WHAT IS SOFTWARE QUALITY?

Software quality is measurable and varies from system to system and program to program. There is no one perfect standard to which all software must

35

adhere. Some software may carry astronauts into space; it will need to be reliable or, better yet, zero fail. Other software might implement a one-shot program for a client or management; it will not require the same investment in quality. An application system with a life span of 10 years will require extensive concentration on reliability, maintainability, and flexibility. If a system is difficult to maintain or enhance, it will eat an IS department alive in maintenance costs over its expected life.

2. SOFTWARE QUALITY METRICS

What are the different facets of software quality that you might want to measure? They are mainly referenced as correctness, efficiency, flexibility, integrity, interoperability, maintainability, portability, reliability, reusability, testability, and usability, and are generally defined as follows:

CORRECTNESS.   The degree to which a program satisfies the user's specifications. (Does it do what you want?)

EFFICIENCY.   The amount of computing resources required to perform a user-defined function. (Does it run on your hardware as well as it can?)

FLEXIBILITY.   How much effort does it take to enhance the program? (Can you change it?)

INTEGRITY.   How well are the software and data protected from security breeches. (Is it controlled and secure?)

INTEROPERABILITY.   How much effort is required to couple this program or system with another? (Will it interface with other systems?)

MAINTAINABILITY.   How much effort will be required to locate and repair errors in the program? (Can you fix it?)

PORTABILITY.   What kind of effort will it take to transfer a program from one machine to another? (Will it run on your micros, minis, and mainframes?)

RELIABILITY.   To what degree can the system be expected to perform its function without failure? (Does it work accurately without failure?)

REUSABILITY.   To what extent can the module or program be used in other applications? (Can it be partially or totally reused in other applications to reduce costs?)

TESTABILITY.   How much effort will be required to test the structure and correctness of the code? (Can you test it?)

USABILITY.   How much effort will the user expend to learn and use the system input and output? (Can the computer center run it? Can the user operate it easily?)

Each of these software qualities describes one facet of quality and is comprised of several underlying metrics. These lower-level metrics, or software criteria as they are sometimes called, are defined as follows.

3.   SOFTWARE QUALITY CRITERIA

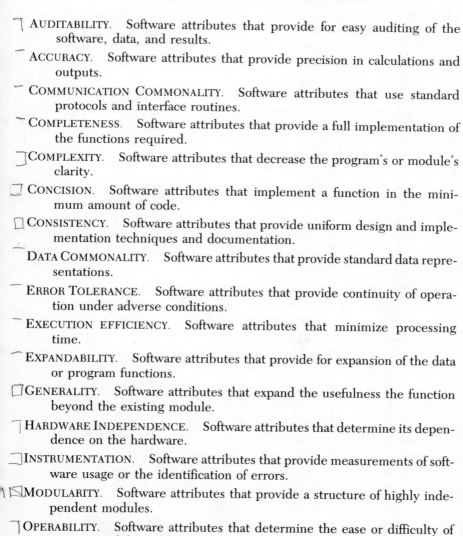

AUDITABILITY.   Software attributes that provide for easy auditing of the software, data, and results.

ACCURACY.   Software attributes that provide precision in calculations and outputs.

COMMUNICATION COMMONALITY.   Software attributes that use standard protocols and interface routines.

COMPLETENESS.   Software attributes that provide a full implementation of the functions required.

COMPLEXITY.   Software attributes that decrease the program's or module's clarity.

CONCISION.   Software attributes that implement a function in the minimum amount of code.

CONSISTENCY.   Software attributes that provide uniform design and implementation techniques and documentation.

DATA COMMONALITY.   Software attributes that provide standard data representations.

ERROR TOLERANCE.   Software attributes that provide continuity of operation under adverse conditions.

EXECUTION EFFICIENCY.   Software attributes that minimize processing time.

EXPANDABILITY.   Software attributes that provide for expansion of the data or program functions.

GENERALITY.   Software attributes that expand the usefulness the function beyond the existing module.

HARDWARE INDEPENDENCE.   Software attributes that determine its dependence on the hardware.

INSTRUMENTATION.   Software attributes that provide measurements of software usage or the identification of errors.

MODULARITY.   Software attributes that provide a structure of highly independent modules.

OPERABILITY.   Software attributes that determine the ease or difficulty of operation of the software.

SECURITY.   Software attributes that provide for control and protection of the software and data.

SELF-DOCUMENTATION.   Software attributes that explain the function of the software.

SIMPLICITY.   Software attributes that provide an implementation of the functions in the most understandable manner.

SOFTWARE SYSTEM INDEPENDENCE.   Software attributes that determine its dependence on the software environment—extensions of the language, operating system, data base management system, and so on.

TRACEABILITY.   Software attributes that provide a link from requirements to the implemented program.

TRAINING.   Software attributes that provide transitions from the current environment to the new system.

Each of the software qualities, important to software developers, is a function of these metrics. The objectives of software quality measurement is to derive the following equations:

$$\text{Correctness} = F(\text{completeness, consistency, traceability})$$

$$\text{Efficiency} = F(\text{concision, execution efficiency, operability})$$

$$\text{Flexibility} = F(\text{complexity, concision, consistency, expandability, generality, modularity, self-documentation, simplicity})$$

$$\text{Integrity} = F(\text{auditability, instrumentation, security})$$

$$\text{Interoperability} = F(\text{communications commonality, data commonality, generality, modularity})$$

$$\text{Maintainability} = F(\text{concision, consistency, modularity, instrumentation, self-documentation, simplicity})$$

$$\text{Portability} = F(\text{generality, hardware independence, modularity, self-documentation, software system independence})$$

$$\text{Reliability} = F(\text{accuracy, complexity, consistency, error tolerance, modularity, simplicity})$$

$$\text{Reusability} = F(\text{generality, hardware independence, modularity, self-documentation, software system independence})$$

$$\text{Testability} = F(\text{auditability, complexity, instrumentation, modularity, self-documentation, simplicity})$$

$$\text{Usability} = F(\text{operability, training})$$

The following chapters will discuss each of these metrics and their supporting criterion. Each of the submetrics is derived from the presence or absence of certain operators, operands, and data types in the code. Unfortunately, there is no one correct equation for the previously described functions; each must be derived from your existing environment and historical data. As the programming languages and applications vary, so must the equations describing them. Perhaps the hardest equation to derive is the one for quality:

Quality = F(correctness, efficiency, flexibility, integrity, interoperability, maintainability, portability, reliability, reusability, testability, usability)

Fortunately, when designing a program or system, the system analyst and project manager can often eliminate some of these metrics and reduce the weight of others. For example, the code to validate a Social Security number should be *reliable* and *reusable*. It may not need to be *maintainable* due to the exhaustive testing normally performed on common routines of this type. In some payroll systems, the time-worked data may be loaded on a distributed processor, so the SSN routine may need to be *portable*. If the front-end is an on-line application, then the code should be *efficient* as well.

4. DESIGN ANALYSIS

The system and each of its components should be evaluated to select the quality required of each. Figure 3.1 shows a basic chart for examining the system's quality needs. It may also be used for each component. Once these are determined, the programmer can code the program toward these goals. An experiment by Gerald Weinberg (1972) showed that programmers can direct their energies toward a desired goal, but usually at the expense of some other quality.

In Weinberg's experiment, five programming teams were given the varying programming objectives of minimizing the core used (efficiency), optimizing output clarity (usability), optimizing program clarity (maintainability), minimizing the number of statements (maintainability, flexibility), and producing the program in the minimum number of hours (productivity). Each team met its primary objective. The results?

1. The team minimizing core usage took the longest time to develop their program and had poor output and program clarity. Efficiency goals caused degraded usability, flexibility, maintainability, and so on.

2. The team maximizing output clarity used the most core and the most statements. They tied, however, with the code clarity team for program clarity. Usability goals caused inefficiency and increased complexity.

Software Quality Metrics	High	Medium	Low
Correctness			
Efficiency			
Flexibility			
Integrity			
Interoperability			
Maintainability			
Portability			
Reliability			
Reusability			
Testability			
Usability			

FIGURE 3.1. System quality analysis worksheet.

3. The team maximizing program clarity took fourth place in development time. Flexibility and maintainability goals decreased productivity.

4. The team minimizing the number of statements had the worst output clarity, but were near the median in other categories. Simplicity goals reduced the program's usability.

5. The team minimizing development time had the worst program clarity (poor maintainability), poor usage of core (inefficient), and second largest usage of language statements (higher complexity). Stressing productivity in the absence of quality goals causes severe degradation of product quality.

Weinberg believes that these findings dispell the "good" and "bad" programmer myths, substituting the idea that programmers may not be coding toward the corporate objectives. Producing a program by an unreasonable due date sacrifices maintainability and efficiency for timeliness. These decisions are made by managers who may not recognize that they are trading anything for this higher productivity. Later, they will not understand why the system that took 10 programmers to build takes 20 to maintain. Careful analysis of corporate objectives should be factored into the overall schedule.

Another advantage of design analysis is that the programmer knows the quality objectives beforehand and, much like management by objectives (MBO), they will attempt to meet those objectives. This allows the manager to evaluate the subordinate on coding skills that produce desired code qualities and to identify weaknesses that can be strengthened through training. This also prevents the programmer from arbitrarily selecting the wrong quality goals.

5. MAINTENANCE METRICS

Perhaps the most important place to apply quality metrics is in the maintenance portion of a system's life cycle. With over 50–80% of the IS budget being consumed by maintenance, quality improvements can help reduce this load significantly. Comparisons of the before and after metrics of a modified program provide a basis for quality analysis. Did the program's maintainability and flexibility improve? Did its complexity increase? What was the nature of the change and how did it affect the program? Were bugs inserted or removed? Perhaps the easiest way to understand software quality is to follow the development of classical quality theory and expand it to encompass software.

6. CLASSICAL QUALITY THEORY

Most of software quality theory has evolved from the existing base of knowledge accumulated in the manufacturing sector. Studying classical theory may give us further insights into the software manufacturing process. The most far-reaching and vital of all quality metrics is fitness for use (Juran, 1974). The basic building blocks of this metric are the quality characteristics: technology, psychology, time relations, contracts, and ethics. These characteristics can be classified into the parameters of fitness for use: quality of design, quality of conformance, abilities, and service.

6.1. Quality of Design

The basic metric of design quality is grade. First class, second class, economy, mid-sized, luxury, and so on are examples of grades. Stocks are graded on their potential earnings. Grade is a term, commonly known to all Americans, that implies a standard of excellence.

This concept of grade is often forgotten when engineering software systems. Does the user need a Volkswagen, Oldsmobile, Cadillac, or Mercedes-Benz? The variance in price is possibly five to one, and yet all of these grades of systems provide the same basic vehicle. We often rush to design a giant on-line DBMS system when the user could buy a microcomputer and some software and be operational by the end of the week. The user sometimes expects luxury at economy prices and is then thoroughly confused when IS fails to deliver. The concept of grade is universal; the user should decide how much they want to pay in advance, and IS should design to meet those needs.

Design quality is measured in three steps: identifying what constitutes fitness of use for the intended user, choosing a product or service to respond to those needs, and translating this concept into a detailed set of specifications that will meet the user's needs.

6.2. Quality of Conformance

Quality of conformance is the degree to which the product meets the original specifications and is a direct result of the machines, tools, management, organization, and workmanship that produced the product. Quality of conformance, as it applies to manufacturing quality, is the same as the concept of software *correctness*.

6.3. Ability

Products that are consumed or have a short life span may have their fitness of use determined directly from the qualities of design and conformance, just as one-shot software projects are measured on their design and correctness. Products with a longer lifetime, however, invoke time-oriented metrics such as availability, reliability, and maintainability to represent their *ability*. Long-term software projects should be measured on the same criteria.

Availability

Availability describes the continuity of service for items like energy, communication, transportation, and so on. The gasoline shortages in the seventies affected availability. The phone system will operate for over 12 hours on battery backup in case of an emergency, providing continuous service to your neighborhood or the nation. Computer hardware availability can be expressed as the ratio:

$$\frac{uptime}{(uptime + downtime)}$$

and similarly

$$\frac{MTBF}{MTBF + MTTR}$$

Software availability is based on the same factors: MTBF and MTTR.

Reliability

Reliability is the probability of a product performing without failure under given conditions for a specified period of time. It is largely determined by the quality of design. Reliability is measured by MTBF.

Maintainability

Maintainability has evolved from the need for continuity of service. Maintenance occurs in two different ways: scheduled or unscheduled service.

1. Scheduled maintenance takes two different forms: enhancement and preventive maintenance. Enhancement maintenance concerns itself with adding functionality to the software product.

Preventive maintenance, on the other hand, helps detect potential failures. A hardware system undergoes monthly preventative maintenance; why are software systems excluded from this common practice? Information systems departments often fail to check their software for potential failures and degradation. Eventually, the programs become too weary from continuous patches and new enhancements; they fail more often than they run. At this point, a manufacturer would replace the machine with a new one; the project manager does not have this choice, only a complete rewrite or continued expense for repair.

But software doesn't wear out like hardware; it simply becomes too hard to repair. Preventative maintenance can catch these problems before they become serious. The code may never need to be replaced.

2.   Unscheduled maintenance, often called repair maintenance, restores service following a system failure.

Common measures of maintainability include MTTR, mean time for scheduled maintenance, and probability of restoring service in the allotted time.

In the manufacturing world, maintainability is affected by the supporting technology: Products are designed for easy access and modular replacement at the customer's premises; special instruments are used to detect and repair the product; and all products come with extensive repair manuals. Software developers have much to learn from these manufacturing lessons. Software products need to be designed for easy access (modularity) and ease of repair (maintainability) or enhancement (flexibility).

6.4.   Field Service

The previous parameters, design quality, quality of conformance, and abilities, all speak to the system or product prior to installation. Field service talks about user's ability to obtain support. The basic factors of field service include promptness, competence, and integrity. The user often measures the IS department not on productivity, quality, or whatever, but on how they perceive the promptness of a response to a system failure or an enhancement request, the competence of the personnel working on the system, and the honesty or integrity of those people.

6.5.   Fitness of Use

Figure 3.2 displays the metric "fitness of use" and the relationship of all of its parameters and factors. To achieve fitness of use requires numerous controls during the development process.

7.   QUALITY CONTROL

Control is the process by which you establish and meet the standards that ensure quality. Establishing control requires seven universal steps.

1.   Select the person, process, or tool to be controlled.

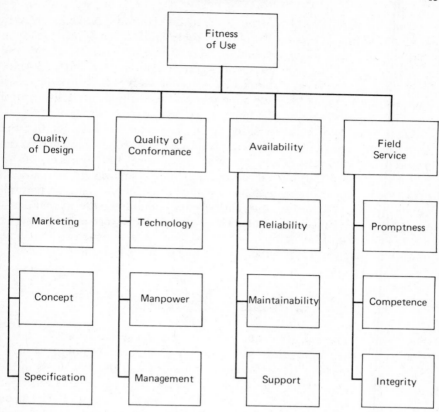

FIGURE 3.2. Fitness-of-use metric and its components.

2. Choose a measurement that can be applied to the control subject.
3. Set a standard value for this measurement that will gauge the presence of the desired quality.
4. Create a measuring device.
5. Conduct the actual measurement.
6. Interpret the differences between the measurement and the standard.
7. Act on this information to improve quality if necessary.

Measurement allows control. This is probably what led Tom DeMarco to say: "You can't control what you can't measure." (DeMarco, 1982) The basis of all control and quality or productivity improvements is measurement.

Quality control sprang from the early process of trying to prevent defects in products. In the 1940s and 1950s, quality control relied heavily on developing statistical methods for determining quality. This led to the term statistical quality control (SQC). SQC was great for numerologists, but failed to consider all of the other means available to help control quality. Pushes for reliability and zero defects in the 1960s further restricted the definition of quality control and caused problems with the human factors of manufacturing.

Once a standard of quality is achieved, employees often assume that the limit has been reached. But this is rarely the case. Someone somewhere in the organization will begin to find new ways to improve. In the process of this investigative work they often discover some tidbit of knowledge that causes a major breakthrough in productivity or quality which, in turn, changes how the employees work, with resulting changes in their cultural patterns that eventually produce changes in results. These changes rarely occur immediately, but take time for new methods or technology to gain acceptance. Finally, a new quality standard is created and the investigators turn their thoughts to other problem areas.

8. QUALITY IMPROVEMENT

The key to quality improvement focuses on maximizing return on investment. This invokes the Pareto principle: 20% of the programs encounter 80% of the costs. This rule states the importance of the few and the trivialness of the many. 20% of your competition gives you 80% of your headaches. The engine in your car generates 80% of the maintenance costs, and so on. Focusing on the few programs, programmers, or whatever that generate 80% of your expense, will lead to a continuing program of quality improvement.

Pareto analysis—determining the few things that affect program maintainability and IS costs—is the basis for designing quality improvement programs. For example, Figure 3.3 shows a chart of the number of design defects by each system analyst. Analyst F may have breakthrough knowledge that Analyst A does not. Similarly, Figure 3.4 shows the maintenance hours worked by program. Programs A−D should be reworked by the preventive maintenance team. Pareto analysis restricts the scope of quality improvement to a select few projects, thereby providing the maximum benefit to the corporation.

9. QUALITY OBJECTIVES

Top management has the ultimate responsibility for software quality as measured by fitness of use. They set corporate policy, and quality should be one of

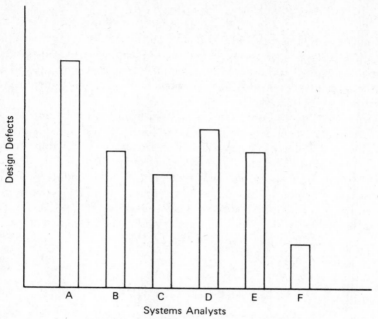

FIGURE 3.3.   Design defects by system analyst.

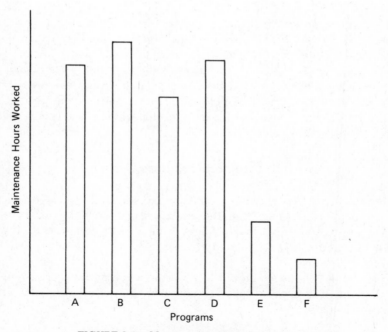

FIGURE 3.4.   Maintenance hours by program.

those policies. Policies are carried out by setting realistic quality improvement goals—these become the objectives. Management by objectives has become widespread because clearly stated objectives serve to unify and direct workers and management alike. Quality objectives serve the same purpose for programmers and analysts.

The need for quality objectives may stem from too many failures in the field, potential cost reductions, or the need for improved user relations, but they can create problems. Managers may seek to avoid quality improvements because: they cost too much; they take away from present performance; they do not feel the need for change; or they feel it would be counterpolitical. In any case, establishing quality objectives requires that they be written into corporate gospel, monitored internally as well as during field performance, and be established by the people doing the work. Quality improvements cost time and money, but reap many benefits and reduce overall costs.

10. THE COST OF QUALITY

Quality is free. It's not a gift, but it is free.

Phillip B. Crosby

Every department in a company is responsible for measuring its cost to the company and justifying its existence with benefits provided. Selling quality control and improvement demands just such analysis translated into the terms that management can understand—money. This idea first appeared in manufacturing when they decided that detecting and preventing defects was a "gold mine" for reducing costs. The potential benefits and costs associated with quality fall into three broad categories: internal failure costs, external failure costs, and prevention costs.

10.1. Internal Failure Costs

Internal failure costs would disappear if programs and systems had no errors in them prior to installation. Often, these costs are ignored in the rush to release a system into production. Internal failures incur costs due to scrap, rework, retest, downtime, and productivity losses.

SCRAP.   Labor and machine time are wasted when portions of systems are thrown away because they are unusable. Rewritten programs replace those scrapped.

REWORK. Labor and machine time are also wasted when a program or module must be changed to make them fit for use. Design and code rework following walk-throughs fall into this category.

RETEST. Labor and machine time are wasted to correct errors in the design and code, while system tests may reject programs that fail to meet the user's specifications.

DOWNTIME. Labor is wasted when programmers and machines are left idle because analysts are still reworking parts of a design or when analysts are awaiting a client's definition of requirements.

PRODUCTIVITY LOSSES. What are the costs of lost manpower and machine resources that could have been productively spent with better controls, methodology, or technology?

Part of the gold mine tapped by quality improvements comes from the reduction of failures encountered internally before the system ever reaches the production environment. These can never be eliminated entirely, but they can be substantially reduced. The benefit derived from quality improvements equate to savings of these failure costs. The other vein in the gold mine is the external failures that often plague software systems.

10.2. External Failure Costs

External failure costs would also disappear if no defects were found in the delivered system. These costs occur after system release and are due to defect investigation, rework, retest, downtime, productivity losses, and possible warranty charges.

DEFECT INVESTIGATION. Once a failure is reported, the maintenance team must determine if there was an error and where to fix it.

REWORK. Aside from rework to make programs fit for use, the operations personnel must also reschedule and run the job, causing further rework.

RETEST. Testing programs following corrections in the design and code causes further productivity loss.

DOWNTIME. In the case of external failure, the user must sit idly by, waiting for the system to be repaired. Depending in the number of users, 1 to 1000 people may be unable to work.

PRODUCTIVITY LOSSES. External failures cause the loss of user productivity, computer usage, and programmer productivity spent on repair rather than new development or enhancements.

WARRANTY CHARGES.   If the software is contractually required to provide a
    certain level of reliability, then penalties may apply if it fails.

External failures are expensive, often two to ten times as much as the same
failure captured before system release. Preventing internal and external
failures can provide excellent benefits, but not without the accompanying
costs.

10.3.   Prevention Costs

Prevention costs seek to reduce or eliminate failures and stem from quality
planning, training, process control, quality assurance data acquisition and
analysis, quality reporting, and improvement projects. Software measurement is intimately linked with each.

QUALITY PLANNING.   Creation of an overall quality, inspection, reliability,
    data acquisition, and improvement plan are quality planning costs. Also,
    the communication of these plans to management and staff are regarded
    as quality costs.
TRAINING.   Not only quality plans, but all process controls and improvement
    projects require training.
PROCESS CONTROL.   The costs of achieving software quality are due to
    process control. Walk-throughs are a form of process control.
DATA ACQUISITION ANALYSIS AND REPORTING.   Quality assurance must col-
    lect, analyze, and report on all data having to do with fitness for use and
    quality costs. This data fuels the development of improvement projects.
    Without such data, it is hard to know where to begin.
IMPROVEMENT PROJECTS.   Each improvement project will incur costs from
    lower initial productivity and possible quality problems. They may not
    work either; so the effort spent only serves to identify what will not help
    improve quality.

10.4.   Cost-Effectiveness

Determination of cost-effectiveness involves many parameters. Figure 3.5
shows these two parameters, total costs and effectiveness, and their submetrics. It may not be cost-effective to make a program highly efficient if it
only runs once a year. It is cost-effective, however, to make aircraft software
highly reliable. Cost-effectiveness is the fulcrum between total costs and
software effectiveness. Take away from one side and something must be
removed from the other. Trying to produce the same product with fewer

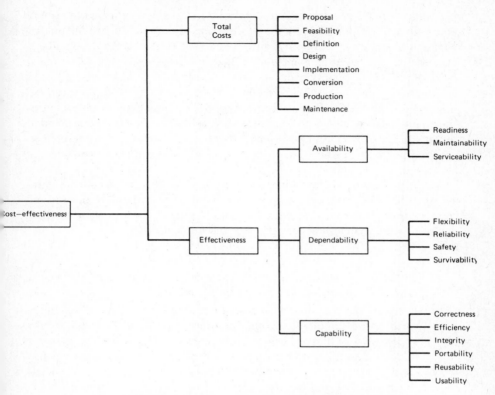

FIGURE 3.5.   Cost-effectiveness metric and its components.

resources means that maintainability and reliability must suffer. The only way to optimize the trade-off between costs and effectiveness is to manage software quality.

11. MANAGEMENT OF SOFTWARE QUALITY

Software quality can be managed to maximize the company's return on investment. Software quality programs, when properly implemented, extend from project proposal to system termination. Much of management's resistance to comprehensive quality programs stems from their lack of awareness that new levels of productivity and quality can only be attained at the expense of new tasks that make improvement possible. Many methods help justify the need for more funds, personnel, and resources to create a software quality program. But all of the documentation and statistics in the world cannot convince management to open the purse strings unless they share the quality analyst's perspective on quality, and the current state of software quality in the organization. Getting management to share these views is often the most difficult part of the quality plan, because without these perceptions, statistics are meaningless. Making management want quality is a highly political and important step. Laying the groundwork for management commitment forces the quality analyst to document software failures that could have been avoided by quality control, to send pertinent software engineering articles to managers who put faith in the written word, and he or she must never become frustrated.

While you are trying to get management on your side, begin collecting the statistics that they will later request to document their perceptions of why software quality is important to the company. Such data serve to validate their decision rather than influence it. There are a couple of different ways to collect such data.

1. Quantify the costs of internal and external failures and show how quality programs could reduce these costs.
2. Estimate the total life cycle costs of new and existing systems under various levels of quality. Then, identify the point of maximum return on investment derived from quality program. This will show management that, unlike other magic wand solutions, quality control has clearly definable benefits up to some point, beyond which, resources should be diverted to other projects.

Once the quality project has been approved, a specialized organization should be set up to handle the quality assurance tasks. Just as programmers should not test their own code, they should not serve as their own quality engineers; they are not objective.

12. VENDOR QUALITY

There is another aspect of quality management: contracting from outside vendors or supplying software to clients. In either case, vendor quality becomes a major management issue. Many organizations do not have the time or staff to handle all of their system work. Consequently, they engage an outside software vendor to do their excess development. But without solid definitions of quality that are contractually stipulated and reviewed, the client is often due for a big surprise when the system is delivered. To overcome these obstacles, you need to assess the vendor's ability to supply quality

software. The vendor should be able to demonstrate their software's ability to
meet quality criteria set forth by clients.

12.1. Vendor Assessment

With a quality program in place, it is possible to review and assess a vendor's
ability to supply quality software at a reasonable cost. The client has several
choices when specifying software quality:

1. Rely on the vendor. Without a specific, contractual quality specifica-
    tion, the client has little other choice.
2. Inspect the system when it is delivered. This prohibits inexpensive
    changes to the software before implementation.
3. Inspect the system at the vendor's premises. This allows a more
    interactive dialog to occur during development.
4. Actively keep the vendor under surveillance. Surveillance requires a
    client representative to be attached to the development project. It can
    help improve the project's quality, but only if major quality problems
    rather than minor errors are discussed and resolved.
5. Certify the vendor's quality assurance program. This eliminates the
    need for extensive surveillance and inspection.

12.2. Vendor Improvement

With quality data in hand, it is possible to help the vendor improve the quality
of the systems produced. There are two approaches:

1. Identify chronic problems encountered with the software. Many prob-
    lems recur in different programs and systems. The vendor, once aware
    of these errors, should be capable of eliminating them.
2. Pareto analysis of major quality deficiencies should identify areas that
    will maximize quality for the resources expended.

Either or both of these two methods will aid both the client and the vendor,
providing better quality to one, while improving the vendor's abilities and
product quality.

12.3. Vendor Quality Rating

Vendors may be rated in several ways. First, examine what percentage of the
total programs or modules were defective when delivered. Then, examine the

vendor rating as the ratio of expected cost of inspection or surveillance in relation to the actual cost. A vendor may also be rated on quality, cost, and service. These ratings provide the vendor with an index of their performance. If they want to keep your business, they know what must be done.

13. SUMMARY

One of the major keys to programmer productivity is software quality. The ability to measure quality brings software development and maintenance one step closer to becoming a profession. The ability to define and measure quality puts IS management in a position to make trade-offs among corporate goals, to take greater control of the development process.

Quality measurement in no way detracts from the "artistic" qualities of programming. The analyst still paints a design. The programmer still creates the program code. Quality metrics merely measure the talent demonstrated by both. All artists have critics; in this case, the computer can perform most of the critique.

The measurement of software quality—correctness, efficiency, flexibility, integrity, interoperability, maintainability, portability, reliability, reusability, testability, and usablity—is the only way to quantify IS's contribution to the corporation. It is an excellent way to hone the skills of the department's analysts and programmers. Finally, it provides a quantifiable method of controlling the products produced. Quality measurement sets the stage for an IS organization to become a software factory.

CHAPTER FOUR

COMPLEXITY METRICS

Complexity conveys a feeling of how hard it will be for someone to pick up a system, program, or module and understand how it works. Simple as that. The harder the code is to maintain or enhance, the more it will cost. Conversely, the simplicity of a program or the system's parts will tend to make the whole easier to maintain. Figure 4.1 shows how productivity and complexity are inversely related. Complexity reduction can tap the potential productivity gains shown. You or your programmers have probably picked up a program listing several hundred pages in length; the sheer bulk is a complexity metric. A listing only five pages long is the essence of simplicity. Other than these standard metrics of weight, thickness, and depth, how do you measure complexity?

There are four prominent complexity metrics for code: executable lines of code, decisions, Halstead's software science metrics, and McCabe's cyclomatic complexity metric. Many other metrics say something about code complexity, but have not received much attention or study. They will be covered as they arise.

System complexity metrics are different from code complexity metrics; they rely on the number of programs, number of modules, number of functions, number of files, and the number of interfaces among programs and between humans and the system. Both system and code level metrics have importance: Each may impact how many programs are affected by a system enhancement and how long will it take to implement the change. Both metrics are required to determine the extent of the change and the time required.

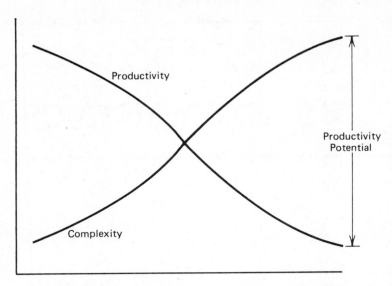

FIGURE 4.1.   Interrelationship of productivity and quality.

1. SYSTEM COMPLEXITY METRICS

When you start to develop a new system or to enhance an old one, the question comes to mind: How big is it? What does it do? How many people will I need? So many questions and so few answers. Determining system complexity from the number of programs, modules, functions, files, and interfaces can help. You may find that by correlating this information with productivity data you will be able to better estimate development resources and costs, bring projects in on schedule, and work enhancements on a timely basis.

1.1. Number of Programs

The number of programs in a system is one indicator of system complexity. I have worked on systems varying in size from one program to over a thousand. The system with over 1000 programs was more than a thousand times as complex as the single program. No one person could keep the system in their head. So, there were multiple subsystems that were the responsibility of specific persons. Each subsystem had groups of programs assigned to specific people, reducing the overall complexity per person. Still, coordinating changes to the system was more complex than with a smaller one.

$$\text{system program complexity} = \text{number of programs}$$

1.2. Number of Modules

The number of modules is another important system level metric. Following structured design, you should end up with one module for each function in the system. Many of these modules are common to all and will be reused rather than recoded for each program. One industry study found productivity increases of 3:1 possible with common code methodology (Stevens, 1982). If you have only one module for each program, complexity will be greater than having separate and possibly reusable modules for each of the program's functions.

$$\text{program complexity} = \text{number of functions/number of modules}$$
$$\text{average program complexity} = \text{number of modules/number of programs}$$

You might expect as the number of modules increases, so will the complexity. To some extent, this is true. There are more interfaces between modules, but there is less likelihood of breeding the kinds of errors that occur in larger, single module programs. This has to do with the functional strength and data coupling of the modules. These two terms come from Glenford J. Myers (1976) and represent the best forms of module coupling and strength.

Module Strength

Module strength states how well the module conforms to a single function. Single function modules typically are preferable to large single module programs containing multiple functions. Single function modules have functional strength.

FUNCTIONAL STRENGTH. A module possessing functional strength performs only one function. When it fails (they rarely do), it will be located easily and repaired. The programmer can go directly to the errant module and perform the repair.

INFORMATION STRENGTH. A module having informational strength may have many functions that operate on the same data. Each function has a unique entry and exit point. For example, a module that updates a data base may collect statistics on the number of additions, changes, and deletions; these are later retrieved by an audit module via a separate entry point.

COMMUNICATION STRENGTH.   A module possessing communication strength performs many functions that are related by their use of data.

PROCEDURAL STRENGTH.   A module having procedural strength performs many related functions in a logical sequence.

CLASSICAL STRENGTH.   A module having classical strength performs many related functions, but in no logical order.

LOGICAL STRENGTH.   A module possessing logical strength will contain many functions, but only execute them one at a time. An input/output module that handles all files would be an example of classical strength.

COINCIDENTAL STRENGTH.   A module possessing coincidental strength contains many different functions that are totally unrelated. The module is a Frankenstein made of parts from unrelated sources. This is the worst form of coupling; functions with nothing in common should not coexist. A maintenance programmer will someday try and mate them, producing varied mutant offspring.

Module Coupling

Module coupling describes how a mainline module talks to its subroutines and how each subroutine talks to its neighbors. The best form of coupling involves an interface where only the required data are passed from routine to routine. This is known as data coupling.

DATA COUPLING.   Only the required data are passed via a parameter list, not by way of common working storage. This is considered the best form of coupling; interfaces between modules are concise and easily tested.

STAMP COUPLING.   Modules are considered to be stamp coupled when one passes the other an entire data structure rather than just the necessary data items. A module that reads a file and returns a record would be stamp coupled.

EXTERNAL COUPLING.   When both modules refer to the same global data item, such as a data item defined as EXTERNAL, they are considered to be externally coupled. This reduces the module's access from all global data to selected global items.

COMMON COUPLING.   When both modules refer to the same global data structure by means of a FORTRAN COMMON statement, they are considered to be common coupled. Common coupling allows any module to access and modify global data, thereby making maintenance more difficult by expanding the number of places that data can be violated. Similarly, COBOL paragraphs that reference the same common data structure can be considered common coupled. This problem with COBOL paragraphs illustrates why small, single-function modules are preferable to large, multi-function COBOL modules.

CONTENT COUPLING. In this last form of coupling, one module directly references data inside of another module. This is the worst form of coupling; any module can violate any other leaving nothing sacred in either. The use of address constants in IBM assembler language allows content coupling.

1.3. Number of Functions

The number of functions in a program or system should correlate with the number of modules, as previously described, for maximum productivity and quality. The number of functions also says a lot about the capabilities provided to the user and has a direct impact on productivity as described in Chapter 2. Each function must interface with one or more neighboring functions, adding some complexity to each interface. If each function is coded as a separate module, the interfaces are defined carefully rather than obscured by the surrounding code.

1.4. Number of Files

The number of files in a system impact complexity. Consider a single program with a single file in and a single file out. It is perhaps the simplest (see Figure 4.2). In the front comes the crude file and out goes the refined data.

Next comes the program with one input and two outputs (Figure 4.3). As the data is refined, the program has to report on the errors it finds, hence the additional output file. This increases the complexity of the program by requiring the detection and reporting of errors. The error file must be examined later by another program or a human to evaluate the errors found.

Moving on to four-file programs, we encounter the common update program, which merges two files and produces a single output file and an error file (Figure 4.4). The two files must usually be in order, implying a prior sort for each file. Whether these are internal (as in COBOL's SORT verb) or external, they add complexity to the system. The program must have additional logic to keep the two files in sync and report errors when they are not, all of which adds complexity to the system.

In fact, the more files there are per program, the more complex the system will be. So as a gross measure of complexity, ask how many files are there in

FIGURE 4.2.   Data flow of a simple module.

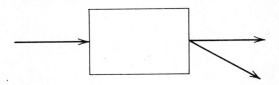

FIGURE 4.3.   Data flow of a module with one input and two outputs.

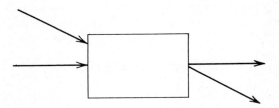

FIGURE 4.4.   Data flow of a module with two input logic.

the system? And as a more refined measure, ask how many files are there per program?

$$\text{system file complexity} = \text{total number of files}$$

$$\text{program file complexity} = \frac{\text{total number of files}}{\text{total number of programs}}$$

In a data-base system, like IBM's IMS, counting each segment accessed should provide a metric similar to the number of files. The important measurement is the number of different accesses to the system's data, not how they are arranged. In a data-base environment, it may be more useful to track the number of data elements, their aggregates, and structures.

$$\text{system data complexity} = \text{number of data elements}$$

$$\text{system database complexity} = \text{number of segments}$$

$$\text{system access complexity} = \text{number of database accesses}$$

$$\text{program access complexity} = \frac{\text{number of data-base accesses}}{\text{total number of programs}}$$

1.5. Number of Program–Program Interfaces

Figure 4.5 shows two programs passing data. There is only one program-to-program interface, simple and easy to understand. Multiply this single interface by several hundred programs and the complexity of who-gives-what-to-whom becomes more difficult and less easy to comprehend. This complexity can weigh heavily on the operations department; if they can't understand the system, how can you expect them to run it reliably? Few systems have the built-in run controls to ensure that the programs run in the proper order with the correct data. They depend on human intervention to certify that the system is ready to continue. This is also a problem: The more human intervention required, the less reliable and continuous the systems is likely to be. These interactions are known as man-machine dialogues.

1.6. Number of Human–Machine Interfaces

How many users will depend on the on-line front end? How many different kinds of users will interpret the reports and take action based on their contents? How many times must an operator communicate directly with the program or inspect the controls output? Each interface allows the human an opportunity to damage the system or for the system to impact the user. Each operational interface can slow the system's throughput and timeliness. Examine the system to identify which programs interface with the user and which with operations. Reducing the complexity of these interfaces will improve the quality and reliability of the system. Each additional interface that requires the user or operations to check the output or input adds complexity to the overall system.

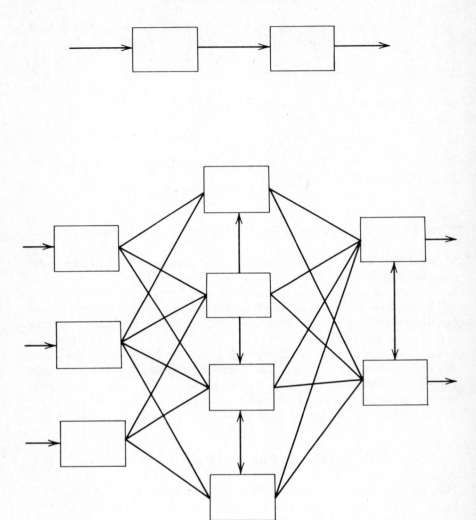

FIGURE 4.5.   Comparison of program interface complexities.

2. CODE COMPLEXITY METRICS

Ever since the first IBM 401 programmer stuck a bunch of wires into a logic board to form a program and another programmer tried to discern what was going on in the mass of wires in front of him, complexity has taken on new meanings. Machine language, assembler language, FORTRAN, COBOL, PL/I, and so on, all have their inherent complexities. Some are easier to use for one application than another. Since the vast majority of a system's costs come from trying to maintain existing code, researchers have invested their energies in quantifying code complexity with excellent results.

There are four major complexity metrics for code: executable lines of code, decisions, McCabe's cyclomatic complexity, and Halstead's Software Science. Halstead's metric is a refinement of counting executable lines of code, while McCabe's is a refinement of counting decisions. Cyclomatic Complexity and Software Science have been shown to be better predictors of complexity than either ELOC or decisions, but ELOC and decisions predate the refinements lending a note of history to the development of these metrics.

2.1. Executable Lines of Code (ELOC)

ELOC has a variety uses: productivity measurement, complexity measurement, and development of other important metrics. From a complexity standpoint, ELOC counts every verb used in the program, forming a basic component of the Halstead Software Science metrics, which will be described further on. Every verb adds an action to the program that the programmer must remember. Every action adds a small amount of complexity to the program.

Research has shown that ELOC has a reasonable correlation to the time it takes to code, enhance, or maintain program code. As such, it is also a reasonable indicator of complexity, but not the best. Its failing has to do with one special type of executable statement: decisions.

2.2. Decisions

Decisions include all of the IF-ELSE, CASE, DOWHILE, and DOUNTIL statements in the program. Each of these has at least two program paths that must be tested, as shown in Figure 4.6. Each test path adds complexity to the program. An IF-ELSE statement is more complex than a simple MOVE or ADD statement: decisions more accurately represent the module's complexity than ELOC; ELOC weights all statements equally.

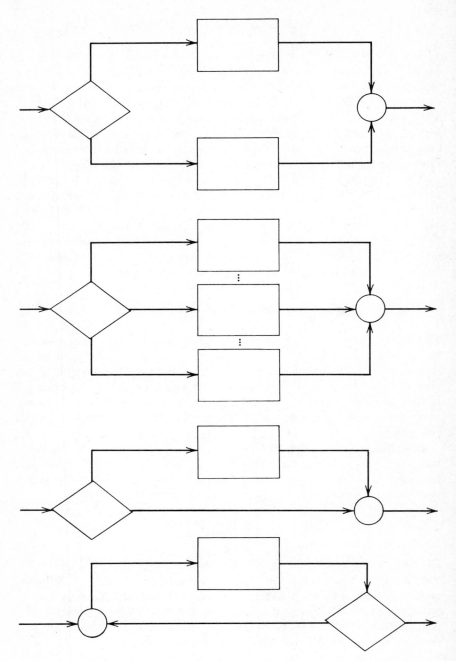

FIGURE 4.6. Test paths in each of the structured decision constructs.

To overcome these problems, use a ratio of decisions to ELOC called decision density to measure code complexity.

$$\text{decision density} = \text{total decisions/ELOC}$$

This metric tells how densely the decisions are packed into the executable lines of code. A decision density less than 5% means that each 100 ELOC has only five decisions; the code should be more easily maintained than a program with 40% decisions.

The number of decisions and the decision density both help clarify the complexity of the module or program. The sum of all decisions is the first approximation of the next metric: McCabe's cyclomatic complexity. It further refines the idea of decisions as a measure of complexity.

2.3.   McCabe's Cyclomatic Complexity

In December of 1976, Thomas McCabe proposed a complexity metric based on mathematical graph theory. The question to be answered was: How to build a modular system with the resulting maintainability and testability? To date, Yourdon had set 50 ELOC as the magical upper limit for program size to limit program complexity, while TRW had fallen on two pages (approximately 100 ELOC) as an upper limit (Boehm, 1974).

McCabe proposed that a program be viewed as a graph with a single entry and a single exit point. Figure 4.7 shows a program with a simple IF-THEN-ELSE construct as a program control graph. Using graph theory, it is possible to state the number of basic paths through the control graph; cyclomatic complexity $V(G)$ becomes:

$$V(G) = e - n + 2p$$

where e = the number of edges in the graph
n = the number of nodes in the graph
p = the number of connected components in the graph

Assuming that p equals one (there is only one module), Figure 4.8 shows the calculation of $V(G)$ for several different control graphs. Note that $V(G)$ does not depend on anything other than the number of decisions. As the number of decisions grows, so grows the cyclomatic complexity. McCabe noted that after viewing a few control graphs, it was possible to identify a programmer's style. Imagine that! Cyclomatic Complexity provides a simple metric to identify style, both its weaknesses and strengths, and suggest improvements. This is a key point of the later chapters on languages and quality.

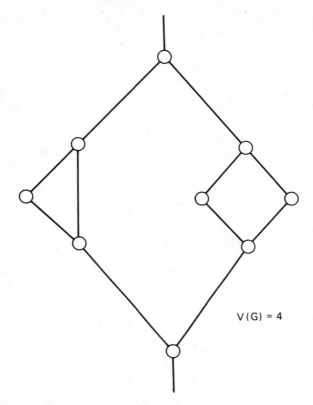

FIGURE 4.7. Example of a control flow graph.

McCabe found that a $V(G)$ less than or equal to 10 seemed to provide reasonably modular programs. Cyclomatic complexities greater than 10 were allowed if the module contained a large case statement: Consider a program that has to anticipate 40 different record types and call subroutines to process each; the cyclomatic complexity would be 41. To examine the complexity of an entire program consisting of many modules, the number of connected components p must equal the number of modules. Or you may sum the complexities of each module to give the same result.

$$V(G) = e - n + 2p$$
$$= V(G1) + V(G2) + V(G3) + \cdots$$

If all of this sounds too complex to calculate, the calculation can be reduced to the following:

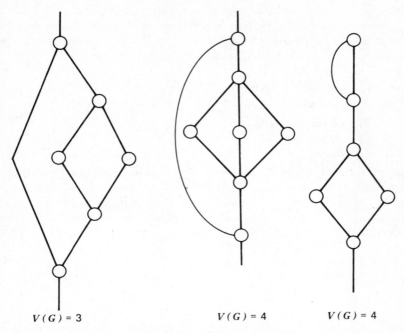

$V(G) = 3$ $V(G) = 4$ $V(G) = 4$

FIGURE 4.8. Cyclomatic complexity calculations for various control flow graphs.

$$V(G) = SUM(\text{Decisions, ANDs, ORs, and NOTs}) + 1$$

"Why the ANDs, ORs, and NOTs?" you might ask. Consider that each may be transformed as follows:

IF A = B AND C = D	IF A = B
	IF C = D
IF A = B OR C = D	IF A = B
	ELSE IF C = D
IF A NOT = B	IF A < B
	ELSE IF A > B

Each AND, OR, and NOT is a thinly veiled IF statement, and as such, each conjunction must be treated as a decision.

The addition of one to $V(G)$ simply implies the existence of the other edge to the program. For example (see Figure 4.9), one IF plus one AND plus one gives a cyclomatic complexity of three—three paths through the module. Graphical analysis of programs has further implications when applied to structured programming. McCabe discovered that there were only four ways to violate structure and produce an unstructured program:

1. Branch out of a decision.
2. Branch into a decision.
3. Branch out of a loop.
4. Branch into a loop.

Each of these are shown in Figure 4.10. What dastardly programming construct allows these violations? The GO TO. So a simple count of the GO TOs in a program will identify the presence or absence of these structure violations. The importance of these structure violations has to do with what McCabe calls reducibility.

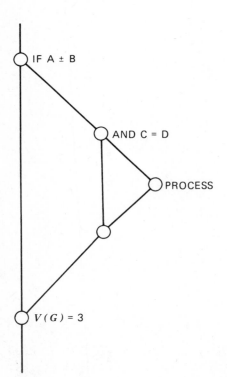

FIGURE 4.9. Effects of ANDs, ORs, and NOTs on control flow.

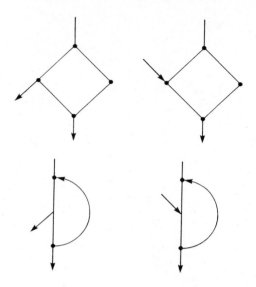

FIGURE 4.10. The four possible structure violations.

When you have a program with a large $V(G)$, it would be good to reduce the complexity of the modules to a $V(G) \leq 10$. This is only possible when the modules have few, if any, structure violations. Figure 4.11 shows a simple flow graph with no structure violations. Its complexity can be reduced if you can draw a circle around any component of the graph that has a single entry and a single exit. This piece can then be moved into a separate subroutine, thereby reducing the complexity of the original module and creating a sub-module of a reasonable complexity. This also forces the creation of a clean interface between the two modules and requires the submodule to have more functional strength. Any structured program can be reduced to a $V(G) = 1$, as shown in Figures 4.12–4.15. The cyclomatic complexity of an unstructured program, on the other hand, must be at least three (see Figure 4.16).

The importance of reducibility has been shown by numerous studies (Baker, 1980; Curtis, 1979). Modules of complexity less than 10 have been shown to contain no errors (Harrison, 1982). By reducing the complexity of your existing modules to values of 10 or less, the maintenance cost of those programs should decrease. Determining the extent of reduction required falls on the presence of decisions and GO TOs in the code. McCabe suggested a metric ev called essential complexity that depicts a module's lack of structure. To determine the essential complexity, you must know the $V(G)$ and the

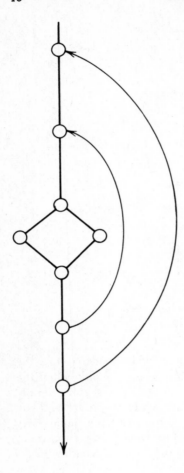

FIGURE 4.11.   Control flow graph of a structure program.

number of subgraphs of a module's flow graph that can be reduced. Figure 4.17 shows an example of an unstructured flow graph with only two removable subgraphs. Essential complexity would be calculated as follows:

$$ev = V(G) - m, \qquad ev = 6 - 2 \text{ (for Figure 4.17)}$$

where $V(G)$ = cyclomatic complexity of the flow graph
        m = number of reducible subgraphs

These two metrics, cyclomatic complexity and essential complexity, tell a great deal about the program or module and its potential maintainability,

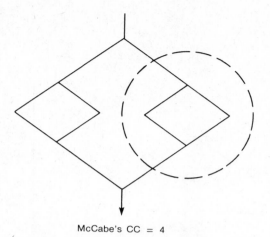

McCabe's CC = 4

FIGURE 4.12. Identifying reducible subgraphs.

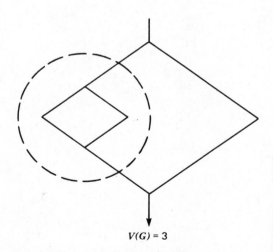

$V(G) = 3$

FIGURE 4.13. First complexity reduction.

71

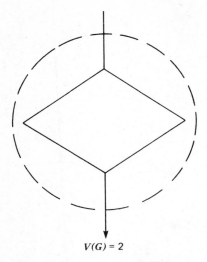

$V(G) = 2$

FIGURE 4.14.   Second complexity
reduction.

$V(G) = 1$

FIGURE 4.15.   Fully reduced flow
graph of a structured module.

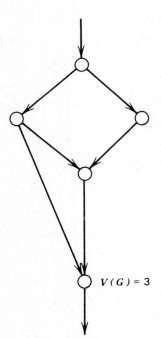

$V(G) = 3$

FIGURE 4.16.   Cyclomatic complexity of unstructured
programs must be at least 3.

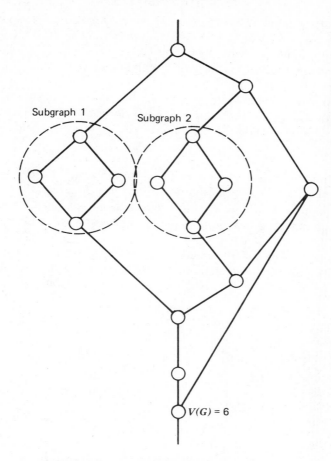

FIGURE 4.17. Determining essential complexity.

flexibility, and reliability. Complexity is the millstone of programming shouldered by every programmer; it should be reduced or eliminated whenever possible.

2.4. Programming's Knotty Problem

Woodward et al. (1979) proposed another method of determining complexity: Anyplace in the program where one control path crosses another, a knot exists. Each "knot" adds complexity to the program that the programmer must untangle to get at the real control flow of the program.

Figure 4.18 shows a COBOL example containing knots. Note that knots come from the use of the GO TO statement. Writing FORTRAN code, in a structured fashion, requires the use of GO TOs, seemingly enforcing the existence of knots. IBM ALC is loaded with branch statements, 15 different kinds.

The number of knots in a program can be calculated fairly easily if you know the beginning and ending line numbers for each branch. Two branches intersect, creating a knot, if their line numbers (a,b) and (c,d) meet the following criteria:

1. minimum $(a,b) <$ minimum$(c,d) <$ maximum(a,b) and
   maximum$(c,d) >$ maximum(a,b) (see Figure 4.18)
2. minimum $(a,b) <$ maximum$(c,d) <$ maximum(a,b) and
   minimum$(c,d) >$ minimum(a,b) (see Figure 4.19)

The knot metric has an advantage over McCabe's metrics in that a simple reordering of the code can often reduce the number of knots, thereby reducing the program's complexity while improving its readability.

```
10 LABEL1.
       statements
50         GO TO LABEL2.
       statements
100        GO TO LABEL3.
       statements
150 LABEL2.
       statements
200 LABEL3.
       statements
```

min(50,150) < min(100,200) < max(50,150) and
max(100,200) > max(50,150)

FIGURE 4.18. Determining knots in code.

```
10 LABEL1.
       statements
50         GO TO LABEL2.
       statements
100        GO TO LABEL1.
       statements
150 LABEL2.
       statements
```

min(50,150) < max(100,10) < max(50,150) and
min(100,10) < min(50,150)

FIGURE 4.19. Determining knots in code.

2.5. Halstead's Software Science

Halstead's software science equations (summarized in Figure 4.20) were introduced as a basis for productivity measurement in Chapter 2. But they are also an excellent indicator of program complexity. The software science metrics that indicate complexity are vocabulary, length, volume, difficulty, language level, and effort.

The *vocabulary* of a program consists of the total number of unique operators and operands. A larger vocabulary means that the programmer will need to learn more words to understand, code, or maintain the program. The African Grey parrot has a maximum vocabulary of 5,000 words; an average human knows 20,000, while the English language contains over 300,000 words. Using words, data names, and literals that the average programmer does not know will make reading more difficult.

The problem with computer programs is that the vocabulary changes from program to program. The basic operators stay the same, but the data names change at the whim of the programmer. That is why data dictionaries are so successful: They restrict the vocabulary of operands the programmers may use to develop a program. By restricting the vocabulary, they help reduce complexity.

n_1 = Number of unique operators (verbs)
n_2 = Number of unique operands (data names and literals)
N_1 = Total number of operators
N_2 = Total number of operands

Vocabulary = $n_1 = n_1 + n_2$

Length = $N = N_1 + N_2$

Estimated length = $N = n_1 \log_2 n_1 + n_2 \log_2 n_2$

Volume = $V = N \log_2 n$

Difficulty = $D = \dfrac{n_2 * N_2}{2 * n_2}$

Language level = $\lambda = V / D^2$

Information content = $I = V / D$

Effort = $E = D * V$

FIGURE 4.20. Calculation of software science metrics.

Length is the sum of all occurrences of the operators and operands. If you were to count all of the words in this book, you would then have its length. I know people who will never pick up a novel in a book store if it is more than 500 pages in length. "Takes too long to read," they say. Or they lose the plot, and so on. The same is true of a computer program; programmers may fail to pick up a program and try to fix it simply due to its size. They too may lose the plot halfway through the module and have to retrace their steps to get back to where they were, and often they end up in some other part of the program. I have entered many a program that others consider impossible to understand or maintain and fixed bugs that have been there since the program was first written. But I also like to read 1000 page novels and am always disappointed when they end.

Length has been studied by numerous researchers (Feuer, 1979; Christensen, 1981). They have all found a correlation between length and the complexity of the program. *Volume* is merely a derivative of vocabulary and length, so it also represents program complexity. Christensen et al. (1981) found that executable lines of code, length, and vocabulary were all equal measures of program size, and size means added complexity.

Difficulty, a function of the vocabulary and total number of operands, expresses the psychological complexity involved in writing or maintaining a chunk of code. Thus difficulty is also a complexity metric. Difficulty is actually the inverse of Halstead's original metric *level*. An increasing difficulty is more easily understood than a decreasing fractional *level* metric.

Assembler language is considered more complex than COBOL. Why is that? Can difficulty provide a way to quantify the difference in complexity? Yes, it can. Consider the equation of difficulty:

$$D = n_1/2 * N_2/n_2$$

The number of unique operators is represented by n_1. IBM assembler language has over 250 operators, while COBOL has only 50. Putting these values into the equation, it is easy to see that an assembler language program could have a complexity five times greater than a COBOL program just by reason of the number of operators. A common reason for increasing difficulty in COBOL program is the use of the GO TO (Christensen, 1981; Fitsos, 1980). Once you have a GO TO that heads toward the end of paragraph, as shown in Figure 4.21, you then need an EXIT statement. You now have two additional operators, the GO TO and EXIT. And then you sometimes find a GO TO modified by an ALTER statement. None of these operators are required in a structured program.

Christensen et al. also found that difficulty increases due to six basic code "impurities": complementary or unnecessary operations, the use of ambigu-

```
PARAGRAPH-NAME.
   statements
   IF EXIT-CONDITION
       GO TO PARAGRAPH-NAME-EXIT.
   statements
       .
       .
       .

PARAGRAPH-NAME-EXIT.
   EXIT.
```

FIGURE 4.21. Example of a GO TO structure violation.

ous operands, use of synonymous operands, reuse of common subexpressions, unnecessary assignment of operands, and the use of unfactored expressions. These impurities can be found and possibly fixed mechanically. Removing these kinds of redundancies is the basis of optimizing compilers. The following examples should help clarify the meaning of each impurity.

Complimentary operation	$A = (C + D) * B/[(E + F) * B]$
	$A = (C + D)/(E + F)$
Ambiguous operands	$A = B + C; A = A + A$
	$A = (B + C) * 2$
Synonymous operands	$A = B * C; D = B * C; E = A * D$
	$E = (B * C)^2$
Common subexpressions	$E = (B * C) * (B * C)$
	$E = (B * C)^2$
Unnecessary assignment	$A = (B * C); E = A * A$
	$E = (B * C)^2$
Unfactored expressions	$A = B^2 + 2 * B * C + C^2$
	$A = (B + C)^2$

Based on what has been shown here, it should be possible to reduce the difficulty, and therefore complexity, of any program by removing GO TOs and the six code impurities. In existing programs that have undergone maintenance for several years, the reduction in difficulty may be as much as $50-75\%$. The number of executable lines of code may be reduced from 10 to 30%. This has been my experience; yours may be different.

The *language level* indicates how well a programmer uses the language at hand. The equation for language level is:

$$\text{language level} = \text{volume}/(\text{difficulty})^2$$

Language level increases as the programmer uses the more powerful features of the language instead of coding the same thing with more simple statements. As an example, a COBOL programmer may code a loop with indexes and GO TOs or he or she may use the PERFORM verb. The loop using the PERFORM verb will have a language level four to five times higher than the hand-coded loop.

A high language level usually indicates that the programmer used the most elegant features of the language, causing the resulting program to be easily read, maintained, and enhanced. A programmer who uses tricky code will degrade the language level metric. Thus this metric helps say something about complexity: a low language level implies a higher complexity, while a high language level implies a lower complexity.

Remembering that the software science equations apply across language barriers, numerous researchers have studied each of the current programming languages. The results, summarized by Christensen et al. (1981) showed that the language level ran from 0.81 to 0.91 for APL and IBM assembler language, to 2.07 for PL/S and COBOL. Fortran's language level was found to be 1.14. PL/I measured 1.53, which is less than PL/S, a subset of the full language. The reduction in PL/I language level is due to the additional operators available to the programmers. Based on these results and given the choice, you should use COBOL, PL/S, or PL/I as your main language because of the reduction in complexity.

Last but not least comes the *effort* metric. The effort metric predicts how many "elementary mental discriminations" a person will have to make to write or understand a program. Since the number of mental discriminations varies from 5 to 18 per second, effort will vary from programmer to programmer, but we already know that. The effort metric,

$$\text{effort} = \text{volume} * \text{difficulty}$$

gives a feeling of program complexity in units of time that it will take to write, modify, or maintain the code. Researchers have found a strong correlation between the effort metric and complexity (Feuer, 1979; Christensen, 1981).

3. SUMMARY

Complexity is the major obstacle facing programmers every day. System, program, and code level metrics can help identify problems and how to go about fixing them.

System level metrics include the number of programs, modules, functions, files, program−program interfaces, and human−machine interfaces. Program complexity metrics include the number of executable lines of code, decisions, McCabe's cyclomatic complexity, and Halstead's software science equations. Collecting each of these metrics will help identify both the existence of complexity and ways to reduce it in future and existing systems.

CHAPTER FIVE

CORRECTNESS METRICS

The correctness metric indicates the degree to which a program satisfies the user's specifications. Does it do what you want? Correctness is a function of three underlying metrics criteria: completeness, consistency, and traceability.

$$correctness = F(completeness, consistency, traceability)$$

To a large degree, correctness can be determined from testing and production use of the system. To a lesser degree, code metrics may provide some information, while definition and design walk-throughs provide the earliest indicators of correctness.

1. COMPLETENESS

Completeness recognizes those software attributes that provide a full implementation of the functions required. At the code level there are numerous measurements that reflect completeness. The primary focus, however, rests in the definition and design phases of development. If the full implementation of a function is not specified early on, then by the time the function gets to the coding phase, no amount of good coding will save the design from failure.

1.1. Error Tracking

One of the best ways to understand and improve correctness is by tracking the number and types of functions either left out, or inadequately defined, during the definition and design phases. What functions should have been in the definition? Which were omitted from the design phase? The definition is the earliest point that the user specifies what needs to be done—what functions need to exist in the system to meet their needs. By tracking omitted and incomplete functions that are discovered during design, code, test, and production, you will probably find a small group of common omissions and a large but infrequent group of dissimilar omissions. The small group can be incorporated into your definition process to eliminate their future occurrence. The infrequent problems may cluster around specific clients: Marketing always forgets that they need 15-minute response on "What if?" queries; Accounting rarely specifies exactly how the inputs and outputs should balance, and so on.

Error tracking can be mechanized; numerous software systems exist to do so. Mechanized error tracking provides the basis for change management. You will know what kinds of problems occur and where they appear in the development process. The same tracking system can be used for controlling change to existing systems, providing data about why programs change. This data can then be enhanced with estimated and actual time worked to resolve the problem in a development environment or to enhance a program in the maintenance environment. Once mechanized, error tracking can be coupled to the other metrics programs, providing a way to correlate the data about a developing system. This will help validate the existing metrics and possibly point out other metrics that indicate correctness.

1.2. Walk-Throughs

Walk-throughs are the inspection procedure that identifies the missing functions in definitions, design, and code. Manufacturing industries review definitions, designs, blueprints, and the like for errors before they enter any form of production. They know that eliminating errors will cut the costs of incorrect production runs, scrap, rework, and general loss of revenue when their products fail to meet the needs of the purchaser. Your inspection teams should be as ruthless as these manufacturing teams are.

Analysts and programmers, however, often invite their friends and neighbors to definition, design, and code walkthroughs. Because they are no more firmly grounded in what is good, bad, or missing from the design, and they don't want to offend us ("We're friends aren't we?"), they simply note the minor problems like typos and sentence structure, completely avoiding the issue at hand. The major value of inspections comes from reducing future costs. The focus of the walk-through is to find everything possible that is wrong. Without proper feedback, programmers and analysts can never improve. By reducing future costs, you improve the company's profitability and increase your chances of greater reward. Conversely, if you are a nice guy to your friend, letting errors slip through, you are contributing to your company's reduced earnings or ultimate collapse.

For these reasons, not only is it important to examine definitions, designs, and code within the work group, but occasionally you will also need quality reviewers to drop in uninvited to audit the reviewers. These quality inspectors show management's support of good quality and the avoidance of rework, scrap, and the other plagues of software development. They are not meant to act as Big Brother, constantly watching everyone for failure.

The quality team must also collect and analyze the error tracking reports to provide a correct picture of the common and infrequent problems that occur during definition, design, and code. These then serve to direct the improvement of these phases of development and to stimulate training for the client and IS department.

1.3. Design

The use of common designs further represents the presence of completeness. Common modules usually are designed to fully and correctly implement the function required; uniquely designed modules and programs may not do this. When measuring design completeness, it would be useful to know the percentage of modules that are generic in the design. As this percentage climbs, the design completeness probably increases as well. If there are reusable modules in the design other than the generic ones, then these should be examined to ensure completeness. A minor investment will reap large gains when the module is included in other programs. The use of common designs also implies that common reusable modules will be used during the coding phase.

1.4. Coding

Completeness comes from a variety of coding techniques. In COBOL, the use of ROUNDED, REMAINDER, and GIVING options of arithmetic statements provides a more complete implementation of these functions. The use of the ON OVERFLOW options of the COBOL arithmetic statements will provide further evidence of completeness. In any language, the use of built-in functions will also indicate completeness. For example, a COBOL SORT will provide more complete implementation of the function than a manually coded sort.

Completeness also depends on the decision structure and error handling facilities of the program. For example, every IF should have a matching ELSE; every READ and SEARCH should have an AT END; and in PL/I, every SELECT should have an OTHERWISE. Each of these examples provides a more complete implementation of the code. The erratic application of these options leads to the next measure of correctness—consistency.

2. CONSISTENCY

Consistency identifies those software attributes that provide uniform design and implementation techniques and documentation. Consistency begins with the definition and design processes. If the client uses hand-written ruled-paper definitions all of the time, then you have consistency. If the client uses a requirements statement language and a computer system to process it, then you also have consistency. The latter may be preferable, but the former still presents a consistent interface to your designers.

2.1. Design

Similarly, do your analysts use a standard design methodology? If one group of analysts uses input-process-output (IPO) documentation and data-flow diagrams, while another group uses Nassi–Schneiderman diagrams, you lack consistency. Standards serve to select a consistent method or way of doing business. Sure, the different techniques may all lead to a working product, but you also lose the freedom of interchanging people to meet your resource needs.

During design walk-throughs, the participants should look for consistent application of common designs, data names, and so on. If these functions are applied uniformly throughout the system, it will improve the comprehension of the system maintainers, thereby reducing the maintenance costs. Inconsistent application of common functions should be corrected to reduce implementation costs: Common designs should have common modules, while unique designs require complete development of new modules—an expensive process that should be avoided as much as possible.

2.2. Code

Coding standards are another necessary ingredient of consistency. In Chapter 18 you will find some beneficial rules that improve programming style and code quality. Incorporate them into your coding standards. Some of these basic rules involve using standard modules for common functions like updates, reports, edits, and data selection; using COPY statements to include common data structures and linkage sections; using compiler formating statements to make the listing more readable; and using consistent commenting conventions to document the code.

If you feel that you need to use only one language, rather than many, to reduce your training costs and to improve consistency, you must answer the following questions: Does it support all of the structured programming constructs? Is it well supported on my hardware? The only language that meets these needs in the IBM environment is PL/I. Assembler language, COBOL, and FORTRAN fail the structured programming question. The new COBOL standard (198X) should pass if it is ever approved. The use of procedural and nonprocedural fourth-generation languages is another matter altogether. Choose these languages based on your need for productivity and flexibility of the new system.

3. TRACEABILITY

For a system to be measurably correct, it must be possible to trace the user's requirements to certain parts of the system. This is imperative when providing contract software. Traceability provides a link from the requirements to the implemented software, a link which has not been mechanized to my knowledge. Requirement statement languages like PSL/PSA and design languages like Higher Order Software (HOS) USE-IT are working toward this goal, but none have arrived. Thus it is up to you to build this into your development methodology.

Why is this important? Well, if you have a problem with the results from program A, then you need to trace back to the design and further to the definition to discover where the error entered the system. Was it a definition error? Did the designer overlook something in the requirements? Did the coder misinterpret the design? Can we prevent this from happening in the future? How?

Furthermore, you will want to keep the system definition and program designs up-to-date; so you will need to go back and correct these when an error is found in the program. Also, if an error is later found in the definition, you will want to look forward into the code to correct the problem or omission.

Error tracking, as described in Section 1, provides a method for documenting troubles and their sources. The problem determination is still left to the analyst or programmer, but the act of tracking each problem will help prevent the same error in the future.

Another method of tracing user requirements involves the use of data dictionaries. Use of this tool from the requirements specification to the final product will ensure consistent naming conventions and allow tracking from the definition phase, through design, to implementation. Data-flow diagrams should provide a visual picture of the data flow and processing—a blueprint of the system's traceability.

The mechanized code analyzers can also be used to extract the data names and literals used in each module or program. This information can be used to verify the information contained in the data dictionary or to create it if none exists. Since these analyzers must look for data names and literals to calculate many of the software quality metrics, they can also write these data items onto a file for further processing.

The mechanized analyzers also provide information about the uses of GOTOs. Is the structure violated by branching into or out of a loop or decision? If so, the traceability of the program's structure decreases. The number of GOTOs, combined with the cyclomatic complexity (described in Chapter 3), will help quantify the traceability of a module's code and therefore the traceability and correctness of the entire system.

4. SUMMARY

The measurement of correctness falls mainly into the definition and design phases of project development. In the absence of mechanized methods of requirements specification, manual inspection by team members, with occasional quality assurance audits, will serve to identify the correctness of the design or definition. The major method of identifying correctness in these early phases involves error and omission tracking with a mechanized system. The results of this tracking, when analyzed by quality assurance will help identify weak spots in the development methodology and implement corrective actions. Analysis may also indicate projects that suffer from too many errors and omissions that may need quality assurance involvement before the system goes into the design or code phases of development.

Once in the coding phase, static analysis of the code can identify the use a language's features to enhance completeness, consistency, and traceability. Coding walk-throughs provide manual inspections of the code to verify its correctness. Error tracking from this phase of development will pinpoint further areas for improvement.

Correctness is one of the most important metrics and yet one of the hardest to quantify. The measurement of correctness will become more exact as the definition and design processes become more automated. But there is plenty of data to collect, measure, and analyze from the existing process.

CHAPTER SIX

EFFICIENCY METRICS

With the declining cost of hardware, efficiency no longer plays the part it did 15 years ago, but it should not be ignored either. It still impacts the user's perception of on-line systems and the expenses involved with running an application system. Efficiency measurement indicates the amount of computer resources required to perform a user-defined function. Does the software run on your hardware as well as it can? Efficiency is a function of three underlying metrics: concision, execution efficiency, and operability.

$$\text{efficiency} = F(\text{concision, execution efficiency, operability})$$

To a large degree, efficiency can be determined directly from the code and only indirectly from the design.

The hardest thing for most people to accept about efficiency is that it doesn't matter that much anymore in business application programming. It is still important in systems programming, but the overriding concern is whether people can maintain the software or not. Efficiency has some bearing on programming for microcomputers, but with the advances in chip and storage technology, this too will pass.

Before proceeding with efficiency enhancements, the programmer, analyst, and manager must determine if the effort is really worthwhile. Using Pareto analysis, they can determine if the program is one of the 20% that generate 80% of the operating costs. If so, they can proceed to expend the programming resources to fix the problem.

To identify these cost-prone programs, the development or maintenance staff should first examine the system log information for all of the programs run in the operating center. Which applications cost the most to run? Which programs run most frequently? Which systems consume the most disk storage? Which ones generate the most paper? And so on. From this information, the managers may choose to invest in efficiency enhancements. The user may also choose to invest in efficiency enhancements based on this information. In the IBM world, products like KOMMAND read the system logs and generate information about all of the jobs and programs run during the month. Extracting the information to identify resource-gobbling programs is simple. CPU and execution time are readily available.

Programmers should use instrumentation of the code or tools like the CAPEX Optimizer III COBOL compiler to determine the exact locations of the inefficiencies. The analyst and programmer then initiate the changes that offer the best possibility of improving the efficiency. These changes should be concerned with concision, execution efficiency, and operability.

1. CONCISION

Concision recognizes those software attributes that implement a function in the minimum amount of code. Optimizing compilers, being what they are, often produce more efficient code from COBOL or PL/I than an average assembler programmer can in ALC; thus there is no reason to code in assembler language unless you want to saddle the company with expensive maintenance costs.

The choice of language can greatly affect concision. A single COBOL or PL/I statement may convert to five ALC instructions; the single COBOL statement is more concise. Similarly, the use of compiler and locally developed functions, such as SORT, MERGE, or SQRT( ), increases the functionality and concision of a program. A SORT statement represents several hundred lines of executable code. Similarly, a RAMIS, FOCUS, or MARKIV program will be more concise than the equivalent COBOL or PL/I code, often by a factor of 10:1. And because of the attention to efficiency in these fourth-generation languages, the program may again execute faster than the equivalent COBOL program coded by an average programmer. So, the use of a language's function statements implies concision and, usually, efficiency. These are easily measured by a static program analyzer.

2. EXECUTION EFFICIENCY

Execution efficiency examines those software attributes that minimize processing time. The use of compiler function libraries will indicate execution efficiency. These routines are usually programmed for maximum efficiency. The presence of these functions can be determined directly from the code. The presence of inefficient compiler functions, like the INSPECT verb, can also be indicated.

2.1. Numeric Data

The next major source of efficiency, at least in the IBM environment, comes from the representation of numeric data. There are three forms of numeric data: display, packed decimal, and binary. Display format should only be used for data directly input by the user or output to the user. In all other phases of processing, it should be retained in packed decimal or binary format. The reason for requiring these formats involves the machine's method of processing numbers: To add two display numbers, it must first convert them to packed decimal, an expensive operation, then add them, and finally convert the result to display (UNPACK) and store the value. Although trivial for a single ADD or SUBTRACT, when multiplied by the calculations in a complex numerical algorithm, these conversions can consume a large quantity of CPU resources. I occasionally find a person using a display item as an index. The compiler has to convert the number to packed decimal and then to binary before it can calculate the index. If you increment or decrement the index, the machine converts the code from display to packed decimal to binary and all the way back again. This is extremely inefficient.

The use of efficient data representations can be obtained by static analysis of the data definitions in the program. In COBOL, the use of COMP-3 (packed decimal) and COMP (binary) in relation to the total number of PICTURE 9 (numeric) data items provides a feeling for the programmer's concern or understanding of efficiency. In PL/I, the use of FIXED DECIMAL and BINARY versus the number of display numeric items will indicate the efficiency of the code.

$$\text{percent efficient data types} = \frac{\text{total(COMP or COMP-3)}}{\text{total(PIC 9)}}$$

I have found a few programs with either very complex algorithms or extensive table, and therefore index, processing that used display numeric data exclusively. A simple transformation of the data items reduced the CPU and wall time by 50−80%. A more detailed examination of data efficiencies can be found in Chapters 19−21 describing efficient methods for each programming language.

2.2. Procedural Efficiencies

Structured programming, much to everyone's surprise, tends to produce more efficient programs than those coded with GO TOs. Intuitively, this seems reasonable because the flow of data and its processing is optimized. Extensive use of GO TOs causes code duplication and often multiple executions. For example, an unstructured program might have five to ten different edits for the Social Security number field, verifying it before each function that uses it. A structured program would have only one such edit.

Another source of procedural inefficiencies involves the loop nesting structure. Loops within loops are executed many more times than their parent loop. Whenever possible, it is helpful to move code out of these loops or rewrite them to improve efficiency.

The best way to locate and control efficiency problems is to first write the program in the most maintainable style possible. Then, once the program is working, examine the workings of the code with an analyzer—Boole and Babbage, or the CAPEX ANALYZER COBOL compiler. These will identify the major resource consumers in the program. Once you know where the hot spots are, you can decide whether or not to spend the time to tune those areas or not. Once the major efficiency problems have been resolved, quit.

3. OPERABILITY

In an IBM business application systems environment, most programs run at the speed of the input and output; the CPU is rarely ever taxed by a complex scientific algorithm. So the efficiencies, in an operational environment, are derived from optimizing the storage and throughput of data. The other major efficiencies evolve from high-quality operational documentation, strong run controls, and a low incidence of failure and reruns.

3.1. Input/Output

Storing data in the most efficient format, as previously described, results in some operational benefits: a seven-place numeric stored as a display item takes up seven bytes; the same packed decimal item takes only four. Storing true/false indicators in bits instead of bytes also reduces the size of the data. This can be done efficiently in PL/I. As a general rule, the most efficient format for data will take up the least space on disk or tape and increase throughput on I/O channels. The presence or absence of efficient data formats is easily obtainable from static code analyzers.

Eliminating redundant data also reduces the amount of storage required. How often do you see data passed from program to program, without change, simply because the report program will need the information? Pass this data to the report program directly rather than through a succession of intermediaries. This will reduce I/O time and prevent the intervening programs from making radical changes to the data or from omitting it completely.

Integrated data bases are another method of reducing data redundancy and inaccuracy. If the accounting and payroll systems use much of the same data, an integrated data base prevents redundancy while ensuring that data need only be entered once, not two or three times to different systems. The inaccuracies from multiple entry points is alleviated. It is worthwhile, however, to increase the amount of validation that occurs—one invalid data item affects not one system, but many.

The use of data control block (DCB) information will also affect the efficiency of a program when using sequential files. First, the blocking factor affects how efficiently the data is stored on tape or disk. There are optimal blocking sizes for tape and disk based on what medium is used. Second, the use of variable spanned (VS) format will ensure that variable records use every available byte of the disk. Finally, the number of main memory buffers available per file impact the program's efficiency. Most of the time, two optimized length buffers are enough, but some programs go through these in no time at all; an additional buffer or two may be needed to maximize throughput. Each of these factors may be determined from static analysis of the job control language (JCL). The optimization of the blocking factors and buffers should be left to the operations personnel. An execution analyzer will help pinpoint many of these problems.

Another method to reduce input/output bottlenecks involves the use of data storage optimizers such as SHRINK and SHRINK/IMS. These can reduce the amount of data stored by 50% or more. This reduction will speed the flow of data over I/O channels and reduce your hardware requirements. The overhead for the package is minimal while the benefits are impressive. There is only one problem: portability. Programs with internal calls to SHRINK or IMS depend on the I/O methodology. Porting them to another type of hardware will be difficult.

3.2. Operational Documentation

For the computer center to know how to run a system and what to do when it breaks down, some form of documentation is needed. The more consistent and informative the documentation, the better the center will be able to run the program or system. Program error messages and their corresponding corrective actions should be clearly stated, while the validation of the run controls should also be described clearly.

3.3. Run Controls

A system without run controls is like an airplane without instruments—it will fly, but I'd hate to fly it at night or in foul weather. Run controls govern whether a program should run, when it should run, and in what sequence it runs in relation to its neighbors. Run controls should print out, in a common format, the number of records read, processed, added, changed, deleted, output, and so on. Furthermore, it should tell the names of each module executed and the release and level number of the source code it was created from and the date compiled. The presence or absence of common run controls and audit trails can be determined by static analysis of the code.

3.4. System Failure and Reruns

Another major operational inefficiency comes from program aborts and system reruns. Program failure is really the domain of reliability analysis (more about that in Chapter 12). But you can collect data on program failures and the cost and extent of system reruns. This data should aid a Pareto analysis of which systems, programs, or whatever are causing the majority of reruns and rework that occurs in the operations environment. Corrective action can then rectify the systems in error.

4. SUMMARY

Efficiency problems involve not only the CPU and input/output activities of a program or system, but also the interface presented to the operations group and the cost of system reruns. The cost of program inefficiency has been long overrated, while the cost of operations productivity and rework has been largely ignored by IS technicians. Careful Pareto analysis of the factors causing inefficiency will lead to improved methodology and technology to reduce or eliminate much of the waste.

Concise languages provide efficiency benefits as do concise statements. Concise functional statements improve maintenance productivity while performing more efficiently than hand-coded loops, sorts, and so on. Concision can be determined directly from the code via mechanized analysis.

Execution efficiency depends on data definitions and procedural flow, both of which, can be largely determined from dynamic analysis with execution analyzers and static analysis of the code.

Operability determines the ease or difficulty of operating the software once it has been placed in production. Much of the inefficiency in existing systems stems from the people who operate the program and the type of hardware it runs on. Operability metrics seek to reduce this inefficiency.

Efficiency can be obtained without sacrificing maintainability or quality in most application systems. This may not be true in the development and maintenance of operating systems or other system software. Efficiency should definitely become an integral part of any quality improvement program.

CHAPTER SEVEN

FLEXIBILITY METRICS

Enhancements are usually 80−90% of the maintenance work done on existing systems. Adjusting this to account for new development work, enhancements generate 75% of the typical costs incurred by an IS department. Understanding what makes programs difficult or easy to enhance will provide significant cost reductions. New programs should be coded to provide flexibility while the existing programs that change continually can be modified to improve flexibility. Software measurement provides the necessary tools to quantify flexibility.

Flexibility metrics indicate how much effort it will take to enhance a module, program, or system. Can you change it? Flexibility is a function of the submetrics that affect program enhancement: complexity, concision, consistency, expandability, generality, modularity, self-documentation, and simplicity.

flexibility = F(complexity, concision, consistency, expandability, generality, modularity, self-documentation, simplicity)

1. COMPLEXITY

Complexity recognizes those software attributes that decrease a program's or module's clarity. The three most important metrics of complexity are Halstead's software science, McCabe's cyclomatic complexity, and ELOC. These three metrics are described in Chapter 4. Code complexity affects its flexibility in many ways.

As a module's complexity increases, the programmer will have increasing difficulty understanding where to place new enhancements. To restrict complexity, you may find it necessary to place upper limits on the major metrics of complexity. I have found modules to be more maintainable when: The software science difficulty metric is less than 10, effort is less than 10,000, the cyclomatic complexity is less than 20, and ELOC is under 100. These are only general boundaries. The actual boundaries will vary from module to module and function to function. For example, the process of editing input data often takes several hundred lines of executable code and at least one decision for each input field. A single function, like editing, can rarely be decomposed into subfunctions, but it may well exceed these general bounds. A well-structured update module should fit these bounds, however. A report program, with header, trailer, and line formatting routines, should easily fit within these bounds. Use your own experience with these metrics to establish some upper bound as a checkpoint; a module whose metrics fall outside this limit should be reviewed.

2. CONCISION

Concision identifies those software attributes that implement a function in the minimum amount of code. Anytime a single statement can represent the equivalent of many lines of code, it becomes easier to grasp its meaning and purpose. Once a programmer can easily understand the code, he or she can also perform enhancements with relative ease.

Take the different languages as an example. A single COBOL statement can easily represent several assembler statements; therefore, it is more concise to write in COBOL than ALC. Similarly, a single fourth-generation statement may equal several hundred lines of COBOL code. The concision of these languages makes COBOL easier to enhance than assembler and nonprocedural languages more flexible than COBOL. Based on this knowledge, you would want to prototype new systems in a nonprocedural language, changing quickly to meet the needs of the developing system. If necessary, you would then want to code the final product in COBOL or PL/I for efficiency and to meet needs not met by the fourth-generation product.

To determine flexibility within a language you would focus on the macros, compiler functions, CALLs, and PERFORM statements that make up the available functions. Function statements act like sign posts to the maintenance programmer; if they need to change some part of the program that deals with editing incoming transactions, then a function will point the way to the correct location to begin work.

CALL 'VALIDATE' USING TRANSACTION-RECORD.

The concise statement directs the programmer quickly to the area for enhancement, no wasted time. Functions statements within the VALIDATE routine will further reduce the amount of code to understand and change. The enhancement may ultimately be restricted to less than 50 ELOC, without the programmer ever needing to know the entire program.

But not all modules of a program should contain function statements. Those modules at the bottom of the hierarchy may not have any functions; they are the drones that do the exacting work. The top module, on the other hand, is the driver; it should call functions to do the work. It is the manager, not the worker. To understand the difference between driver and subordinate functions, it is useful to look at a metric that I call function density.

$$\text{function density} = (\text{number of functions} / \text{ELOC}) * 100\%$$

As the number of functions per 100 ELOC increases, the flexibility of the code also increases. A driver module may have a high function density and the worker module may have a low value. Figure 7.1 shows how function density changes throughout a program's structure. The driver module has a large

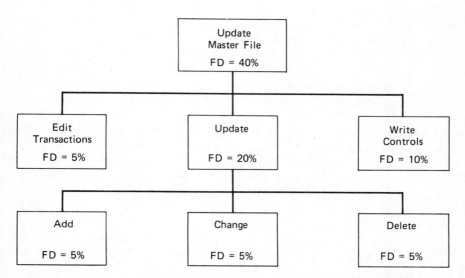

FIGURE 7.1.   How the function density metric varies within a module or program.

number of function statements in relation to its total ELOC. The sub-modules—edit, update, select, and report—have lower function densities because they do more work. Finally, the add, change, and delete modules have the lowest function density, because they are doing all of the detailed work. Function statements concisely represent what the code is going to do; function density reflects how concisely an entire module or program states what it is going to do. Function density is a good indicator of a program's flexibility.

3. CONSISTENCY

Consistency provides uniform design and implementation techniques and documentation. If programmers all follow the same programming style and data-naming standards, you will observe consistency. If the analysts use a select group of design documentation standards and tools, you will also experience consistency. Flexibility benefits accrue from this common approach to doing: Programmers need only learn a select group of design documents; their comprehension is increased simply by the use of a selected few design techniques. The programmers who maintain and enhance the code also experience better understanding from a common coding style.

You should use design and coding standards. Adherence to standards that can be measured either manually or mechanically indicates consistency; in turn, consistency represents flexibility. Design consistency tells whether you use data-flow diagrams, IPOs, structure charts, Warnier–Orr diagrams or whatever uniformly throughout your department. Coding standards may require specific ways of coding the five structured coding constructs, methods of indenting code for readability, and other commenting and formatting restrictions that improve the flexibility of the code.

If you use standard designs and code for most newly developed programs, these too represent consistency. Their absence implies a nonstandard, and therefore suspect, module or program. Consistency may extend into testing and conversion. Is regression testing possible? Can you recreate any test, over and over again, and compare the outputs mechanically for correctness? Do you always release and install the new system in the same way, or is it done haphazardly? Each of these questions reflects a degree of uncertainty about consistency. You can probably think of dozens more. Why do you think structured programming and project management have been so successful when developing new products? Consistency. And this same trait carries over into the enhancement of the software; consistency improves flexibility.

4. EXPANDABILITY

Expandability recognizes those software attributes that provide for expansion of the data or the program's functions. Enhancements are an expansion of the program's capabilities, so flexibility goes hand in hand with expansion. As a module becomes larger and more complex, expanding its function becomes more and more difficult. It is like loading a camel: At first it is easy; then, it becomes harder to find a place to strap on more cargo. Finally, the camel collapses from the sheer weight of its burden. Your programmers are tired of playing the camel.

In ALC, the program may run out of base registers and available storage. In COBOL, the program may be too large to compile, or your data records may exceed the limits of the machine. No more expansion is then possible.

4.1. Data Expansion

The use of a data dictionary and data-base management system usually increase the ability to expand a program beyond its current data requirements. Data dictionaries provide common naming conventions and data descriptions. These are then combined to form the record structures required by all of the system's programs. If field X needs to increase to seven numeric positions, you change the data dictionary, generate the revised data structures, recompile and relink the system, and you are done.

Data-base management systems allow relatively simple expansion of the data structures it contains. Supplied conversion programs transfer the data from the old structure to the new structure without significant programming. Sequential files, on the other hand, have to be updated by a special, hand-crafted conversion program, thereby reducing the productive hours available for meaningful work.

4.2. Functional Expansion

The use of generic designs and code indicates the capacity for further expansion—the new function may be CALLed from an existing routine without much work. Fourth-generation languages provide for simple expansion: Just add another line or two, each containing a function, and the program is functionally greater than before. In COBOL or PL/I the expansion requires coding of the new function, unit testing it, interface testing, and finally system testing. The new function may be coded in-line or as a separate module.

Once the program has been expanded, metrics should indicate whether the difficulty, effort, cyclomatic complexity, and ELOC have increased beyond approved limits. If so, the program or module should be examined and subdivided into smaller functions. If the metrics are not out of bounds, then the expansion was successful.

5. GENERALITY

Generality specifies the ability to expand the usefulness of a given function beyond the existing function and its present scope. Generic program skeletons possess generality. They can be enhanced easily to meet the custom requirements of the design; all the programmer must do is flesh out the skeleton. Similarly, a module that converts Gregorian date to Julian date should be easily enhanced to reverse the conversion. Edit, update, data selection, and report modules should all be general in nature and easy to enhance.

Driver modules, with a high function density, should also be fairly general, and therefore flexible. Adding a new function to the existing control logic is a simple process. Once again, programs with a high complexity are probably less generic and therefore harder to enhance.

6. MODULARITY

In a manufacturing environment, designers and workers use interchangeable components to increase flexibility. A typical car, when it rolls along the assembly line, can be fitted with several different engines, transmissions, wheels, hubcaps, radios, stereos, and so on. For software to be truly flexible, it needs the same flexibility which comes from modular, interchangeable components.

Modularity provides a structure of highly independent modules, having sharply defined interfaces that are tolerant of external changes. A module possessing functional strength and data coupling has little to fear from the outside and its internal logic is often so easily understood that enhancing the module becomes simple.

To measure modularity, you must examine the module's structure chart and code. A program consisting of only one module is not modular, unless it performs only one function, and these are rare. More often, a single-module program may have three or more functions intermingled it its logic. In COBOL and PL/I, you can identify these extra functions by extracting the paragraph and procedure names from the module; a quick review will usually point out three to five major functions (see Figure 7.2). To be truly modular, each function should be in its own module.

```
UPDATE-MASTER-FILE

    EDIT-TRANSACTION-RECORDS

        SORT-TRANSACTION-RECORDS

    UPDATE-MASTER-RECORDS

        ADD-MASTER-RECORD

        CHANGE-MASTER-RECORD

        DELETE-MASTER-RECORD

    WRITE-CONTROLS-REPORT
```

FIGURE 7.2. Simple display of program structure.

Once each function resides in its own module with carefully designed interfaces, the program's flexibility improves, allowing the maintenance programmer to move functions around, adding, changing, and deleting them at will. The driver module will have many CALLs that should increase the clarity of the logic, showing the order in which functions are performed. Modularity is the cornerstone of flexibility. Without it, your enhancement costs will continue to soar.

7. SELF-DOCUMENTATION

Self-documentation identifies the software attributes that explain the function of the software. For programmers and analysts to maintain the program's external documentation is so rare and seemingly painful that I have found the only solution is to extract the documentation from the code mechanically. Thus the most likely place to document a program and to have that documentation maintained is in the code itself.

Comments are essential in assembler language, while COBOL and PL/I both need to be explained at times. The comments in each program should help increase the understanding of the logic flow and what happens at each step along the way. Without them, the maintenance programmer will find it difficult to grasp complex algorithms and fancy uses of the language. Without a clear understanding of the code, the programmer will have a hard time identifying where to insert new functions or to change or delete old ones. Self-documentation is measured by the comment density—the number of comments per 100 lines of code.

7.1. Comment Density

Dividing the number of comments by the number of total lines of code, gives a percentage of comments in the code:

$$\text{comment density} = (\text{number of comments} * 100)/\text{TLOC}$$

This number may vary from 10% for COBOL and PL/I to 80% for ALC. By examining your code, you will determine a percentage that represents self-documenting code. This should become a guideline for your developers and maintainers. Too high a percentage for COBOL and PL/I will tend to obscure the code and make it less flexible. Establish these ranges for commenting and factor them into your flexibility metric.

7.2. ALC

In assembler language, there may be comments that take one whole line and others that sit on the same line as a statement. Comments that take an entire line are easily counted. Comments on actual statement lines, however, must be differentiated from the operands and operators and then be evaluated for clarity:

```
*
*   CALCULATE MONTHLY SALES
*
    MVC     SALES,TSALES        REPLACE SALES WITH
*                               TRANSACTION SALES
    MVC     SALES,TSALES        MOVE TSALES TO SALES
```

Which comment is clearer? All comments are not created equal, but a mechanized analyzer can spot the presence of both kinds and report them for further evaluation. The sum of these two kinds of comments divided by the total lines of code gives the comment density. In ALC, a 50% or better comment density indicates good self-documentation.

7.3. COBOL

COBOL has a REMARKS section to describe the function of the program and single-line comments to do the rest of the documentation. COBOL was designed to read more like English, so it tends to be self-documenting.

Consider the last ALC example when compared to the equivalent COBOL statement:

MVC SALES,TSALES
MOVE SALES OF TRANSACTION-RECORD
   TO SALES OF MASTER-RECORD

COBOL can say more than the equivalent assembler language code. Single-line comments can be used to clarify the code wherever the code doesn't adequately describe itself. Normally COBOL comment density should be between 10 and 20%.

7.4. PL/I

PL/I allows both full-line and on-the-line comments. So it is equivalent to the other languages in its ability to be self-documenting. PL/I allows 32 character data names like COBOL, so it can be clearer than either ALC or FORTRAN.

    PL/I comments can be counted as the number of lines included between the beginning of the comment "/*" and the end "*/". The comment density for PL/I should run higher than for COBOL, but less than ALC.

7.5. Data Names and Literals

As previously mentioned, COBOL and PL/I both allow 32-character data names with 32-character qualifiers like:

SALES OF TRANSACTION-RECORD
TRANSACTION＿RECORD.SALES

while ALC and FORTRAN only allow seven- or eight-character names. These abilities and limitations affect the code's self-documentation and therefore its flexibility. One of the things the metrics analyzer can do is to determine the lengths of the data names and the use of qualifiers. In a COBOL program, it could report that the shortest data name was only two characters in length, while the longest was 31. The shorter data name could be expanded easily with a full screen, on-line editor to something meaningful. The metrics analyzer could also write out the names that are shorter than 10 characters, giving the programmers a list of data names to improve. It could also determine the usage of qualified names. For example, what if only 10% of the data names were qualified? These 10% are probably inconsistent with the rest of the module. A module that has 70% of its data names qualified will be consistent. Whether these qualified names are any better than a single descriptive name has not been studied.

Literals in the procedural part of the code pose another problem; no one knows exactly what they represent. For example:

SET STATE-INDEX TO 1.
SET STATE-INDEX TO ALABAMA.

The literal "1" is not explicit about what it means; ALABAMA is specific and better self-documentation. Now suppose that the maintenance programmer is trying to make an enhancement to how ALABAMA's data is handled. Which of the two statements will improve the module's readability and therefore flexibility?

Furthermore, literals may be changed by future enhancements to the system. Would you want the programmers to research every occurrence of the literal "1" or just change the definition of ALABAMA and recompile the program? Which one allows more flexibility? Metrics analyzers should count the number of alphabetic and numeric literals in the text. Each literal can be counted and summarized so that the programmer knows where to take corrective action. In the example in Figure 7.3, the programmer may want to invest the time to change the occurrences of "1" to ALABAMA, but not spend time on moving the alphabetic literal "ALABAMA" to the data division. It can and should be argued that the state names should be in a table referenced by

```
Literals for Program XYZ
```

Number	Literal
5	0
23	1
23	2
23	3
1	"ALABAMA"
1	"ARIZONA"
1	"ARKANSAS"

FIGURE 7.3. Extraction of literals with a code analyzer.

the state index, but if there is only one occurrence of a literal, it may not make sense to spend the time to define it elsewhere. Reducing the number of literals will improve the module's self-documentation and flexibility.

8. SIMPLICITY

Simplicity recognizes those software attributes that implement a function in the most understandable manner. Simplicity is the opposite of complexity; the presence of one implies the absence of the other. The size of the program in ELOC, the use of function statements, the absence of GO TO statements, and the use of high-level languages all indicate simplicity. Consider the nonprocedural language statement:

> List monthly sales by state, city, and salesperson
>> summarized by state and city
>> for montly sales > quota.

and then compare this to the equivalent 400-line program in COBOL or ALC. The difference in simplicity is astounding. So why don't we just write everything in a nonprocedural language? Because to implement detailed user requirements for large systems, not one-shot what-if problems like this one, is not possible in the existing nonprocedural languages. But IS management would like the user to write all of these smaller reports so that IS can carry out the major needs of the corporation. This is what I call the Tom Sawyer effect—let someone else do the simple work for you.

But how do you measure the simplicity of the code produced by IS? The size of the program in executable lines of code gives a metric of simplicity: the larger the program, the more difficult or complex it will be to maintain. The absence of complexity, therefore, indicates the presence of simplicity. Looking at Halstead's software science and McCabe's cyclomatic complexity, low values of either of these two metrics would further indicate the presence of simplicity. As described under concision, function statements like CALL and SORT increase the code's simplicity by substituting preprogrammed code for extensive, hand-coded routines.

Concerning the GO TO, Christensen (1981) found that the major reason for large difficulty and effort metrics in software science was the presence of GO TOs in the code. So the GO TO should also be considered the antagonist of simplicity.

The language used also indicates the degree of simplicity. COBOL will be more flexible than ALC. PL/I will be more easily enhanced than either of these, and nonprocedural languages normally will be much simpler for small systems. Simplicity is not only a function of the code, but of the language used.

9. SUMMARY

The ability to modify and enhance a module or program depends on many metrics that can be extracted directly from the code. The significant metrics of flexibility are ELOC, cyclomatic complexity, software science, function density, and comment density. From these, it is possible to predict the flexibility of the code.

A large part of the code's flexibility depends on the language used. COBOL and PL/I are more flexible than ALC, and fourth-generation languages are more flexible than any of the procedural languages.

System enhancements consume over 70% of the IS budget. Flexibility metrics help determine why and where that money is going. They help quantify where to make improvements in the code to reduce these ongoing costs. It is worth every penny to collect, analyze, and apply these metrics to the maintenance process.

CHAPTER EIGHT

INTEGRITY METRICS

Data continues to increase in value to the corporation. Theft or loss of that data could crush a business. The metric integrity measures how well the software and data are protected from security breaches. Is the software controlled and secure? Integrity is a function of auditability, instrumentation, and security.

$$\text{integrity} = F(\text{auditability, instrumentation, security})$$

As systems increase in complexity, it is no longer possible for humans to audit and control the entire process. So the system and application software must do most of the work. To facilitate auditing, the application software must have internal controls to track the processing, commonly known as instrumentation. The system software must control who has access to the data and who may update or delete it. Each of these metrics tells something about the system's integrity. Accounting and payroll systems will need to achieve integrity, while minor reporting programs can often do without these controls. Ultimately, all systems will need to be incorruptible and you will need a way to measure these traits.

1. AUDITABILITY

Auditability identifies those software attributes that provide ease of auditing for the software, data, and results. Sources of auditing data include the operating system, data-base management system, data security packages, source code control libraries, compilers, and software metrics static analyzers.

1.1. Operating Systems

Operating systems collect accounting information by user. They can show a potential violator trying over and over to gain entry by the repetition of different passwords. They show which users are applying which commands and how often the commands are used. Each item of information makes auditing easier; programs to examine the accounting data can be devised to track fraudulent activities.

1.2. Data-Base Management Systems

Data-base management systems allow the data administrators to specify data access down to the element level, restricting who can update a field and who may only read it. Data-base management systems often keep their own audit trails in the form of log files that are accessible to auditing programs. The presence or absence of this control in the data base helps indicate its auditability and integrity.

1.3. Data Security Packages

Data security packages also provide security and auditability benefits. They provide reports of which users tried to access data that was not available to them. The protection of application files with this kind of system implies auditability and integrity.

1.4. Source Code Control Libraries

Some programmers keep their code in personal libraries; others keep it in controlled libraries like PANVALET. The control library should know who checks code out and who updates it, providing audit trails as the programmers work. In UNIX™, the source code control system (SCCS) may interface with the change management control system (CMTS) to prevent programmers from checking out code without an approved change request, further ensuring that changes to the code occur in a controlled environment. Source code control systems typically provide reports of the modules changed during the month. This should agree with the manager's knowledge of what work is being done.

The UNIX SCCS system allows programmers to embed key words in their source code that are later expanded by SCCS. The programmer can use these keywords to drive auditing reports of the source modules executed, their release number, the level number of the source changes, the data extracted from SCCS, and so on. The mere existence of these key words as data items in the code ensures that they will serve as audit trails; if the program ends abnormally, these expanded key words will show up in the dump. SCCS is only source code control system that provides these mechanized audit trails.

1.5. Compilers

Compilers can add identification records to each object module and the production programs. These marked modules can later be identified by system utilities to ensure that the correct version of a program is operational. The identification records provide another audit trail that indicates the presence of integrity.

1.6. Software Metrics

Static code analyzers can look for the existence of specialized audit modules and internal audit trails that should be included in each program. The use of generic or standard audit code may also be identified.

2. INSTRUMENTATION

Instrumentation measures how well the software measures itself. Does the software count how many times it added, changed, or deleted a transaction or master file record? Does it identify errors as they occur? Some compilers allow the presence of code that is compiled only when specifically needed; so you could insert special code to examine the user's transactions or data handled by the program. Auditing code could be inserted to measure specific activities of interest. In "C" language, specialized code can be added and compiled when needed. For example:

```
#ifdef AUDIT
    printf("%s, %s, %s\n", module, release, date−compiled);
#endif
```

When compiled with the AUDIT trails requested, the program will print the module name, release and level number of the code, and the date compiled. The PL/I preprocessor also supplies this facility.

The use of generic designs and code will automatically include this kind of instrumentation with the new program. Collecting and reporting the information can be done by a generic audit module. The existence of generic designs, code, and audit modules can be detected easily by a code analyzer.

3. SECURITY

Security provides control and protection for programs and data alike. As previously mentioned, operating systems, data-base management systems, and data control facilities indicate the presence of security. The use of passwords in the operating system, of data access control in the data base management system (DBMS), security packages, and source code control systems help secure the company's data resource. No amount of security is foolproof, but the absence of security is foolhardy. Source code should contain a proprietary information statement, something to the effect that this code is the property of the XYZ company and is not to be released, copied, or whatever, under penalty of law. Inputs and outputs of critical programs should have similar statements included. Application system reports should explicitly state their readership. Application system reports should explicitly state their readership. Although this is only a mild deterrent to information theft, it is at least visible.

4. SUMMARY

Integrity should be designed and built into a system; it can only be added later at considerable expense. There are a few ways to extract and measure the auditability, instrumentation, and security of system and application software and data. As more systems come to depend on system integrity, additional measures will surface from the fertile minds of researchers in the field. It is a fertile field for future study because of the growing complexity of software systems and the need for control of this corporate resource.

CHAPTER NINE

INTEROPERABILITY METRICS

As software systems continue to grow, expand, and multiply, they require more and more data, most of which can be obtained from other systems. Unfortunately, most systems were not designed to deliver or receive data from other systems. The metric, interoperability, indicates how much effort it will take to couple this program or system to another. Interoperability is a function of four underlying metrics: communications commonality, data commonality, generality, and modularity.

interoperability = F(communications commonality, data commonality, generality, modularity)

To a large degree, interoperability can be determined mechanically from existing code. Interoperability should be specified during the definition and design phases of development. Selection of communications and data-base software during these phases can impact the future ability of the system to operate with other newly developed systems. Design choices also impact the generality and modularity of the code. Let's look at each underlying quality metric and how to measure it.

1. COMMUNICATIONS COMMONALITY

Communications commonality recognizes the use of standard communication protocols and interface routines. If two computer systems, existing at opposite ends of the country, can communicate via the same telecommunications package, then they can share data. If they exist in the same room but cannot communicate, their communications commonality is zero. With personal computers, and the movement to put data into the hands of the user, communications and transfer of data takes on great significance. The various machines will need to work together to meet the user's needs. The system designers should identify the need for communications between two computer or application systems during the definition phase of development.

1.1. Definition and Design

During the definition and design phases of development, measurement of communications commonality rests entirely with the review teams. They should examine not only the required interfaces among systems but fantasize about future requirements, and enhance their definitions to anticipate those needs. No system lives in a vacuum for very long; the user soon sees new and intriguing ways to tie their systems and data together. Developers must ensure that the emerging system can interface with the other systems.

1.2. Code

Communications commonality depends on programs and systems sharing the same technology. In COBOL, consistent applications of communications techniques in the procedure division will provide communication commonality. The use of a DBMS that handles data transfers and telecommunications will indicate communications commonality.

Measuring the communication abilities of systems has not been studied. Measuring interface complexity among programs and systems is a possible method of identifying commonality and that means looking at the data.

2. DATA COMMONALITY

Data commonality provides standard data representations. If the data is a standard format, then it will be more easily accessible to other modules, programs, or systems. Common data naming standards and their application across developing systems will provide data commonality. The tools that mechanize data commonality are data dictionaries and data-base management systems. To have maximum impact, they need to be applied during from the beginning of the definition phase.

2.1. Definition and Design

Data dictionaries provide a common interface to all systems that need to describe data and its attributes. Once defined, the data can be more easily accessed by other programs or systems; the data dictionary develops data structures based on the logical data-base design and the data elements. Other systems that need access to the data can then collect the data structure from the dictionary and select methods of retrieving it.

2.2. Code

The presence of COPY statements in COBOL indicates a degree of data commonality. The use of data dictionaries to define the structures contained in the COPY statement indicates the next level of data commonality. Finally, the use of a DBMS, which can be determined from examination of the code, indicates the final degree of data commonality among programs and systems.

Programs in different systems that both use the same record structure from a COPY statement and the same DBMS, possess data commonality. Two modules that have an interface defined by a COPY statement also possess data commonality. Again, little research has gone into the measurement of data commonality, but it is possible.

3. GENERALITY

Generality identifies the software attributes that expand the usefulness of a function beyond the existing module and its current scope. Data-base management systems are a good example; they can handle different kinds of programs, systems, and data. Sequential systems that use common modules for input or output of records also possesses generality. Some FORTRAN math libraries can be ported from machine to machine, compiled, and reused. Software that can be used in the sending *and* in the receiving system, helps provide interoperability.

Code generality demands that only standard versions of the programming languages be used for its development. Extensions to the language affect the code's generality. Unfortunately, DBMS systems are an extension to any language, but they provide a data and communication commonality that would not be possible otherwise. Generality remains unaffected by the use of data-base management systems as long as the data doesn't need to move from one type of hardware to another.

4. MODULARITY

Modularity provides a structure of highly independent modules, as described in Chapter 4. Independent modules tend to be easily enhanced to access data other than they were originally designed to handle. It is this flexibility that makes it possible for these systems to be easily enhanced to operate in conjunctions with other systems—interoperability. Modular systems may not be directly operable with others, but they can be enhanced to meet these needs. And judging from the current trends, the systems of benefit to the corporation will need these abilities.

5. SUMMARY

The ability for systems to share information—interoperability—is almost a commandment. Look at the problems faced by personal computer pioneers that wanted to interface their DBMS software to their spreadsheet to their graphics package to their word processor. It was difficult, if not impossible. The systems of the future will need to integrate these needs if they are to be useful to the employees that use them.

Interoperability is not the most easily measured metric of quality, but it is important and bears further investigation, research, and refinement.

CHAPTER TEN

MAINTAINABILITY METRICS

Maintenance is a problem dating from antiquity. The first stone tool that man ever fashioned soon became dull, causing someone to put a new edge on it. The extent of the problem has grown phenomenally since the industrial revolution; maintainability is a major force in achieving productivity in factories. Machinery downtime decreases productivity and increases unit costs. The maintainability of manufactured goods also has a bearing on productivity and quality; the cost of product maintenance over the life of a new car or computer may easily exceed the original price.

In response to these problems, most companies have formed maintenance departments to improve effectiveness and to provide feedback to designers and parts manufacturers. Service organizations have sprung up to meet consumer needs. Researchers and designers have developed maintenance-free designs, materials, components, and assemblies to reduce maintenance. When this was impossible, designers created plans for new products that facilitated easy access to the major parts to reduce maintenance costs.

In contrast to reliability, which is concerned with the causes of product failure and removing those problems, maintainability examines the effects of product failures and ways of minimizing those effects. Many manufacturing organizations have created a separate discipline for maintainability engineers, who play an integral role in product design. This is the person most often missing from software design teams.

113

Software maintenance consists of three activities: adaptive, corrective, and preventive maintenance. Adaptive maintenance enhances a product. The measurements for the ease of adaptive maintenance were given in Chapter 7, Flexibility Metrics. Since enhancements are usually 70–90% of the maintenance workload, concentrating on flexibility should be a company's primary concern.

But errors do happen, so corrective maintenance comes into play. Somebody has to fix the error and, more often than not, it is not a new kind of error, but rather one of the common ones. There should be a way to determine recurring errors and to prevent their insertion in new programs. And there is, but first you must be able to identify what kinds of errors occur, their associated costs, and what can be done to prevent them. Obtaining this information and translating it into dollars and cents requires the establishment of a maintainability program.

Maintainability programs are widely used in manufacturing industries to identify ways to reduce maintenance and the related costs. In a software environment, a maintainability program will focus on reducing the mean time to repair (MTTR) software and on eliminating the need for maintenance. Once this ongoing examination of software errors and correction is undertaken, then not only the new programs, but also the existing ones, must be upgraded to make use of the findings. Since most of your programs are already in system maintenance, the logical place to apply maintainability changes is in the existing code. The process of upgrading existing code is known as preventive maintenance. To maximize the return on investment provided by preventive maintenance, the maintainability program must be in place and functioning.

1. MAINTAINABILITY PROGRAM

Assuming that the maintenance of existing systems is 75% of the work performed in an IS organization, reducing that effort rather watching it grow seems like a pretty good idea. Formal maintainability programs assume that ease of maintenance can be programmed in the same way that user requirements are designed and coded into a program or system. A software maintainability program consists of four phases:

1. *Planning* ensures that maintainability requirements are specified and translated into design criteria.
2. *Program or module design* establishes the functional and physical characteristics that provide maintainability.
3. *Software measurement* verifies that quantitative and qualitative maintainability goals have been met.

4. *Performance reviews* evaluate the definition, designs, code, and results, providing feedback to management, analysts, and programmers about the success of the maintainability program.

The absence of a maintainability plan or requirements should provide the first metric of system maintainability. Metrics in subsequent phases of development are needed to ensure conformance to the plan or requirements.

2. SOFTWARE MAINTAINABILITY METRICS

Software maintainability measures the effect of errors and the effort required to locate and repair them in a program. The major industry metric of maintainability is MTTR. Can you fix it in a reasonable length of time? Software maintainability is a function of six underlying metrics: concision, consistency, instrumentation, modularity, self-documentation and simplicity.

maintainability = F(concision, consistency, instrumentation,
modularity, self-documentation, simplicity)

These metrics can be mechanized to a great extent. Designs should also reflect the need for maintainability.

2.1. Concision

Concision recognizes software attributes that implement a function in the minimum amount of code. Read a record, format status report, sort input transactions, and display input screen are all examples of functions that can be easily described in one line of code—a CALL or PERFORM. The concise representation of these functions gives the maintenance programmer a signpost to follow when tracing errors or locating potential enhancements.

The number of function statements used in the module and the function density are the major metrics of concision. The function density represents the number of function statements in relation to all other executable statements.

function density = (number of functions) $*$ 100% / ELOC

As the function density increases, the overall concision of the module also increases. Each incremental CALL, PERFORM, or whatever adds another signpost for the maintenance programmer. A module that drives the processing of all other modules in the program should have a high (20—50%) function density. A module that edits date fields should have a low (0–10%) function density.

Concision is also a function of the language used: COBOL is more concise than assembler; PL/I is more concise than COBOL; and nonprocedural languages are more concise than any of the second- or third-generation languages.

The conciseness of the design can be evaluated as the number of pages of documentation per 100 ELOC. Too few pages of documentation typically cause maintainability problems. Too many pages of design documentation may cause similar problems. How many would be just right? That depends on your design techniques and application. Study of these factors under the maintenance plan should provide the answers that best suit your organization.

2.2. Consistency

Consistency provides uniform design and implementation techniques and documentation. The existence and use of design and code standards is the first metric of consistency. The use of common design techniques and development tools provides the next metric of consistency.

The use of standard design techniques and representations makes the programmer's job easier. The uniformity of system, program, module, and function documentation simplifies the process of isolating, repairing, and testing the errant code. Unfortunately, little work has been done, in the software arena, to quantify design consistency as a contributor to maintainability.

Coding standards help ensure consistency. Chapters 18 through 21 provide some basic rules for writing more maintainable code and ways of measuring the benefits derived from improved programming style and coding standards. The use of a standard programming language throughout a system or subsystem further improves consistency and maintainability. Use of standard commenting techniques and naming conventions provide uniform coding styles that make code easier to maintain.

2.3. Instrumentation

If a program terminates because of an error, that is one thing. If it recognizes an error and either tolerates it or terminates, that is another. If it recognizes the error and puts out meaningful error messages to direct the programmer to the source of the error and the potential problem, then the code is said to have instrumentation.

Even copying machines can determine when they have paper jams or they have run out of copier fluid or whatever. Most programs, however, are less than profound when they detect an error. A simple example involves a division by zero in an IBM machine: The operating system gives some exotic IEF????? code and a system OC7 return code. Then it is up to the programmer to read through pages of hexadecimal dump to determine the location of the error, what actually happened, and what can be done to fix it.

Properly instrumented programs detect these errors before they occur and deal with them rationally. But instrumentation is often costly. It is one more function that must be designed and built into the code. It can even contain errors. But it can improve maintainability in critical on-line applications.

Instrumentation can only be measured when you know what kinds of code provide these functions. In PL/I, the ON ERROR conditions provide instrumentation. In COBOL, the ON OVERFLOW conditions provide error detection capabilities. In any language, testing for zero divisors or nonnumeric data usage in arithmetic operations shows the presence of instrumentation. The use of generic program error reporting modules should also show the use of error detection and reporting code. The use of common data validation modules indicates not only instrumentation, but reusability and reliability.

Instrumentation can also be provided externally. The CAPEX OPTIMIZER III COBOL compiler can determine how many times a statement was executed and the CPU time used, providing an excellent method for detecting execution errors and program inefficiencies.

Program instrumentation provides the programmer with the means to get right to the heart of maintenance problems, cutting out wasted time and effort often spent on wild good chases throughout the rest of the code. Error detection, correction, and reporting will help reduce maintenance costs and improve programmer productivity. But it is not necessary in most programs. Only 10–20% of the programs incur 50–80% of the program errors. Instrumentation can be added to these modules at a substantial cost, or it can be built into all of the programs as they are developed for a reasonable cost. The choice is yours.

2.4. Modularity

Modularity provides a structure of highly independent modules, as described in Chapter Four. Modularity begins in design and continues into the coding process. Once completed, maintainability is often fixed by the component orientation of structured design. A program that contains many interwoven functions will be difficult to repair while the modular program makes problem isolation easy and repair simple.

Design

In design, there should be three levels of detailed documentation for each program: program, module, and function specifications. A simple examination of the documentation will verify the existence of modularity. Then the structure of the program and each module should be examined. Does one driver handle more than seven subordinate functions (as shown in Figure 10.1)? Or are the levels of loop nesting too deep (e.g., more than three, as shown in Figure 10.2)? Analysis of the data flowing over the structure chart should indicate modules and functions that do not possess "functional strength" and "data coupling"—two metrics of module/function independence that determine much of the future maintainability.

Next, examine the actual specifications that are normally some kind of pseudocode, IPO, or whatever. Does the description of a function or module exceed a page, two pages, or ten pages? The larger the description of a single function, the greater the chance that the function is not one function, but many, which violates the basic standards of modularity. Any module that tries to handle more than one function often does a few fairly well and the rest poorly. Modularity and precise packaging of the program design help ensure cost-effective maintenance. Leaving this task to the whims of an undisciplined programmer can result in expanding rather than reducing the maintenance burden.

Code

The modularity of a piece of code is based on four metrics: ELOC, cyclomatic complexity, Halstead's programming effort, and manual verification. A module containing only one function, which possesses functional strength and data coupling, often consists of fewer than 100 ELOC. The cyclomatic complexity will number less than $10-15$ and the software science programming effort (E) will be less than 10,000.

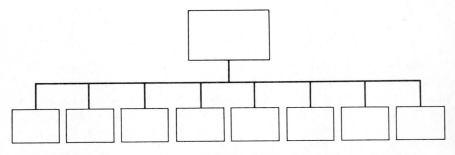

FIGURE 10.1.   Structure of a program or module with span of control problems.

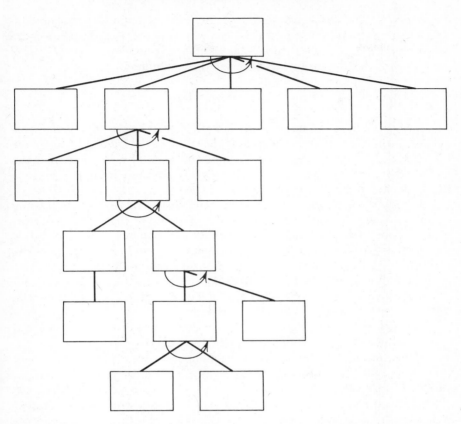

FIGURE 10.2.   Structure of a program or module with nested loop complexity.

If any of these metrics raise a question about the module's modularity and therefore maintainability, then a manual review is required to determine the presence and extent of any potential problem. This review and revision may be carried out by the "preventative maintenance" team responsible for improving the maintainability of a program already under maintenance or by the programmer writing new code.

2.5.   Self-Documentation

Self-documentation identifies software attributes that explain the function of the software. Self-documenting code uses meaningful data names and comments to describe its actions. Languages like COBOL and PL/I are designed to provide more descriptive actions than assembler language. Self-documenting code is more readable, understandable, and therefore more maintainable. Comment density—the number of comments per 100 lines of code—provides the major metric of self-documentation.

2.6. Simplicity

Simplicity assumes the implementation of the functions in the most understandable manner. The presence of simplicity can be detected by means of the executable lines of code, cyclomatic complexity, and software science metrics. When these are less than the prescribed levels indicated in Chapter Four on Complexity Metrics, the module has simplicity.

A study of factors affecting corrective maintenance (Vessey, 1983) found that complexity and programming style as measured by the number of errors found were statistically significant predictors of maintainability. The study covered two groups: one Australian company and two U.S. companies. The study covered a total of 447 COBOL programs among the two groups.

The study actually found a correlation between complexity and maintainability only in the Australian group. The complexity of the American programs was typically less than the Australian programs, however. Complexity was defined as programs having over 300 source statements (medium complexity) and over 600 source statements (high complexity).

In the American test groups, only the number of times a program had been released was found to be statistically significant as a predictor of maintainability. Intuitively, programs that are released more often probably are changed more often. The chances for error increase with each successive change.

The study also found that corrective maintenance was not a major portion of each company's activities, only 10% in most cases. And not all programs were involved in corrective maintenance: 55—72% of the programs in the three organizations incurred no repairs at all. Of the remaining programs, 13—22% had only one error, and 7—16% had just two. In all companies, these programs accounted for 90% of the total code. Only the remaining 10% incurred 3—22 errors. Thus Pareto analysis comes into effect.

3.   PREVENTIVE MAINTENANCE

In IS, it is possible to do as mechanics do, perform maintenance before it is needed. Computer systems have monthly preventive maintenance. Systems engineers check for potential hardware failures and correct or replace the defective parts. The same can be done for computer software.

Following the Pareto analysis to identify the problem programs, programmers and analysts can look into a program to determine its weaknesses and strengths. They can perform preventive maintenance, changing the existing code to anticipate common errors: division by zero, subscripts out of range, invalid data, or whatever. The techniques for preventive maintenance are described more fully in Chapters Eighteen through Twenty-one.

4. PERFORMANCE REVIEW

The metrics described thus far can only be used to predict maintainability. Once a program or system has been put in production, the actual metrics of maintainability can be collected:

1. MTTR.
2. Downtime per unit time (total downtime per release cycle).
3. Availability per unit time.
4. Maintenance cost per unit time.

MTTR describes how long it takes to fix the program after it fails. Some programs fail infrequently and take a short time to repair. Others fail quite often and take much longer to repair. The latter programs are prime targets for preventive maintenance.

Downtime per unit time helps identify those programs that are easily repaired, but fail frequently. They fail so often that their total downtime is greater than the programs that have a high MTTR.

Availability per unit time describes those programs that are constantly in use. An on-line update or inquiry system is one of the obvious contenders for maximum availability.

Maintenance cost per unit time factors the analyst, programmer, and manager time as well as support resources into the cost of maintaining a piece of code. Programs that consume the largest amount of maintenance resources are also prime candidates for preventive maintenance.

5. SUMMARY

Maintainability is a key issue when examining software quality. Only 5–10% of all work performed by IS involves correcting software errors. But understanding the code attributes that affect maintainability will help reduce the chances of building similar errors into developing systems. A far greater percentage of IS work comes from enhancements. Since the same metrics that affect maintainability also affect flexibility, it behooves you to examine and understand the factors that affect over 70% of your costs.

Many of the metrics that affect maintainability also affect reliability. In on-line systems or systems that could impact human life, reliability and maintainability take on great significance. What happens if the software controlling a nuclear reactor fails and we can't fix it in a short period of time? What happens if aircraft or space shuttle software fails? What happens if a totally automated assembly line goes berserk? No one wants these things to happen. That is why elaborate backup controls are built into each of these systems. But as software controls more and more things, even the temperature of your house, the manual controls will begin to disappear simply to reduce costs. Maintainability will play a key part in everyday life and the benefits derived from computer applications.

CHAPTER ELEVEN

PORTABILITY METRICS

The metric, portability, measures what kind of effort will be required to transfer a program from one machine to another. Can it run on your microprocessors, minicomputers, and mainframe machines? Portability gains importance in a varied hardware environment or in the situation that you want to market your software to the largest possible hardware base. Portability is a function of five underlying metrics: generality, hardware independence, modularity, self-documentation, and software system independence.

portability = F(generality, hardware independence, modularity, self-documentation, software system independence)

Each of these metrics can be derived from the code and are specified by design choices. The original requirements play an important part in specifying the need for portability.

1. GENERALITY

Generality recognizes the software attributes that expand the usefulness of the function beyond the existing module and its current scope. In the current environment, where every market is opening to the use of computers, generalized application software will be usable in virtually all environments. Look at the success of spread-sheet packages: They were born in the microprocessor environment and have migrated to minis and mainframes. Graphics that were expensive last year are easily affordable today. Software that combines both word processing and graphics is usable in any environment.

Generality should be specified in requirements and design and then built into the code. As the distinction between micros, minis, and mainframes blur with the increasing power of chip technology, programs may be built entirely on micros and then transferred to the mainframe for production. Conversely, some microprocessor software is built on minis and mainframes and then down-loaded into the microprocessor. Generality will help provide opportunities for software in each of these environments.

1.1. Requirements

Early in the requirements phase is the time to determine whether the software has applicability in more than one market. Businesses that build their own software may sell it to other noncompetitive businesses to help lower their development and maintenance costs. If this sounds attractive to you, then the software will need to be general enough to meet the varied needs of other companies. The only available metric of portability is a manual sign-off of the definition document by the quality assurance group.

1.2. Design

In the design phase, the use of standard, generic logic designs should indicate generality. Forbidding the use of nonportable languages like ALC should be specified at this time.

1.3. Code

The generality of the code can be determined either from manual inspection or from the programmer's use of generic code. Generality can be predicted from the number of executable lines of code (less than 100), the number of decisions (fewer than 10), and by the number of functions (greater than 10% of the ELOC).

Code that contains input or output statements typically lacks generality. Modules that receive all of their parameters from external sources, on the other hand, are often more general. The use of input and output statements often raises the issue of hardware independence.

2. HARDWARE INDEPENDENCE

Hardware independence determines ability of the software to compile and run on varying kinds of machines. The dependence or independence from the hardware should be specified in the requirements phase and implemented in the design phase. The software metrics of code portability can be determined by answering the following questions.

1. Is the language portable? Fortran and COBOL typically are. Assembly-level languages are rarely portable.

2. Are the nonstandard features of the language, like IBM's Report Writer, avoided completely? The presence of any extension to the language indicates hardware dependence and a lack of portability. Language extensions normally are implemented to discourage the user from purchasing another vendor's hardware.

3. Do any of the features of the language depend on the hardware? Does the hardware have one-byte instead of two-byte words and how does the compiler handle the difference? Are numerical calculations handled differently? Does one round up while the other rounds down?

3. MODULARITY

Modularity provides a structure of highly independent modules. Independent modules are less likely to have input/output statements that are one of the banes of portability. It seems that every system has a different form of input and output or data-base management system. Instead of having the I/O buried throughout the program, it is often contained in fewer than 10% of the modules; the other 90% are often easily compiled in the new environment. Thus modular programming can reduce the work to just 10% of the code. Consider the UNIX^{TM} system, that has been ported from PDP 11/45s to IBM and Amdahl mainframes and also to virtually every microprocessor. The original system was designed to isolate the I/O in just a few machine language modules that would have to be recoded on the target machine. The remainder of the operating system and all tools were written in a portable language called "C." The modular implementation of the operating system and its toolkit can be experienced in an excellent book on programming: *Software Tools*, by B. W. Kernighan and P. J. Plauger.

The measures of modularity—ELOC, cyclomatic complexity, decision density, function density, and software science—have been discussed in previous chapters and will be expanded in Chapters 18–21, the programming language metrics.

4. SELF-DOCUMENTATION

A program with good informative comments will further improve the portability of the code. The person porting the code probably has little knowledge of the original application development, but does know the new machine. Clear, self-documenting code and good comments will speed the transfer of software from one machine to another. Comment density (the number of comments divided by the ELOC) gives a reasonable metric of self-documentation. The length and descriptiveness of data names and literals should also be examined to predict a module's self-documentation.

5. SOFTWARE SYSTEM INDEPENDENCE

Software system independence determines the application program's dependence on the software environment: operating system, data-base management system, telecommunications system, extensions to the language, and so on. Developing software system independence depends on the definition, design and code.

It may not be useful or necessary to legislate the necessity for portability, but if it is needed, the definition phase is the time to do so. The program or system may need to be connected to another system that uses a specific nonportable DBMS. Portability may no longer be possible. The only metric of portability available this early in the development process is the client, IS, and quality assurance sign-off.

Once specified in the requirements definition phase, hardware and software must be selected carefully to meet the portability needs. Programs must be designed with portability in mind. Again, the only available metric of portability is the client, IS, and quality assurance sign-off.

Once in the coding phase, however, the use of nonportable language statements, input/output statements, DBMS calls, and so on can all be counted by a static code analyzer. The use of nonportable statements varies from machine to machine and language to language. In IBM COBOL, the language reference manual gives a list of the key words supported by the various standards and those used as extensions to IBM COBOL. Every language reference manual should have this information in one form or another. Seek it out and measure your portable programs accordingly.

6. SUMMARY

Portability may be required when a system will run on various kinds of hardware or if it may be advantageous economically to sell it to other users. The major factor that determines portability is the code's dependency on the system hardware and software. Special extensions to the language must be avoided if at all possible. Input and output differences among machines can also cause a large amount of grief and should be isolated, as much as possible, from the majority of the code by modular programming.

The future hardware environment will blur distinctions between micros, minis, and mainframes, providing opportunities for companies to down-load their processing into other machines if their software is portable. The potential benefits of this are unknown, but believed to be worthwhile: When a mainframe goes down, hundreds of people are suddenly out of work; when a microcomputer breaks down, you wheel in a spare and the person goes on working. Portability may well play an important part in software's, and therefore metric's, future.

CHAPTER TWELVE

RELIABILITY METRICS

The metric reliability determines to what extent the module, program, or system can be expected to perform its function without failure. Does it work accurately without ending abnormally? Reliability is a function of six underlying metrics: accuracy, complexity, consistency, error tolerance, modularity, and simplicity.

$$\text{reliability} = F(\text{accuracy, complexity, consistency, error tolerance,}$$
$$\text{modularity, simplicity})$$

Reliability is determined by the requirements and program design. It is then cast in concrete by the programmers. Reliability can be measured mechanically from the code and by means of walk-throughs during the definition and design phases of development. Measurements taken early in the development process predict the actual reliability of the software. Once the system enters the testing phase, actual metrics of reliability become available. Further metrics of reliability are collectable once the system goes into operation. Predicting program or system reliability as early as possible allows for corrective action. Measuring actual reliability from testing and production information will provide quantifiable verification of predictive metrics. For example, Glenford J. Myers (1977) found that as the number of errors in a program increased, the chances of the program having more errors *increased*. You might expect that as errors are found and removed, the probability of finding other errors would decrease, but this is not the way program bugs work. If there is one termite, there may be a few more; but if there are dozens of termites, the whole house is probably infested. The same rationale seems to work with program bugs.

1. ACCURACY

Accuracy implies the presence of software attributes that provide precision in calculations and outputs. One creative story of applied accuracy centers around a programmer in a bank. This programmer changed the dividend calculations to summarize the fractional cents on each dividend calculation and place them into his own account. In the space of six months, the programmer had accumulated a little over $400,000, which was unfortunately brought to the attention of the bank's management. Fractions of a cent, when multiplied by millions or billions of transactions can equate to a small fortune. AT&T handles over a billion long distance calls a day. The loss of one hundredth of a cent per call would equal one million dollars a day or $365 million per year. This is only a fraction of its gross income, but it would hire an army of programmers to prevent such losses.

Accuracy is concerned with the accuracy of data, computed results, and the avoidance of error buildup in iterative routines. Accuracy is best legislated during the definition and design phases of development. Accuracy is also hardest to measure during these early phases.

1.1. Definition

The definition phase is the earliest point in the development cycle to begin specifying the required accuracy. Does the system need checks and balances to ensure its internal workings? In most cases, the answer is yes. Financial algorithms should check and double-check themselves. Common modules should tolerate few errors. A simple marketing analysis program may forecast 100,000 sales rather than just 10,000 wreaking havoc with production and sales forces alike. A simple table lookup program may error thousands of transactions by failing to check the last entry in a table, causing hundreds of lost programmer and end-user hours.

Two simple metrics of accuracy are the existence of an accuracy specification and the accuracy of the definition itself. The existence of an accuracy specification is relatively easy to determine. The client should specify the accuracy required, and the checks and balances necessary to ensure the system's reliability.

The accuracy of the definition is not determined so easily. Preliminary metrics of its accuracy come from the definition review. Each error should be tracked and repaired. Errors uncovered during design, code, test, and conversion that stem from the definition phase should be tracked as well. Although tracking will not eliminate the errors in the current system, it will show the types of inaccuracies and ways to prevent them in future projects. Improvements in accuracy are just one of the ongoing means to improve computer system reliability.

1.2. Design

During the design phase, the accuracy of the program design falls on the shoulders of the systems analysts. They must carry out the needs of the user, ensuring the system's "fitness for use." The major source of accuracy measurement is the design walk-through. Errors in the design that affect the program's or system's accuracy should be documented and tracked to eliminate errors.

The design document should specify the ranges for all numeric data items, the size of tables, and the accuracy of all numerical calculations. If the user needs four decimal places, the design should say so. If the result of a calculation should be rounded up or down, the design should say so.

With products like the Writer's Workbench (UNIX), systems analysts can mechanically evaluate their definition and design documentation. The package will identify the reading level required to understand the document, misspelled words, erroneous punctuation and grammar, and propose improvements. Documents that exceed a readability of about eighth or ninth grade level are suspect. Their readability may affect the accuracy of the design and its conversion into code.

1.3. Code

Accuracy can be examined directly in the code. In every language there are ways to ensure accurate calculations. In COBOL, the use of GIVING, ROUNDED, ON OVERFLOW, and similar keywords will affect accuracy and reliability of calculations. The COBOL keyword GIVING ensures that intermediate results are stored in a variable other than the two used as input. For example, ADD A TO B causes the original value of B to be replaced with A+B. B no longer represents its original value. A programmer tracking a program error cannot determine its original value from a core dump. The statement ADD A TO B GIVING C, however, does allow A and B to remain the same. The variable C represents the sum of the other two.

The COBOL keyword ROUNDED ensures that fractions of a decimal point are not truncated but rounded properly up or down. For example:

MULTIPLY ACCOUNT-BALANCE BY PERCENT-INTEREST GIVING
DIVIDEND.

This statement would give any fractional cents back to the bank. GIVING DIVIDEND ROUNDED would round the dividend up or down as required.

ON OVERFLOW is only useful when the program generates a resulting value that is greater than the size of the receiving field. But this is a frequent occurrence. The sum of two numbers may be greater than the receiving field; the leading digit is clipped off. And the leading digit is often the most significant.

Most compilers identify arithmetic statements that have receiving fields smaller than one of the two operands. Some compilers identify mixed mode arithmetic (integer with floating point, etc.) These warning messages should be removed from the program to help ensure accuracy and reliability.

2. COMPLEXITY

Complexity measures an increase or decrease in the program's clarity. A module or program with a high degree of complexity is more likely to have reliability problems. Complexity metrics exist for documentation, systems, and code.

2.1. Documentation

As previously described, software like the Writer's Workbench (under UNIX) can determine the complexity of user, analyst, and programmer documentation. If the documentation is hard to read and understand, the resulting system will be vulnerable to reliability problems.

2.2. System

At the system level, complexity can be measured using the work of Alan Albrecht as described in Chapter 2. The number of programs and modules gives one metric of overall system complexity. The number of files or interfaces between programs and modules gives another. The number of external interfaces (to users and other systems) provides a further metric of system complexity.

In the Function Point section of Chapter 2, there is a list of factors that affect system complexity. These serve as useful metrics of complexity at the design level.

2.3. Code

Module by module, the complexity metrics described in Chapter 4 can determine code complexity. The modules that show abnormally high complexity should be examined for reliability problems. Pareto analysis also comes to bear on reliability analysis: The modules or programs that have a high complexity may never exhibit reliability problems, or they may only run once a month and do not deserve a lot of scrutiny. The programs that do run and fail most frequently are candidates for evaluation and repair.

The major code complexity metrics are executable lines of code, cyclomatic complexity, software science, and interface complexity. The boundaries for what should be considered complex and what shouldn't varies from installation to installation, but 100 ELOC, a $V(G)$ of 10, and an effort metric of 10,000 should provide a meaningful starting point for complexity comparisons. Interface complexity is based on how the module communicates with the outside world, how independent it is, and so on. The metrics of interface complexity are module strength and coupling as described in Chapter 4.

3.   CONSISTENCY

Consistency provides uniform design, code, and test techniques as well as uniform system user documentation. Standards for design techniques, coding, naming, and documentation all serve to improve consistency.

In a manufacturing environment, consistency helps ensure reliability. Making a component exactly the same way each time helps prevent errors. Consistency in the design and manufacture of components helps the repair personnel know how and where to find and fix problems that do occur. Consistency can aid software manufacturers and maintainers in the same ways.

3.1.   Design

In the design phase, consistency is measured by the use of a standard set of design tools: IPOs, data flow diagrams (DFD), pseudocode, structure charts, or whatever. Design consistency improves with the application of reusable designs: edits, update, data selection, reports, and so on. Design consistency can only be measured manually in walkthroughs, but as design documentation becomes more widely implemented on word processors and computer-aided design (CAD) packages, consistency measurement will become easier to extract mechanically.

3.2.   Code

Code consistency depends on the use of reusable code and the application of standard programming techniques and styles. Reusable code, to match the reusable designs, will further increase consistency throughout a system. One validation routine for the Social Security number should be sufficient for an entire system. One reusable routine can be tested exhaustively, while many uniquely coded routines leave the system open to reliability problems.

Consistent programming techniques and styles involves things like only coding one statement per line, initializing all variables, verifying input parameters, and so on. These techniques are fully described in Chapters Eighteen through Twenty-one.

3.3. Testing

To ensure reliability, the testing phase must be capable of repeating each test over and over again exactly. Regression testing gives consistent results that can be examined for erroneous results. To provide this kind of testing environment, each test case must be fashioned for a specific purpose. The test cases should remain standard and reusable. Only the programs should change. Without this kind of consistency, it will not be possible to repeat an error condition, identify its source, and ensure that the problem is corrected.

4. ERROR TOLERANCE

Error tolerance provides continuity of operation under adverse conditions. Software development methodologies simply do not provide a basis for developing error-free software. As a matter of fact, managers, analysts, programmers, and users have come to take software bugs for granted. Status quo. As a group, we have accepted software errors as a fact of life. We expect errors not only in software we develop, but in the operating systems, compilers, and other software testing tools we use. As users of software, we have become tolerant of software errors.

Error tolerance relies on three types of detection and correction techniques: mutual suspicion, fault containment, and fault tolerance. Mutual suspicion requires each module to examine all data passed from other modules or programs and especially any data contained in common areas. Fault containment tests the reasonableness of any computed results prior to overwriting a previous result or releasing an output. Fault-tolerant software will call on another routine that uses different data to provide the required output or will take some intelligent default action.

Error tolerance has one basic problem: If you can anticipate an error, you should be able to avoid it without all of the additional code required to implement error tolerance. Error-tolerant code may be error-prone as well. It may add unnecessary complexity to the program. Error tolerance is an unpleasant but necessary method of improving system reliability. But there is always one more bug.

4.1. Definition

During the definition phase, the user should specify the need for error-tolerant software. Maybe it is an on-line system for 2,000 users; if it breaks, the hourly cost for wasted user time is prohibitive. On the other hand, it could be a year-end report that has no time critical data. It can fail and still be fixed in time to run the report. The only metric of error tolerance during the definition phase is the user's specification for error tolerance.

4.2. Design

During design walk-throughs, attendees should look for references to routines that perform abnormal terminations. They should also check for tests of interface data, range checking, and similar fault containment and tolerant routines. The use of fault detection, correction, containment, and tolerant routines should be specified in the design.

The problems found with the design should be documented and tracked. Error tolerance must be designed in; it rarely can be added later and only at great expense.

4.3. Code

Static analyzers can locate uses and features of the language that handle error conditions. PL/I provides excellent error-handling features with the ON conditions: AREA, CHECK, CONDITION, CONVERSION, ENDFILE, ENDPAGE, ERROR, FIXEDOVERFLOW, KEY, NAME, OVERFLOW, PENDING, RECORD, SIZE, STRINGRANGE, STRINGSIZE, SUBSCRIPTRANGE, TRANSMIT, UNDEFINED FILE, UNDERFLOW, ZERODIVIDE. Each of these conditions allows the programmer flexibility in detecting and doing something about errors as they occur.

COBOL has similar operators such as ON OVERFLOW, AT END, and so on. Each of these error-handling statements provides fault tolerance. These are somewhat limited in their scope, however. ALC has no such error-tolerant code.

Static analyzers can also identify the use of mutual suspicion. A module that checks all of its inputs for reasonability shows its concern with error tolerance.

Fault containment tests the reasonability of calculated results. Following each calculation, a module can examine the results before proceeding to the next step, preventing errors from creeping into the far reaches of the program before they are discovered. Mechanizing the measurement of fault containment is also possible.

Error tolerance can be determined directly from the code, but only after the fact. Since coding is a trivial part of the development expense, fault tolerant, mutually suspicious, and fault containment code can be added to the code before it moves on to unit and system testing. Once the code has been tested and delivered, however, the cost of making these changes increases radically.

As on-line systems replace existing batch ones, the need for error tolerance will increase dramatically. Understanding and measuring the attributes of error tolerance will provide the information necessary to increase reliability at a minimal cost.

5. MODULARITY

Modularity provides a highly independent structure of modules, which can improve reliability. One of the keys to manufacturing reliability is modularity. Small, modular components can be easily tested, repaired, or replaced. The same is true for software. Modularity, when represented by functional strength and data coupling as described in Chapter 4, reduces the possibility of errors in designs and programs.

5.1. Design

Software companies are working to mechanize the design process to provide provably correct programs. The Higher Order Software (HOS) Company's product USE-IT is one such product. But for most IS organizations, the walk-through is still the major source of information about modularity. Attendees should examine the design for functional strength and data coupling. Structure charts help with the analysis of data coupling and module strength. IPOs or functional specifications provide a basis for detailed analysis. Modularity violations should be identified and corrected before coding.

5.2. Code

Static analyzers can determine code modularity from the ELOC, cyclomatic complexity, software science metrics, and data coupling. The first three metrics examine the size of the program in lines of code, operators, operands, and decisions. Data definitions give clues to the type of data coupling used. The use of these metrics is described in Chapter 4.

From a reliability standpoint, the number of bugs in the code can be estimated through the use of these estimators. Using software science, the number of bugs can be calculated as:

$$bugs = volume/3000$$

where 3000 is the number of mental discriminations between the insertion of bugs in the code.

Halstead also observed that the total number of operators and operands N is a function of the number of executable lines of code (P):

$$N = KP$$

where K is a constant relating to the type of language used. For ALC, $K = 2.7$ and for FORTRAN and other high-level languages, $K = 7.5$. (Ottenstein, 1979) From this, it is possible to calculate the error rate B/P as:

$$B/P = A0 + A1 \ln P + A2 \ln 2 \, P \qquad \text{(Lipow, 1982)}$$

For

ALC	FORTRAN, COBOL, PL/I
A0 = 0.001184	A0 = 0.005171
A1 = 0.0009749	A1 = 0.002455
A2 = 0.00001855	A2 = 0.00004638

It seems obvious that the error rate for high-level languages will be higher than for ALC, but more executable lines of code (P) are required to implement the same function in ALC. Given two equivalent programs, one written in ALC and one in a high-level language, the number of faults might be calculated as follows:

ALC fault rate $= 400(0.0077) = 3.1$ faults
COBOL fault rate $= 100(0.0175) = 1.7$ faults (Lipow, 1982)

The study (Lipow, 1982) showed that modularizing programs decreased the predicted error rate. The reduction in the number of predicted faults varied from 7 to 11% for two-module programs compared to equivalent single-module programs. For five modules versus a single module, the expected number of faults declined from 16 to 28%.

The fault-rate metric gives a convenient way of predicting the number of errors in the code *before* testing. After testing has been completed, however, it may not be useful unless the number of bugs found during testing is known. Then, the predicted number of bugs found, minus the number of bugs found, gives a metric of the number of bugs still remaining in the code. A testing confidence level might be established as:

$$\text{confidence} = \text{bugs found/predicted bugs}$$

Testing might continue until 95% of all predicted bugs are found. The opportunity lies in applying this metric to increase modularity and improve reliability.

6. SIMPLICITY

Simplicity implements the software functions in the most understandable manner. Simplicity is the opposite of complexity. Thus the metrics ELOC, cyclomatic complexity, and software science will indicate simplicity. The measurement of simplicity is much the same as the measurement of modularity. Small, concise functions will be simple, easy to understand, and easy to repair. They will rarely break down.

7. SUMMARY

As software systems grow and proliferate, reliability will become an absolute necessity. Movies like *2001—A Space Odyssey* and *The China Syndrome* paint futuristic pictures of computers and computer-controlled systems gone haywire. As computers take over more of the drudgery of human labor, as artificial intelligence increases its abilities, as computers move into every home and workplace, reliability will determine much of our future society—the productivity and quality of life.

CHAPTER THIRTEEN

REUSABILITY METRICS

The metric reusability examines the extent to which a module or program can be used in other applications. Can it be partially or totally reused to reduce costs? An on-line update program is fairly general, but not directly reusable. A header routine for an reporting system may be reusable throughout the system without a single modification. Reusability is a function of five underlying metrics: generality, hardware independence, modularity, self-documentation, and software system independence.

> reusability = F(generality, hardware independence, modularity, self-documentation, software system independence)

Reusability is a direct result of the design and code produced for a given module or program. Reusable designs are checked during walk-throughs. Code reusability may be checked either manually or mechanically.

It has been repeated for over a decade: We should build on the backs of our predecessors. Reusable designs and code provide the foundation for that construction to begin. Measuring and quantifying the reusability of systems will point the way to further improvement. With the proliferation of hardware—from micros to mainframes—reusable designs and code are essential to reducing development and maintenance costs.

Reusable code not only speeds the development, but also the maintenance process. Reusable modules are easily understood, maintained, and enhanced because of their generic logic and design. Logic errors discovered by future maintainers may be tracked easily to all reused modules. Enhancements to the design and code may also be propagated into existing reused modules. Reusable designs and code are the cornerstone from which you may erect a software factory. Measuring reusability will help identify modules that are candidates for inclusion in the factory toolkit.

1. GENERALITY

Generality is the primary requirement of any reusable module. Generality measures the software attributes that expand the usefulness of the function beyond the existing program and its scope. Table 13.1 shows numerous designs and modules that can be built as generic logic for future development. Use of these designs and code in a software system will indicate generality. One study (Kapur, 1980) found that out of 1600 programs, 40% were reports, 27% update, 21% data selection/edits, and 12% data extraction. Generic logic could have been the basis for all of these programs. Usage of generic logic in new development efforts achieved productivity increases of 50−80%.

Modules that perform functions like date conversions and so on, are also general; each module has a specified common function and a well-structured interface. The use of these modules in a program speak of its generality. Similarly, a project may develop many common modules to handle specific

TABLE 13.1.   Generic logic modules.

```
1.  Edit and Data Validation (dates, Social Security Number, etc.)
2.  Update
    a.  Two input sequential file update
    b.  VSAM access update
    c.  DBMS update
3.  Table handling
    a.  Table loading and unloading
    b.  Table searching
    c.  Table sorting
4.  Reporting
    a.  Headings and Footings
    b.  Pagination
    c.  Control breaks
    d.  Margin control
    e.  Formating lines
5.  On-line
    a.  Data collection
    b.  Data validation
    c.  Data inquiry
    d.  Data reporting
6.  Security
7.  Integrity
```

activities: writing header and trailer records on sequential files, writing report headers and footers, writing audit trail records, and so on. The use of these submodules tells more about the program's generality.

During design walk-throughs, the participants should be on the lookout for generic designs that should be incorporated throughout the project. The development and application of this common design will help reduce costs and bring the project in on schedule. The measurement of design generality should be based on the use of existing generic designs in the proposed design and on the potential generality of the program's modules.

During code walk-throughs, participants can measure the use of generic modules and common code: record structures, system constants, and so on. Mechanized analyzers can also scan the code for the presence of COBOL COPY statements and CALLS to common modules. Each use of generic code indicates the existence of generality.

2. HARDWARE INDEPENDENCE

Hardware independence measures the program's dependence on the hardware it runs on. Modules written in assembler language are rarely reusable on another type of hardware. Modules written using the full features of a language are rarely reusable on a machine that only supports a subset of the language. In this way, reusability and portability are synonymous.

Design walk-throughs should check for hardware dependent restrictions. In a mechanized documentation environment, with office automation running rampant, design documentation can be scanned for hardware and software references like IBM, IMS, COBOL, and so on. Unless there is only one kind of hardware available, the presence of hardware or software references in the documentation can reduce the reusability of the design.

Static analyzers can detect what kind of language a module is written in—ALC automatically receives a failing grade for reusability. Use of compiler extensions to a language or the use of the full language when the program may run on a machine having only a subset of the full language, can also be detected mechanically. The correction of the code usually is handled by conversion programs.

Code walk-throughs should examine the software metrics produced and choose a course of corrective action if required.

3. MODULARITY

Modularity provides a structure of highly independent modules. Typically single-function, well-structured modules possessing functional strength and data coupling are reusable. Modules performing more than one function often have intertwined logic that makes reuse of the separate functions difficult if not impossible. Programmers and analysts have to experience this phenomenon several times to gain this knowledge; corporations do not have this time to waste.

The design walk-through provides the first opportunity to ensure modularity. Each participant must evaluate the design's modularity and demand that it be correct before any further work is undertaken. Information Systems management thinks that because everyone has been trained in structured design they are generating structured programs. Nothing could be further from the truth. The analysts and programmers are producing better programs than the spaghetti code of yesteryear, but not the highest quality code possible.

Code modularity can be measured most easily by a static analyzer that collects the four major metrics of size and difficulty: ELOC, McCabe's cyclomatic complexity, Halstead's difficulty, and programming effort. Executable lines of code in the 50–100 range, cyclomatic complexities less than 10, difficulties less than 10, and programming effort metrics less than 10,000 are all quantifiable measures of modularity. These boundaries are somewhat arbitrary, although they have been proven in industry studies. Your own requirements may vary.

4. SELF-DOCUMENTATION

Self-documentation helps explain the function of the software. For any software to be reusable, it must be documented. First, it must have good design documentation showing the exact interface to the module and then it must have internal documentation about how it performs its function. Looking at the idea of generic logic modules, comments will help programmers flesh out the program more quickly, while also providing guidelines for good commenting. The code in reusable modules should not use cryptic data names; they are an invitation for the programmer to propagate their use. Reusable modules should be as error-free and perfect as possible, otherwise programmers will discard them.

Static code analyzers measure self-documentation by the use of comments, the length of data names, and the absence of literals. Cryptic data names can be found and rewritten quickly with any editor. Literals in the code have no name to guide the programmer; their presence reduces the module's self-documentation and therefore its reusability.

5. SOFTWARE SYSTEM INDEPENDENCE

Software system independence determines the application's dependence on the software environment: operating system, data-base management system, programming language and its extensions, and so on. Software system independence only becomes a factor in reusability when the code must move from one software environment to another. For example, microcomputer software vendors want their programs to run under CP/M, the 8-bit standard operating system, and MS−DOS, the 16-bit standard. Independence from the operating system becomes very important. On the other hand, you may have only large IBM mainframes, in which case, software system independence loses its priority.

Again, during design walk-throughs is the time to build software independence into the application if it is required. If you are designing a large IBM−IMS application, you are already tied to an operating system and a DBMS, so why worry about software system independence?

Software system independence can be easily measured directly from the code. The use of embedded or external CALLs to a data-base management system indicate software system dependence. Use of compiler extensions to the language also indicates dependence. The use of languages that are only supported in the existing software environment indicates complete software system dependence. CALLs to IMS, or the data compression facility, SHRINK, or whatever indicates the module's dependence on some external software to allow it to work correctly. None of these things are necessarily bad; they just limit your future opportunities.

6. SUMMARY

Software reusability is the foundation of building the software factory and increasing productivity. This idea is not new; it has been around since 1969 or earlier. Yet few information systems organizations have developed the concept of reusable designs and code. Software measurement provides an opportunity to begin to enforce the generality, modularity, self-documentation, hardware and software independence that will bring about the reuse of software rather than its recreation. Recreation is expensive; reuse costs half as much, if not less. Rigorous measurement of reusability has not been undertaken, but the need for good metrics will continue to grow as the amount of software development increases each year.

CHAPTER FOURTEEN

STRUCTURE METRICS

Structure metrics determine the degree to which a program has a good structured design and implementation. Are the functions implemented in a correct hierarchical tree with properly defined and restricted interfaces? Structure is a function of three underlying metrics: data commonality, expandability, and modularity.

$$\text{structure} = F(\text{data commonality, expandability, modularity})$$

Structure metrics can be extracted from either design documents or code to examine the framework, organization, and anatomy of the module, program, or system. Measuring structure can provide timely meaningful feedback to the system designers, analysts, and programmers, increasing the viability of the system, program, or module structure prior to implementation. This will, in turn, improve the project's chances for success and reduce development and maintenance costs in the bargain.

1. SYSTEM STRUCTURE METRICS

Measuring a system's structure depends on an analysis of the data flows in the system. On a positive note, these metrics of system structure can be determined early in the system design phase, but mainly from manual inspection. Requirement statement languages (RSL) are working toward quantifying and refining the design of the system's structure, but they are not 100% correct as yet. Most of the promising metrics of system structure are based on information flows.

1.1. Information Flows

Information flows can be determined from automated analysis of existing systems while the major components of these flows are available for manual inspection early in development. The availability of system information flows and their impact on system structure allows inexpensive correction of the system design. Once the system design migrates into the program design phase, the costs of redesign increase radically.

Information flows, depicted by data-flow diagrams, often reveal more about the connections between system components than studies of the hierarchy and so on. Defining the way components communicate allows the definition of complexity, module coupling, module strength, level interactions, and stress points. These critical metrics of system structure cannot be obtained from a simple lexical analysis of single modules; they must be extracted from design documents and the whole system.

The work done by Henry (1981) shows a method for first defining types of data flows and their impact on structure. There are three types of information flows: global information flows, direct local information flows, and indirect local information flows. A global information flow exists between two modules that access the same global information structure; one updates the structure and the other retrieves data from it. The FORTRAN COMMON statement or the use of a data-base management system implies the presence of global data flows.

Local information flows occur between calling and called modules. A direct information flow exists between modules A and B if module A calls B, passes it information, and B does not return anything. An indirect information flow exists between the modules A, B, and C if A calls B and B returns data that A uses, or that A passes to C for its use. Information flows are represented as follows: A→B, B→C, and so on. The use of information flows, which can be determined from static analysis of the code, give insight into not only the physical structure of the program, but also the inner workings of the program. A structure chart shows only the skeleton of a program. Data flows show the arteries and musculature of the program.

1.2. Data Dictionaries

Data dictionaries provide another tool for analyzing data flows in systems. Each element, group, or structure of data should be traceable to the programs that will either pass or modify the data. Data dictionaries provide data commonality—common data names and data attributes. The generation of all data structures from the data dictionary also ensures the expandability of the system; changing the data definitions propagates the expanded data structures into all programs that access the data.

2. PROGRAM STRUCTURE METRICS

With a touch of toolsmithing, you can create a program to extract the CALL-ing structure of a program. Along with this information, you can gather the parameters passed, how they are passed, and their attributes. The structure may be displayed simply, as shown in Figure 14.1, or in graphical form, as shown in Figure 14.2.

Knowing the calling sequence and the parameters passed, you can determine the functional strength and module coupling present in each module and at each interface. Data commonality, expandability, and modularity are also easily determined.

2.1. Data Commonality

Data commonality implies that the parameter names and attributes on both sides of an interface are the same. If not, the commonality has eroded to some extent. The first order of priority involves the data attributes (alphabetic or numeric, length, and format); if they are equal, then commonality is preserved. If even one of the attributes is incorrect, potential problems may occur. Next, the data names should be the same. When calling general modules, this is not often possible: Consider a date routine that converts today's date, last revision date, and a host of others. It is possible, however, to evaluate the original data name to determine if any part is in the subordinate module's data name: DATE in TODAYS-DATE and CONVERSION-DATE.

```
Create Year End Report
    Write Report Headings
    Read First Record
    Format Report
        Format Report Line
        Write Report Line
        Read Next Record
        Write Report Footers
        Write Report Headings
    Format Summaries
    Write Report Footers
```

FIGURE 14.1. Simple structure of a report program.

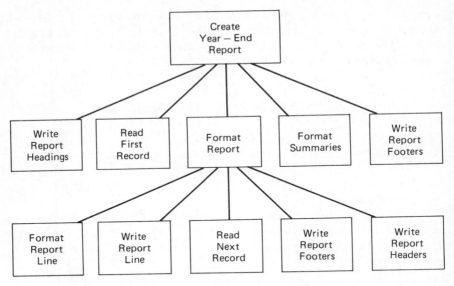

FIGURE 14.2.   Hierarchy chart for a report program.

Data commonality depends on the use of COPY statements in COBOL, DSECTs in ALC, and %INCLUDE statements in PL/1. These statements virtually assure data commonality for modules that use them.

2.2. Expandability

Expandability relies on the ability to stretch a program's data structures as well as its capabilities. Increasing the size and content of data structures and parameters depends, in turn, on the use of data dictionaries and common copy libraries. Expanding a record structure, when the data definitions are all contained in a single copy library member, is simple; just change the structure and recompile all of the affected programs.

Expanding a program's logic depends on its functionality. The function density metric provides a basic metric of expandability: a program with a high function density is easier to change and enhance than one that does detail work.

2.3. Modularity

Modularity depends on each module's ELOC, cyclomatic complexity, difficulty, and programming effort. More about these metrics in the next section.

3. MODULE STRUCTURE METRICS

The module level is perhaps the easiest place to determine structure. Data commonality, expandability, and modularity are directly obtainable from the code. Once again, you will need the department toolsmith to create the tools to analyze the code, build structure charts, and take all measurements.

3.1. Data Commonality

Data commonality is easily measured from the use of COBOL COPY statements and similar features in all languages. Use of global data definitions, like the FORTRAN COMMON statement, are also easily collected. Use of references to single-element data items can be found from the use of EXTERNAL data statements. References to the inside of another module can be determined in ALC from the use of address constants. Each of these statements points out the type of data coupling the module employs and documents the module's vulnerability to external changes.

3.2. Expandability

Expandability is also a function of the number of COPY statements and the use of CALLs and compiler functions within the program. Expanding the program's function requires the existing function to be clear and concise. The antithesis of clarity and concision is the lowly GO TO. Comparing the number of GO TOs (hopefully none) to the number of ELOC gives a metric of expandability: GO TO density.

$$\text{GO TO density} = (\text{number of GO TOs} * 100\%)/\text{ELOC}$$

I have seen programs measuring as high as 10%—one GO TO for every 10 lines of code. In these spaghetti programs, expandability is a forgotten dream. The code can be enhanced, but the change takes many times longer than it would for an equivalent GOTO-less program.

Another metric of expandability is the number of knots in the code. These were described in Chapter 4. As the number of knots increase, the code's Medusalike qualities come into view, until finally there remains only a swirling, twisting mass of snakelike code that every programmer fears to enter.

3.3. Modularity

Modularity depends on the metrics: ELOC, cyclomatic complexity, difficulty, and programming effort. The ranges for these metrics is shown in Figure

14.3. Once these limits are exceeded, managers, analysts, and programmers need to look at the code to determine if the module is growing beyond its function. Often, the module will have been designed to include several functions. Sometimes the programmer lacks the skill to use the best features of the language to make the code concise. Whatever the problem, now is the time to identify and fix it, not later.

One of the primary metrics of modularity is whether the module contains a single entry and exit statement. In COBOL, the entry point can be either the PROCEDURE DIVISION or an actual ENTRY statement. The module's exit can be either a GOBACK, STOP RUN, or a call to an abnormal termination routine. The presence of more than one entry or exit should be cause for alarm. A module with more entries than exits, or the reverse, potentially has extensive structure problems: It can enter at two points and only leave at one, or it may enter at one point and leaves at several others. Modules with two or more entry and exit statements may have informational strength, the next best module strength compared to functional strength. These modules need to be examined to verify their structure.

Similarly, a COBOL paragraph has a single entry and exit unless the PERFORM THRU option is used or the paragraph contains an embedded GO TO. The THRU option of COBOL allows the program to PERFORM multiple paragraphs. The problem with the THRU option is that maintenance programmers can add PERFORMs of the middle paragraphs or GO TOs that branch into or out of the range of the original PERFORM THRU. Either of these creates additional entry and exit points for the original function. A GO TO, branching out of a paragraph to a totally unrelated place in the program, adds an exit to the paragraph's original single entry and exit point. Maintaining or enhancing the structure of these distorted modules becomes increasingly difficult with the increase in the number of entries and exits. Measurement of these anomalies should be mechanized and reviewed.

| | | Complexity | |
Metric	Low	Medium	High
Executable Lines of Code	100	500	> 1000
Cyclomatic Complexity	10	50	> 100
Difficulty	<10	< 25	> 50
Effort	10,000	100,000	>100,000

FIGURE 14.3.   Acceptability ranges for complexity metrics.

4. SUMMARY

Similar, but different metrics of structure are used at the system, program, and module level. Tools to measure structure vary from lexical analyzers, at the module and program level, to requirement statement languages and manual review at the system level. Work by Henry (1981) and a few others has broken the ground in this important measurement arena.

Once analysts and programmers know which metrics of structure are the best, and which structures provide the maximum benefit to themselves and the corporation, they will begin to move toward these goals. Metrics provide quantifiable measurements of structure and facilitate feedback to the developers.

CHAPTER FIFTEEN

TESTABILITY METRICS

Testability identifies how much effort it will take to test the structure and correctness of the code. The question, in some cases, is: Can you even test it? Testability is a function of six underlying metrics: auditability, complexity, instrumentation, modularity, self-documentation, and simplicity.

$$\text{testability} = F(\text{auditability, complexity, instrumentation, modularity,}$$
$$\text{self-documentation, simplicity})$$

Testability is designed and coded into a system—it cannot be added later.

1. AUDITABILITY

Auditability recognizes software attributes that contribute to the ease of auditing of the software, data, and results. As mentioned in earlier chapters, auditability is first set down in the requirements phase, signed and sealed in the design phase, and finally cast in concrete during the implementation phase of system development. Manual inspections of the requirements and designs provide metrics of the developing system's auditability. Once in the implementation phase, however, mechanized code analyzers can indicate the presence of audit software and the extent of audit trails throughout the system.

Metrics of each module should indicate the existence of a security or proprietary information statement. One day, the code may be copyrighted and metrics will have to check for these notices in the code. Next, the code should contain version information: module name, the release and source code level of the software, the date compiled, and whatever other factors are important. This information can be used later with a generic audit trail module to produce an audit report of which modules were executed during a given program run. The presence of generic audit modules can be determined by the code analyzer as well.

At the object level, identification records should be embedded in each object and load module to allow external verification of the module names, release and level numbers, compilation date, and so on. In the IBM environment, these are known as IDR records and can be extracted with a utility program. Using these records, Operations can verify that the programs they are running are the same ones released by the IS department. Further audit trails are available from the operating system log and the data-base management system, but these are usually beyond the study of the programmers, analysts, and managers of an application system.

Each of these metrics helps the unit, system, conversion, or integration testing teams identify whether: the correct modules are being tested; the basic audit functions of the system are performing correctly; and the system's auditability meets the requirements specification. Without these basic audit trails, testing a system can quickly degenerate into chaos.

2. COMPLEXITY

Complexity measures the increase or decrease in a program's or module's clarity. How complex is it to test a given piece of code? Well, it depends on the following metrics: cyclomatic complexity, difficulty, programming effort, the ELOC, the number of knots, and the number of GO TOs.

2.1. Cyclomatic Complexity

McCabe's cyclomatic complexity gives the number of structural testing paths in the program, but it cannot measure all of the testing paths. Often a single GO TO can cause the total number of testing paths to increase exponentially. But component testing should be satisfied with having tested all of the structural paths at least once. So cyclomatic complexity indicates how many test paths must be executed to fulfill this unit testing requirement. Also, remember that studies (McCabe, 1976) have shown that an optimum size for a module has a cyclomatic complexity of less than ten. Modules possessing a low $V(G)$ have been shown to be highly reliable and easily tested. The cyclomatic complexity metric should aid in predicting the time and costs associated with software testing. Little research, however, has been done to examine the effects of $V(G)$ on testing costs.

2.2. Software Science

The software science metrics difficulty and programming effort are derived from the number of operators and operands. In effect, testing must exercise each of the operators and operands to ensure that the module or program has been tested adequately. Since both difficulty and programming effort are strongly correlated with the actual time required to implement a program, and testing is often 40% or more of total development time, they should both be reasonable predictors of the amount of time it will take to test a given module, program, or system. These metrics focus not only on the logic complexity—the number of operators, but also on the manipulation of data, which the cyclomatic complexity metric ignores completely. Not only must the logic be correct, but the data must be transformed correctly to fulfill the system requirements. Studies have examined the programming effort in relation to reliability and correctness, finding that an effort of less than 300 will indicate that the modules have no errors. The testability of these modules should be very high.

2.3. ELOC

The ELOC measures testability similarly to the software science metrics, although it focuses on only one of the four foundations of software science— the total number of operators. Again, this metric includes not only the decisions, but all of the data manipulation and function calls. It helps indicate how many lines must be exercised to completely test the structure of the program. Working in concert with the cyclomatic complexity, ELOC helps describe structural testability.

Along with the overall ELOC metrics, a count of each statement in the program will provide insights for the unit and system testers. For example, a count of the number of DIVIDE statements could indicate a possible test case for zero division. The number of arithmetic operators should demand that the testers try and populate those fields with nonnumeric data and see how the program performs, and so on.

2.4. GO TOs

The GO TO is the only way to violate structure in most programming languages. McCabe described the four ways to violate structure: branch into, or out of, a loop or a decision. Because GO TOs facilitate structure violations, they also make the code more difficult to test. The number of GO TOs and the density of GO TOs in the code provides a further metric of testability.

GO TOs are also one of the few ways to create knots (see Chapter 4). Knots cause further difficulty for system testers. Complex logic is often as difficult to test as it is to maintain.

2.5. Decision and Loop Nesting

Decision and loop nesting complexity are two more code level metrics that help indicate the difficulty involved in testing a piece of code. Decision-nesting complexity measures how deeply IF statements are nested in the code. Nesting levels of three or more are difficult to understand and, therefore, difficult to test. Similarly, loop-nesting complexity measures the number of loops nested within one another. In COBOL, a programmer may PERFORM a paragraph that PERFORMs another, which PERFORMs another, and so on. Designing test cases to handle the more complex loop structures is not easy and often leaves portions of the code untested. Again, the maximum nesting level should be three or perhaps four. Beyond this, the code should be split functionally and placed in a separately called module, gaining the benefits of increased functional strength and data coupling.

3. INSTRUMENTATION

Instrumentation accounts for the software attributes that provide measurements of software usage or the identification of errors. A program containing its own instrumentation will contain code to detect errors and correct them. For example, the ON conditions of PL/I provide a facility to detect software errors such as overflows in mathematical operations and to correct those errors when they occur. The use of execution counters can provide further tallies of the records read, written, and processed. When looking at a data base, counters can track the number and type of data-base accesses, potentially providing information to detect logic and data manipulation errors that might otherwise go unobserved.

The use of generic run control modules can help determine if the program is scheduled to run or if it is accidentally being run out of order. These run controls can also verify that the proper data are used as input by keeping track of the audit stamp from the previous program's execution. Similarly, any new files written by the current program should cause an audit stamp to pass back to the run control modules.

The presence of any of these types of software—error detection, execution counters, or run controls—indicate the presence of software instrumentation.

Just as simple instruments in a car measure the engine temperature and oil level, software instruments help pinpoint problems as they occur, not afterwards, when the module cannot be easily repaired. These instruments also provide the testing organization with built-in tools for testing the system.

Some compilers allow portions of code to exist in the module that provide further instrumentation. Using the "C" language, a testing organization might insert the following:

```
#ifdef TEST
    fprintf(stderr, "Loop Control Variable = %s\n", loop_variable);
#endif
```

This code would only be included in the compiled module if the compiler flag TEST was used during the compile. Thus the testing organization could include all of the testing instruments required and then compile their own version of the system to facilitate testing. The presence of this code as well as all of the other software instrumentation is easily obtained by mechanized analysis of the source programs.

4. MODULARITY

Modularity provides a system of highly independent modules. Small single-function modules not only take less time to compile at a terminal, but they can also be easily unit tested with interactive testing facilities available on most large systems. Once unit testing is complete, integration test is easily performed, focusing on just the interface between modules, not the function of each; each module's function has already been satisfactorily tested, so only its interface to its neighbors needs to be tested. Similarly, the interface between programs can be tested without regard for the other aspects of the program's performance. Finally, the system testing group is responsible for determining the product's fitness for use. Does it meet the user's requirements? Usability will be examined in the next chapter. The measurement of modularity depends on three main code metrics: ELOC, cyclomatic complexity, and programming effort. Two minor metrics further quantify the modularity: single-entry, single-exit and GO TO usage. Modularity is also a function of the module's functional strength and data coupling.

As described in Chapter Four, Complexity Metrics, the ELOC metric should be less than 100 ELOC per module, if modularity is to be maintained. The cyclomatic complexity should be less than or equal to 10, except when the module contains a large CASE statement, such as an edit module. The programming effort should be kept under 10,000. These are good starting ranges for these modularity metrics. With experience, you may find the ranges need to increase or decrease to meet your corporate quality goals.

The other metrics of modularity are based on good programming techniques and structure. A module should have a single entry point and a single exit point; otherwise, the testing group may not test all entries and exits, or they may fail to catch an incorrect exit. Similarly, the presence of GO TOs implies some form of pretzel logic, no matter how the GO TOs are used. This makes definition and creation of meaningful test cases more difficult and makes the program more difficult to test exhaustively. Next, the modularity may also be measured as described in Chapter Fourteen, Structure Metrics. The module's functional strength and data coupling can be determined from manual or mechanized review of each module's function and interface to the outside world.

5. SELF-DOCUMENTATION

Self-documentation identifies software attributes that help explain the function of the code. The comments embedded in the code provide the testing group with insights into the program's processing that may enhance or conflict with the original definition or design. Comments often provide insight into the logic and data manipulation that feeds the tester's imagination and creation of test cases. Comments are easily tracked and counted in the source code. A previously mentioned metric of self-documentation was the comment density:

$$\text{comment density} = (\text{number of comments} * 100)/\text{total lines of code}$$

This metric shows how many comments there are per line of code. Ten percent is customary in COBOL programs. The absence of comments may be acceptable in a modular program, since the code is easily understandable. In larger programs, the absence of comments is unforgivable. On the other hand, too many comments can obscure the code, preventing complete testing. A module with a 50% comment density will have so much documentation that some of the executable code will disappear in the forest of comments.

6. SIMPLICITY

Simplicity provides an implementation of the functions in the most understandable manner. If the functionality is clear, then creating test cases becomes much easier. In effect, simplicity represents not only how under-standable the code is, but how easily it can be tested.

Simplicity depends on the use of function statements and the absence of complexity. Function statements, like PERFORM, CALL, SORT, SQRT, and so on, give a concise explanation of what the program will do next. These statements serve as signposts, pointing the tester toward the action, allowing him or her to build proper test cases for each piece of the processing.

Complexity depends on high values of the ELOC, cyclomatic complexity, and programming effort metrics. Simplicity, therefore, is represented by lower values of these metrics. When the number of ELOC is less than 50 or 100, the module is easily understood and proper test cases are easily built. Similarly, when cyclomatic complexity is less than 10, the decision logic is simple and easily understood. And when the programming effort is less than 10,000, the testing effort should be minimal. Low values for these metrics implies that unit testing can be done on-line, at the terminal, with minimal machine or programmer effort. Similarly, testing the interfaces between modules possessing simplicity should be accomplished easily.

7. SUMMARY

The ability to test a module, program, or system depends on metrics that can be obtained from definition and design walk-throughs and the source code. Knowing the metrics of each module and program can dictate where to put most of the testing resource to maximize the return. The highly complex, not easily testable programs, which number perhaps 10−20% of all programs, will require perhaps 80% of the testing resource to verify that they work correctly. Typically, the remaining 80% of the programs can be tested easily. Remember, however, that software metrics can only predict testability, experience with testing each system will show a few complex programs that are easy to test, and a few simple ones that seem to defy proper testing.

Software metrics provides a means to anticipate the resources needed to test a module, program, or system. This metric, testability, gives program-mers, analysts, and managers a tool to plan their time accordingly. They may also choose to change modules or programs with a poor testability, expending only 10% of their effort to recode, while reducing the 40% required for testing. Since testing is often a large percentage of total development effort, redesign and recode of the offending module or program will be less costly than the testing costs over the system's lifetime.

CHAPTER SIXTEEN

USABILITY METRICS

How much effort will the user expend to learn the system's inputs and outputs. Can the user operate the system successfully? Can the computer center run it easily? Usability is a function of the underlying metrics operability and training.

$$usability = F(operability, training)$$

Usability is perhaps the most important metric of quality. It does not matter if the system is reliable, maintainable, flexible, efficient, and so on if the user cannot work the system successfully. Usability depends on the type of system being used. In an on-line system, screen formats and help facilities are the major components of usability. Outputs from an on-line system may take the form of other screens, paper, or microfiche. In an automatic teller machine, simple inputs yield money or bank transactions. In a batch system, the criteria of operability may be quite different. In a micro-based application, usability will determine whether a professional worker, unskilled in microcomputer usage, can apply the package, or if the application will require a microcomputer wizard to understand its operation.

No matter what kind of system is built, humans will have to be trained to use it. The training may vary from weeks of classroom instruction to a simple user's guide for a micro-based application. Training may also be included in the system itself—computer-aided instruction (CAI) as it is commonly known.

1. OPERABILITY

Both the end-users and the operations personnel need to be able to operate the system. The ease of operation determines the productivity and quality of work possible.

1.1. Users

Users are becoming more sophisticated in their understanding of what computer systems can, and cannot, do. Only a few years ago, they filled out forms that had 80-column representations of their data. These were then key punched and used as batch input to their systems. The feedback loop for input errors often took several weeks. In an on-line environment, the user expects systems to provide simple, easy-to-use menus for input processing. Input validation happens in seconds, instead of weeks. The user expects the system to provide help whenever its messages or input requirements are not clear.

Every user seems to have learned to like system menus. They prefer to see one simple menu at a time, and then be led through progressively more detailed menus to do what needs to be done. There is no mechanized way to examine a system's menus to determine their usability. The presence of menus, however, does indicate the developer's concern with human factors. Menus are prime candidates for reusable code, and as such, their presence can be detected with mechanized analysis.

Help facilities provide another tool for creating system usability. Most systems should provide some level of help processing for any situation. Again, help facilities are prime candidates for reusable code. So, investment in usability can be held to a minimum while still providing the user with a more friendly and helpful system.

A system's usability, from the end-user's perspective, is only as good as its inputs and outputs. The insides of the black boxes that process the data may be of high quality, but the outside interfaces may be atrocious. The only way to quantify the usability of the system's input processing is through a study of the user's likes and dislikes. The same is true of the system's outputs.

1.2. Operations

Some of the largest problems with computer systems occur in a production environment. When the system aborts, it gives no meaningful error messages; it fails to suggest a course of action other than to call the programmer; and the runbook is worthless. Operational error messages are another function that could be provided with reusable code. Only the error messages need to be changed. The presence of reusable error modules can be detected with code analyzers. Operational considerations like these should be specified in the definition and design documents. They are a price of running a productive, high-quality system.

Operational documentation can be examined for readability with mechanized analyzers. The presence of data flow diagrams (DFD) and flow charts also indicate a concern for providing high-quality documentation. Only the operations group, however, can pass final judgement on the usability of the documentation.

2. TRAINING

End-user and operator training are both parts of providing usable systems. Without sufficient training, users often fail to use the system at all, use it incorrectly or incompletely, or use it inefficiently. The most promising methods of training are CAI, classroom instruction, and step-by-step user guides.

2.1. On-line Tutorials

Computers are rapidly becoming an inexpensive way of training anyone in their use. Each new microcomputer software product comes with some form of tutorial that steps the user through its basic functions. Large mainframe systems should consider the same approach. Employees are constantly moving from job to job, and training them in a classroom environment grows increasingly more expensive with each passing year. Tutorials offer a means to reduce the cost and get the user familiar with the computer from the start. Tutorials help the user learn the system and also help prevent user resistance—the computer is perceived as a friend and not as an enemy.

2.2. Classroom

The effectiveness of user training can be determined partially from studies of the types of errors that occur during processing. If the user always has problems entering a certain kind of master record, the training is probably weak in that area. Conversely, if the user can always enter some series of complex transactions, the training is probably particularly effective. Analysis of user errors must come from the system routines that edit each transaction. Collecting this information adds overhead and costs to the development and operation of the system, but it can give a handsome return when the user's productivity improves due to specialized training suggested by the transaction metrics.

2.3. User Guides

The usability of the system documentation can be determined with the aid of products such as the Writer's Workbench (to describe readability, etc.). The content of the documentation can only be determined from user surveys.

3. SUMMARY

If it were any friendlier, it would be illegal.

a VisiOn™ advertisement

User friendliness seems to be the watchword for the eighties. Usability is the key. But there are few ways of determining usability. Most software measurement theory has been directed at the development and maintenance processes. Little work has gone into the ergonomics of software. What makes a system usable? Is it a "mouse?" Is it graphic displays with icons? What makes the system easy to learn and use? It is a difficult question, but one that will receive more attention as the cost of people increases while the cost of hardware declines.

CHAPTER SEVENTEEN

APPLICATION OF SOFTWARE METRICS

Software metrics are only useful if presented in a format that lends itself to the person's job. Managers needs differ from systems analysts, and systems analysts focus on different productivity and quality items than programmers. Each of these people should be concerned with productivity and the different quality metrics: Complexity, correctness, efficiency, flexibility, integrity, interoperability, maintainability, portability, reliability, reusability, structure, testability, and usability. But each person will need these metrics selected, summarized, and presented in different ways to aid and improve their jobs. Let's examine the different jobs and potential ways of presenting software metrics to aid decision making, productivity improvement, and quality control.

1. MANAGEMENT

Whether programmers and analysts care to admit it or not, managers play an important role in determining productivity and quality. So, managers should be measured on the same things their troops are measured on, creating an environment that stimulates the achievement of quality and productivity goals through constant innovation and improvement.

Excellent company managers are constantly concerned with both productivity and quality, knowing that the corporation stands to gain a great deal from both. Excellent company managers constantly look for new ways to improve productivity, quality, and the quality of work life. Software metrics is a tool for these managers to gain a better insight into the development and maintenance of software and to implement improvements.

There are managers, however, whose sole purpose in life is to advance in the corporation. All they want is the ability to show increased productivity. By the time the problems from this sort of management style show themselves, the manager has normally moved on to another job or to a higher position. He or she rarely suffers the consequences of their actions. I only mention these few managers because they can spoil the benefits of a measurement program; their people come to resent measurements and they pass that attitude on to the rest of the corporation. Suddenly, you could find your whole IS organization becoming less productive and producing lower-quality systems. Productivity does not come from measurement, but from concern for eight basic goals of excellent companies (Peters, 1982): maintaining a bias for action, staying close to the customer, fostering autonomy and entrepreneurship, encouraging productivity through people, being value driven, doing what you know how to do, having a simple form and a lean staff, and maintaining simultaneous loose-tight properties and controls. Software measurement is simply a tool to quantify your progress toward these goals.

1.1. Productivity

Productivity metrics should be summarized by work group within the IS organization. Each higher management level should receive summaries of the metrics collected for each management level underneath. Summarizing productivity metrics helps prevent their use at a programmer level, where they have little meaning. The productivity of development programmers is usually a function of the analyst's design; high-quality designs are easier to develop. Similarly, simple programs often are easier to develop than complex algorithms. The productivity of maintenance programmers depends on the quality of the existing code; spaghetti code is more difficult to fix or enhance.

How should managers look at productivity? Back in Chapter 2, I suggested that managers need to see a network of input/output ratios: rate of profit to fixed investment, capacity utilization, productivity of fixed investment, functions per person-day, and so on. Managers also need to know their unit costs, cost proportions, input prices, and input productivity, and input proportions—also described in Chapter 2. The most critical factors affecting productivity, such as employee morale and client concern, will be the most difficult to measure.

Management metrics should be summarized from system, design, and code productivity metrics. These metrics should be combined with budget and payroll information to reflect costs. The more useful metrics are as follows:

1. Number of people working on the system.
2. Number of person-days (including overtime) worked per month.
3. Total monthly cost for the system's development or maintenance.
4. Cummulative costs for the system's development and maintenance.
5. Wage costs.
6. Material costs.
7. Computer costs.
8. Wages to total costs ratio.
9. Materials to total costs ratio.
10. Computer to total costs ratio.
11. Number of programs delivered or maintained.
12. Number of modules delivered or maintained.
13. Number of functions delivered or maintained.
14. Number of ELOC delivered or maintained.
15. Person days per program, module, function, or ELOC.
16. Cost per program, module, function, or ELOC.
17. Computer time per program, module, function, or ELOC.
18. Computer time per person.
19. Computer center measures like jobs run, compiles, tests, connect hours, and CPU hours per person-day, program, or ELOC.
20. Schedule overruns, employee turnover, and absenteeism.

Each of these metrics tells something about productivity at a system level. At a design level, a manager may need to know the number of programs, modules, or functions designed per analyst day.

These measurements should also include the Albrecht function metrics described in Chapter 2: number of user inputs, number of user outputs, number of user inquiries, number of files, and number of external interfaces per program, module, or function. These numbers are tempered by the complexity adjustment described in Chapter Two to arrive at the number of function points, which should in turn be compared with person-days, costs, and so on. The number of pages in the definition document compared to the number of functions and programs may be of interest. The number of pages of design documentation per design function may also shed some light on the development process (Walston, 1977).

At a coding level, a manager may find use for the number of programs, modules, and functions delivered or modified. The number of developed or changed ELOC should also provide crude metrics of development and maintenance productivity. The software science metrics—length, volume, and effort—should provide another metric of productivity. How many operands and operators are used in the entire function, module, program or system? The cyclomatic complexity metric (based on the number of decisions in the code) provides another input to the measurement of productivity.

Each of the productivity metrics—system, design, and code—provide information about the development and maintenance of systems. They should be summarized for the appropriate level of management. A project leader will want to see statistics for his or her project, while the director of IS wants to see the department as a whole. These metrics tell a manager where the work group has been. He or she should be able to identify release cycles (see Figure 17.1) and the effects of new technology and methodology (Figure 17.2). Using the productivity metrics, management may be able to see a trend in productivity improvement over many months as new technology or methodology are installed. They should be able to see a dip in productivity for the first few

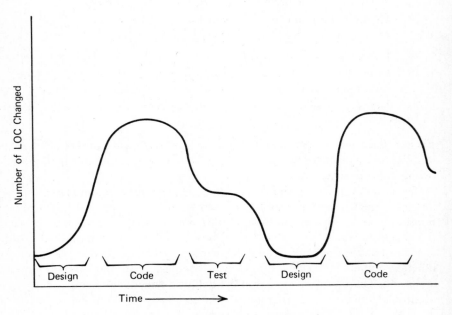

FIGURE 17.1.   Release cycle identification.

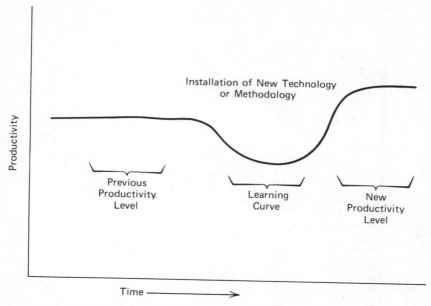

FIGURE 17.2.   Effects of new methodology and technology on productivity.

months while their people are learning and starting to use the "breakthrough" technology. But they should also be interested in quality.

1.2.   Quality

Quality is free (Crosby, 1979). Figure 17.3 contains the questions to ask yourself about where your department stands on quality, its development, and control. Quality helps reduce development and maintenance costs. It helps reduce operational costs. And yet, these savings are difficult, if not impossible, to quantify.

Each improvement in quality comes from some breakthrough in knowledge. One analyst or programmer may discover ways to reuse existing designs or code. This knowledge then spreads from person to person, or the analyst may covet the knowledge because it makes them more productive than their neighbors. Programmers always seem to know who produces the best designs, and maintenance programmers always know which programmers produce the best code. System test personnel can anticipate which programs will need special consideration because they know which maintenance programmers have "breakthrough" knowledge about testing their programs. Signifi-

QUALITY MANAGEMENT MATURITY GRID

Rater _____   Unit _____

Measurement Categories	Stage I: Uncertainty	Stage II: Awakening	Stage III: Enlightenment	Stage IV: Wisdom	Stage V: Certainty
Management understanding and attitude	No comprehension of quality as a management tool. Tend to blame quality department for "quality problems."	Recognizing that quality management may be of value but not willing to provide money or time to make it all happen.	While going through quality Improvement program learn more about quality management; becoming supportive and helpful.	Participating. Understand absolutes of quality management. Recognize their personal role in continuing emphasis.	Consider quality management an essential part of company system.
Quality organization status	Quality is hidden in manufacturing or engineering departments. Inspection probably not part of organization. Emphasis on appraisal and sorting.	A stronger quality leader is appointed but main emphasis is still on appraisal and moving the product. Still part of manufacturing or other.	Quality department reports to top management, all appraisal is incorporated and manager has role in management of company.	Quality manager is an officer of company; effective status reporting and preventive action. Involved with consumer affairs and special assignments.	Quality manager on board of directors. Prevention is main concern. Quality is a thought leader.
Problem handling	Problems are fought as they occur; no resolution; inadequate definition; lots of yelling and accusations.	Teams are set up to attack major problems. Long-range solutions are not solicited.	Corrective action communication established. Problems are faced openly and resolved in an orderly way.	Problems are identified early in their development. All functions are open to suggestion and improvement.	Except in the most unusual cases, problems are prevented.
Cost of quality as % of sales	Reported: unknown Actual: 20%	Reported: 3% Actual: 18%	Reported: 8% Actual: 12%	Reported: 6.5% Actual: 8%	Reported: 2.5% Actual: 2.5%
Quality improvement actions	No organized activities. No understanding of such activities.	Trying obvious "motivational" short-range efforts.	Implementation of the 14-step program with thorough understanding and establishment of each step.	Continuing the 14-step program and starting Make Certain.	Quality improvement is a normal and continued activity.
Summation of company quality posture	"We don't know why we have problems with quality."	"Is it absolutely necessary to always have problems with quality?"	"Through management commitment and quality improvement we are identifying and resolving our problems."	"Defect prevention is a routine part of our operation."	"We know why we do not have problems with quality."

FIGURE 17.3.   Quality management maturity grid (© 1979 Philip B. Crosby).

cant productivity and quality improvements come from identifying these individuals and spreading their knowledge across the entire organization.

One of the ways to distribute this knowledge is by development of software metrics. As each of these subject matter experts identifies what they do to improve quality, measurement tools can be built to track the use or absence of these techniques. Measurement tools help each manager to focus training on weaknesses and to identify strengths.

Measuring Design Quality

Certain products that help analysts produce "provably correct" software designs are available (Martin, 1982). In the absence of these kinds of tools, managers must rely on walk-throughs and error tracking to determine design quality.

Walk-throughs are the heart of most design quality improvements. Design inspections were the practice of manufacturing industries long before they were adopted by software engineers. Managers should be aware of any problems found during design walk-throughs. They should also keep a lookout for common problems and direct training at eliminating them.

Design errors found in walk-throughs and in later stages of development or maintenance should be tracked by a mechanized tracking system like the UNIX™ Change Management Tracking System. The errors should be summarized and presented by development phase. For example, you might discover that nine programs have no audit trails, but not until the implementation phase. The coding and unit testing of these programs is complete. Now the design has to be modified, coded, and tested again. Based on this knowledge of audit trail omissions, audit trails should become a part of an analyst's checklist for new programs. Design walk-throughs should then determine the need for audit trails and enforce their inclusion.

Errors that are unique to the design should be excluded from this quality improvement plan, however. Otherwise, analysts would not know which items on the checklist carry the most weight. Remember, the object of quality improvement is to make the changes that generate the best return on investment.

Management should also be concerned with specifying quality objectives. Figure 3.1 showed a form for specifying design and code qualities. Analysts and programmers can provide the desired quality when they know the goals. The importance of each software quality can be stated at each level of management. At a department level, flexibility, maintainability, and reliability may command the most importance because that is where 80% of the budget is spent. At lower levels, a user might want a program that runs for eight hours every day to be more efficient.

Design and code quality begins with corporate goals, which must be translated into software quality goals by management.

Measuring Code Quality

Code quality depends on many things. Chapters 4–16 described the major software quality metrics. Based on the needs of your corporation, some of these may be applicable; others, unnecessary. But one choice that weighs most heavily on code quality is the selection of languages. When it comes to *flexibility* and *maintainability*, assembler language is far behind COBOL or PL/I. Fourth-generation languages are equally far ahead of COBOL or PL/I, but fourth-generation products do not currently have the capabilities to meet extremely detailed requirements. PL/I is ahead of COBOL because it has implementations of each of the five structured programming constructs: sequential, IF-THEN-ELSE, CASE, DOWHILE, and DOUNTIL. PL/I can also handle bits, where COBOL has trouble with anything smaller than characters.

When it comes to *portability*, FORTRAN and C are among the most widely ported languages. But they both have restrictions in data naming, readability, and support of structured programming.

Most of the fourth-generation products require the use of their language interpreters on the target machine, enforcing *software dependence*. If you have five different computer centers, having a copy of the fourth-generation software on each machine can be expensive. Some products, however, produce COBOL code that can be compiled and maintained even if the fourth-generation product goes away or is replaced by later products.

So the type of language used is the first metric of quality. Next, a manager should be concerned with programs in development and maintenance that are exceeding established boundaries for complexity, flexibility, maintainability, costs, and so on. The following boundaries are somewhat arbitrary and vary from language to language. Assuming a COBOL development environment, managers should look at programs that exceed the following limits:

1. 100 ELOC.
2. Cyclomatic complexity $> 10-20$.
3. Difficulty > 10.
4. Effort $> 100,000$.
5. Decision density $> 20\%$.
6. Function density $< 10\%$.
7. Comment density $< 10\%$.
8. More than one entry and exit.
9. High monthly maintenance cost.
10. High monthly operational cost.
11. Extensive design, code, test, or operational errors.

There are exceptions to these limits, but with experience the variations can be identified easily. For example, editing input data requires many decisions and lots of exception processing logic. These designs could easily exceed the ELOC and cyclomatic complexity limits. Report modules, however, should rarely exceed these limits. Printing a heading, formatting a report line, summarizing data, and writing a report are all simple functions that should fit these criteria easily. Modules that fit these criteria should also exhibit functional strength and data coupling. They should be reusable and reliable.

Managers that directly supervise programmers should be conscious at all times of their programmer's concern for the company's quality objectives and their achievement of those goals. The manager must ensure that those objectives are met. Managers should also be on the alert for programs that incur excessive development, maintenance, or operational costs. These programs should be examined for potential quality improvements that will ultimately reduce costs.

Without good designs, the programs produced will require significant enhancements to meet the user's needs. But without good code, the costs of maintaining and operating a system will choke the corporation and negate the benefits derived from the system. Productivity of both IS and the client, will decline as a result. Managers stand in a position to identify such problems before they occur and to correct them with the greatest cost-effectiveness as possible. But analysts and programmers have a hand in productivity and quality improvements too. How can they help?

Analysts and programmers should be in a better position to help the manager identify quality problems and solutions. They are closer to the designs and code. They know more about the program. Their input should substantiate what the software metrics tell the manager. How should analysts use metrics?

2. SYSTEMS ANALYSTS

Systems analysts are given the rare opportunity to create new systems. On their shoulders rests the fate of the entire enterprise. A project may succeed, breaking all productivity and quality records, or it may fail. Structured programming improves productivity by improving design quality. Systems analysts should be concerned with quality more than quantity. They need to keep ahead of the programmers, but they also realize that a good design will make the programmers more productive and reduce costs for the system's lifetime.

2.1 Analyst Productivity

More than anything, an analyst needs better methods of estimating development time and costs. The Albrecht *function point* method described in Chapter 2 is a good foundation for estimation. With some experience, the analyst will become surprisingly accurate with function point estimation.

In a maintenance environment, the analyst may need to know how many enhancements they designed, the complexity of those modifications, and the success of those changes. This knowledge should help each analyst document their contribution to the system and corporation. Again, the number of functions modified and the function point metrics should help quantify analyst productivity.

2.2. Analyst Quality

Design quality is difficult to quantify, but better tools are on the way. An analyst should be concerned with the following metrics:

1. Use of reusable designs.
2. Module strength and coupling.
3. Design readability.
4. Design errors.

Use of existing designs not only improves productivity, but helps ensure better quality. Reusable designs should have incurred more scrutiny than unique designs. Reusable designs also affect programmer productivity; programmers can more readily convert the reusable designs into code.

Module strength and coupling, as described in Chapter 3, provides a way of quantifying the functionality of the design and its data independence. Modules of the highest quality will have functional strength and data coupling. Design readability is measurable as long as the design has been entered into a word processor. The UNIX Writer's Workbench provides metrics of readability such as the *fog index* (Gunning, 1966), finds punctuation and grammatical errors, and checks for spelling errors.

Finally, error tracking provides metrics of the kinds of errors found in the design. Tracking design errors helps identify potential improvements in design methodology to eliminate future errors. Once analysts become aware of the errors they normally insert in their designs, they are able to eliminate them from future designs.

As more of the design process is mechanized, the ability to measure design quality will improve. But it is hard to beat design inspection as a method of quality measurement and improvement. Walk-throughs are still the analyst's prime source of feedback.

3. PROGRAMMERS

Programmers are concerned with productivity and quality: meeting due dates, testing their code, and so on. But they should be more interested in producing high-quality code than in producing huge volumes of the stuff. By working smarter instead of harder, programmers can be highly productive (in terms of functions produced) and still produce high-quality code; reusable code provides both high productivity and high quality.

3.1. Programmer Productivity

Programmers are pretty sharp people; they couldn't do their jobs without a lot of know-how. They are smart enough to figure out how they are being measured and how to meet the acceptable limits. Taxpayers and accountants play the same game with the Internal Revenue Service every year. Managers have to be extremely careful what they decide to select for performance measures. A manager who wants productivity at the expense of everything else, will get it in spite of the detrimental effects on quality. A manager who wants high quality and fair levels of productivity will also get it.

Programmers should be aware of their productivity. They should know their productivity measured in ELOC, functions, cyclomatic complexity, and software science metrics. Programmers should determine the validity of each metric for the type of project under construction. They should be aware of other programmers' productivity as well. I remember noticing that one of my fellow programmers was coding circles around the rest of us. I took her to coffee one day and asked how she was able to produce so many tested programs. She went into a short explanation of how she worked that would later be popularized as structured programming. She had breakthrough knowledge that everyone else needed. I was fortunate enough to ask for her help. Programmers should always be on the lookout for new techniques and methods to produce more functions for the company at a lower cost. Productivity measurement is one of the ways to identify "superprogrammers" and to tap their knowledge.

3.2. Code Quality

Programmers should request quality goals as a portion of the program design. What levels of flexibility, maintainability, reusability, and reliability are needed? Does the program need to be efficient? Portable? Armed with these goals, programmers can code the program to meet the required quality levels.

Throughout the development and maintenance of a program, the programmers should measure the code's complexity, correctness, efficiency, flexibility, integrity, interoperability, maintainability, portability, reliability, reusability, structure, testability, and usability. They should bring errant programs to the attention of the analyst and manager. Programmers should work on quality improvements. They are the software mechanics that keep the company's information moving.

Chapters Eighteen through Twenty-one describe code quality in detail. Programmers should apply the measurement of quality at the module level. Software metrics provide the programmer with a tool to constantly monitor software quality and to do something about it. Measurement helps the programmer identify his or her weaknesses and to correct them. Measurement helps the programmer detect hard-to-find quality problems. Mechanized code analyzers incur continuous enhancement to improve their measurement accuracy and to identify newly discovered quality problems. A programmer armed with software quality metrics will spend less time testing and maintaining code. More time can be spent developing new, high-quality software.

Chapters 3−16 describe each of the software qualities in detail. A programmer should refer to these chapters to develop familiarity with each. Once aware of the benefits derived from software quality, each programmer should strive to provide the maximum benefit for the corporation.

4. SUMMARY

Programmer productivity and software quality is measurable from the lowliest module to the largest system. To use this information, programmers, analysts, and managers will need different views of the information. Managers need the information summarized by work group. Analysts need the information for each system, program, or module design. Programmers need the information presented by module. Chapters 19−21 give specific examples of metrics for programmer usage. Chapter 22 will describe how to mechanize these measurements and present them to all levels of management.

CHAPTER EIGHTEEN

PROGRAMMING STYLE

The gem cannot be polished without friction, nor man perfected without trials.

CONFUCIOUS

Programming style brings to mind the ways that a creative programmer brings clarity, maintainability, testability, reliability, and efficiency to the coding of a module. But is one programming style better than another? Is there one best approach to coding a specific structured programming construct or implementing a specific function? Yes, there is.

Based on proven metrics, the difference between two coding styles can equate to as much as a 4:1 difference in the time it takes to write, repair, or enhance a module. Your staff could potentially produce systems at four times their current rate by simply educating all concerned in the ways of style. Existing systems could be maintained with a quarter the number of people currently required, freeing the remainder to work on desperately needed new projects.

Mastery of programming style is not the creation of elaborate schemes of code, but rather the simple implementation of complex algorithms so that anyone can understand them. The essence of programming style is simplicity. Obviously the antagonist, constantly at war with simplicity, is complexity.

Industry studies have shown Halstead's software science and McCabe's cyclomatic complexity to be the leading indicators of program complexity—

the amount of effort required to code or understand a statement, function, module, program, or system. This effort directly impacts how long it will take to code, repair, or enhance a module, which directly affects the costs associated with software and the user's perception of the Information System department's responsiveness to change.

The objective of every programmer, analyst, and manager is to provide the highest-quality software at the minimum costs, thereby directly impacting the corporation's bottom line—return on investment. This is the ultimate goal of following the way of programming style: to produce the best code, in the shortest time, at the least cost. An advantage of developing an optimal programming style, by means of measurement and feedback, is that programmers gain a sense of self-worth by quantifying their programming abilities and their contribution to the company.

Software metrics can help select the best style for coding a structured construct or a given function. Similarly, they can help select the best language to implement a function. The following three chapters will discuss this in greater detail.

1. THE CREATIVITY MYTH

But if we can quantify the best coding style for all possible code implementations, won't this reduce or eliminate the creativity of the programmer's job? If you are willing to allow creativity to saddle you with less than maintainable code and at greater expense, by all means ignore the next few chapters. Consider that metrics only quantify why your best programmers code certain structures or functions in a specific way. Are these people more creative or just more knowledgeable? I propose that they have simply acquired a better programming style; their experience has led them to select one style over another.

Isn't this the essence of quality improvement? One person has some secret knowledge that enables them to outperform the rest. Once you identify the roots of this secret knowledge, why not train all your programmers to use better techniques and coding styles rather than waiting years for them to gain this understanding through osmosis?

There is a famous story about Hemingway rewriting and editing the end of one novel 37 times to "get the words right." In programming, the same two processes are needed. First, the programmer writes the code in a burst of creative brilliance. Then, in a cold calculating session, the programmer must edit the result, removing redundant code, reducing complexity, polishing and polishing to make the result more perfect. Sometimes, the programmer must throw the code away and begin again as Hemingway did, simply to make room for a better algorithm or expression of the function.

Just like a writer, a programmer will learn from each editing session what to avoid, how to write clearly, and so on. Most superprogrammers have already made most of the mistakes to be made; as a result, they avoid them. New programmers are like new writers; they have never made any of the mistakes and the training process is often insufficient.

In classrooms, programmers are taught coding languages and try them with simple examples, much as first graders learn to spell, read, and write. But they do not learn to write effectively. They rarely learn to criticize their own writing and so fail to expand their abilities. The same is true of programming. Walk-throughs provide some feedback, but rarely enough to cause major changes in coding style. Programmers must go back to school to learn not advanced coding techniques, but coding style.

2. CODING STYLE

I first fell on the idea of quantifying programming style while reading McCabe's paper on complexity (1976). He said that he could identify a programmer's style from looking at a few of his or her flow graphs. Then I went back to my trusty style guide: *The Elements of Programming Style* by Kernighan and Plauger (1974). They *felt* that one example was better than another and gave an explanation of why. I felt that if software metrics held any validity that I should be able to quantify their feelings with measurements. So I took the first example (see Figure 18.1) and measured each of their three algorithms and compared the results. Eureka! It worked. Feverishly, I compiled metrics of the next example and then the next. It always worked. To date, I have not found a single instance where the metrics did not bear out what the superprogrammers know: There is one best style for every occasion. At most, there are two equally good styles. At this point you simply choose one style and stick with it. No point in spending your time learning two ways when one is perfectly OK.

So consider that there are at most two best ways to code any structured programming construct, any function, any module, or any program. Pick one and stick with it. Train everyone to code it the same way. In the case of functions, modules, and programs, create skeletal versions of each that can be copied and then fleshed out to fit the needs of the application.

```
C  CREATE AN IDENTITY MATRIX
   DO 14 I=1,N                  Unique Operands   =    5
   DO 14 J=1,N                  Total Operands    =   13
14 V(I,J)=(I/J)*(J/I)           Unique Operators  =    4
                                Total Operators   =    6
                                Vocabulary        =    9.0
                                Length            =   19.0
                                Volume            =   60.2
                                Difficulty        =    5.2
                                Effort            =  313.0


   DO 14 I = 1,N                Unique Operands   =    7
      DO 12 J = 1,N             Total Operands    =   12
12      V(I,J) = 0.0            Unique Operators  =    2
14      V(I,I) = 1.0            Total Operators   =    4
                                Vocabulary        =    9.0
                                Length            =   16.0
                                Volume            =   50.7
                                Difficulty        =    1.71
                                Effort            =   86.9


   V = 0.0;                     Unique Operands   =    5
   DO I = 1 TO N;               Total Operands    =    9
      V(I,I) = 1.0;             Unique Operators  =    2
   END;                         Total Operators   =    3
                                Vocabulary        =    7.0
                                Length            =   12.0
                                Volume            =   33.7
                                Difficulty        =    1.8
                                Effort            =   60.6
```

FIGURE 18.1.   Software metrics applied to programming style.

3.   STRUCTURED PROGRAMMING CONSTRUCTS

The following three chapters will tell you many things about style; one of these is how to code the five structured programming constructs:

1. Sequential.
2. IF-THEN-ELSE.
3. CASE.
4. DO WHILE.
5. DO UNTIL.

Each language, whether you use COBOL, FORTRAN, ADA, or PL/I, has a best way to implement each of these structures. Following the *way* of programming style will improve the maintainability, reliability, flexibility, and cost-effectiveness of the code.

4. FUNCTIONS

Function statements normally are supplied by the language compiler in a subroutine or macro library, but it is often beneficial to build your own specialized function library. Following the credo of programming style, there is one best way to code these functions to gain the maximum cost benefit: The functions must be as reusable as possible.

5. MODULES AND PROGRAMS

Modules not taken from your special function library are specialized functions. If they fall into one of the categories listed in Table 13.1, they should be easily coded from a skeletal module that you should have created long ago, but probably haven't. If not, create the skeleton first, using the principles of programming style to obtain the maximum reusability and then copy the skeleton to create the required module. This serves two purposes: to create the desired module quickly and to provide a generalized module for future cost savings.

Programs are made up of modules and functions. So, designing the interfaces between the modules, as described in Chapter Two, and copying the skeletons and required functions to create the basic working program should not be difficult.

6. A NOTE ABOUT PRODUCTIVITY

Once your work group subscribes to one programming style, common designs, and the use of functions, modules, and program skeletons, the productivity of designers, coders, and testers increases dramatically. In my own experience at Bell Laboratories, these standard practices increased productivity from 100−200%. The resulting code was easier to maintain and enhance as definition changes arrived. The common functions and module skeletons made coding new programs a piece of cake. Why is coding style important to you? It will save you enormous amounts of time and effort.

7. DEVELOPMENT AND PROGRAMMING STYLE

If high-quality programs incur fewer lifetime costs, it makes sense to ensure that all new development produces the highest quality possible. I have found metrics invaluable when writing new programs. Whenever the metrics start exceeding my subjective limits for good quality, I assume that something is amiss, for example, the algorithm I am using may be too complex or perhaps the programming style is too difficult.

Before coding the next statement, I take off my creative hat and put on an editorial one. I review the code for obvious redundancies, complexities, or whatever helps me take immediate corrective action. During coding, a programmer needs to wear the hats of both the creative coder and the critical editor. The following paragraphs describe the mental editing process used and potential actions based on the metrics. You should note that only one editing process should be done at one time for the simple reason that people are much more effective when working on one change at a time.

The first thing that normally exceeds its bounds is the executable lines of code metric. Once this metric exceeds 100 (for COBOL or PL/I), I assume that code has been duplicated in many places in the module or that there are multiple functions. An editorial scan of the code for duplications will identify code that can be PERFORMed, CALLed, or converted into a function. Once these are removed, a new metrics analysis may indicate that module has been reduced within limits. If not, another editorial look at the code may discover several unique functions that can be separated from the existing module to form new ones. The only exception to this size limitation is an edit module. Edit modules may examine hundreds of input fields with hundreds of ELOC. Error reports, simple field edits, cross field edits, and similar functions can and should reside in separate modules.

The next group of metrics to watch are the decision count, cyclomatic complexity, NOT count, GO TO count, IF-THEN-ELSE nesting, and loop nesting. The complexity of decision logic greatly affects maintainability, reliability, and testability. The simplest transformation is to restructure NOT conditions into positive statements as described in Chapter 3. Next, I find it useful to examine the decision logic to see if there is some way to reduce the number of decisions. The following is a simple example:

```
IF A = B                          IF A = B AND C = D
    IF C = D                          ACTION1;
        ACTION1;                  ELSE
    ELSE                              ACTION2;
        ACTION2;
ELSE
    ACTION2;
```

Following these reductions and restructuring, I try to add an ELSE for every IF, an AT END for every READ or SEARCH, and so on. In so doing, the default logic path is identified clearly for the future maintenance programmer. Each of these actions reduces the number of decisions, nesting levels, and test paths in the module. The resulting reduction in complexity helps clarify the code to the point that it is often easy to identify potential reliability problems.

If there are any GO TOs, I try to transform the logic to eliminate them. Removing GO TOs tends to clarify the decision logic and improve the module's efficiency. It also clears the way to further reduce complexity.

Next, I apply McCabe's concept of reducibility to reduce the decision and loop nesting levels, often moving whole sections of complex decision code into separate modules. In the process, I usually discover duplicated decision logic that can be PERFORMed, CALLed, or moved into another module.

Next, I look at the number of files used by the module. If it has more than one input and two outputs, I assume that it has multiple functions. Often the complexity of the module can be reduced by isolating the processing of the additional files in separate submodules. Next, I eliminate all occurrences of alphabetic literals and most of the numeric literals. Only ZERO (0) and 1 are spared. Using meaningful data names in place of the literals reduces the software science metrics and improves maintainability.

Once all these corrective activities have been performed, many of the reliability, testability, efficiency, and reusability qualities will have been optimized in the process. Reliability of financial modules can be further improved by examining the processing of all numeric data, the rounding that occurs, and the actions taken with nonnumeric data or zero division. Efficiency can be optimized if an execution analyzer has pointed out specific deficiencies. Other than these small enhancements, the only remaining questions involve stylistic problems.

Anytime I am trying two different stylistic variations of the code, I examine the ELOC, cyclomatic complexity, and software science metrics. Sometimes, the ELOC declines marginally, cyclomatic complexity remains the same, but Programming Effort increases radically. In this case, the fewer number of executable statements required the use of many additional data fields. Stylistically, the change was a failure. All of these metrics should decline if the change is justified. The same editorial process can be performed in a maintenance environment.

8.   MAINTENANCE AND PROGRAMMING STYLE

Traditionally, software maintenance has focused on repair and enhancement maintenance. When a module becomes too complex to be properly maintained, IS junks it and builds another one (which may or may not be maintainable). Even though studies have shown that it is rarely cost justifiable to replace an automobile with a new one, countless millions of people do so every year. The cost-effective method of handling old cars and old software is to employ preventive maintenance.

Preventive maintenance uses diagnostic equipment (software metrics) to identify weak and error-prone parts of the code. The potentially defective parts of the code are improved before they fail. Unfortunately, in most IS organizations these weakened programs already incur most of the maintenance costs. They demand immediate attention.

Preventive maintenance varies little from the editorial process described for developing new programs. Due to the constraints on maintenance programmers, only one editorial pass of the program may be possible during each release of the program. Little by little, however, the old code can become a classically restored program. Modernizing existing programs requires four steps:

1. Select the programs or modules that will benefit most from modernization. Pareto analysis will identify the 20% of the programs that require 80% of the maintenance; they are the top candidates for preventive maintenance.

2. Get a clean compilation and metrics of the existing code, saving a copy of the inputs and outputs for testing.

3. Structure and document the code. Mechanical structuring engines and documentation tools exist for most languages.

4. Modernize the program or module to reflect current programming standards and documentation. Then test the code to ensure compatibility.

Another option is to empower a preventive maintenance team of diagnosticians thoroughly conversant in the restoration of old, clunky code. They identify the programs for revision and work through them rapidly, often more quickly than any programmer could. As editors, they can examine the code more freely and correct it without hesitation.

Whether the programmers or special groups do the changes, software metrics serves as a guidepost for corrective action and as a method of measuring the success of the improvements. Quality has been hard to quantify, but metrics tools will allow programmers, analysts, and managers to set measurable objectives.

9. SUMMARY

Programming style is ballet, where mere programming is hockey: brute force combined with a time clock to score points in whatever way possible. Programming style is the essence from which software quality can arise from the murky depths.

Although distantly related to the topic of programming style, let me relate a parable from the story of the seventh century samurai Musashi, a master of strategy whose text on the subject, *A Book of Five Rings*, is still widely used in Japanese business. Musashi had received an invitation to visit an important Lord. With it, he received a flower. Upon examining it, he found the stem had been severed raggedly, obviously the work of someone untrained in the use of the sword. Musashi declined. The Lord, old as he was, was not offended, but instead sent the courier back with a flower he had cut himself. Irritated, but none the less interested, Musashi took the message and sent the man off. Later he examined the flower. The cut was not only perfect, but it seemed to enhance the flower, which indeed had not wilted since it was plucked. Using his short sword, Musashi tried in vain to match the cut. He soon accepted the invitation; he knew he had found a master of the way of strategy and the sword.

I often pick up a program listing and think of the wilted, raggedly chopped flower Musashi received. Only occasionally do I find a program that demands my interest; a program as fresh as the day it was written. But they do exist. I will admit that as often as I have tried, my code still seems roughly hewn. But it is superior to any I have produced before and to most that I see every day. I continue to improve and develop an optimum programming style. You can too. It will be the most important step you take for yourself and your company.

Improvement is something we often ignore. Status quo. That's what we like. But without progress and growth, we rust; our minds solidify and getting them rolling again takes time.

The next three chapters deal with programming style, metrics, and quality in IBM assembler language, COBOL, and PL/I. If you use some other language but are familiar with at least one of these languages, most of the concepts can be transferred directly to the new language. You should be able to extract the chapter, changing the names of verbs and the examples, to show how each of the universal software metrics—ELOC, cyclomatic complexity, and software science—can be used to measure programming style. A few of you will read the next few chapters and see only what you already know. The rest of you will learn a great deal and some of you will reject every word. This information, however, was garnered from over 14 years of programming and working with the best programmers. It will help you master programming style.

CHAPTER NINETEEN

IBM ASSEMBLY LANGUAGE CODE (ALC)

In his book *The Mythical Man Month*, Frederick Brooks said that he could not imagine coding an application in assembly language. Obviously, you wouldn't be reading this chapter if you didn't have at least some to maintain, so I will try and help you out.

Because no one ever told you the basic ways of writing the structured programming construct and improving the readability of ALC does not mean that you don't need to know them.

1. BASICS

IBM ALC has a wealth of operators. The more operators you use, the higher your metrics of difficulty and programming effort will be (see Halstead, Chapter 2). So if you can use the same simple instruction rather than one of the more complicated variants on the theme, you will be better off. First, consider the number of ways to move data in Assembler: MVC, MVI, MVO, and so on. Consider the number of ways to operate on numeric data: AP, ZAP, AR, and so on. Doing things one way in one place and another somewhere else leads to confusion. Each of these operators is useful and necessary in certain situations. Make sure you understand where they should be used.

1.1. Registers

Another simple technique that can save a lot of work uses the EQU statement to define your registers.

```
R1              EQU         1
```

This allows you to find all references to the registers in the cross-reference listing. Finding all register references by hand is time-consuming and error-prone at best. Let the compiler do some of the work. The metrics analyzer can also pinpoint how many times each register is used.

1.2. Literals

You will find yourself tempted to use literals throughout the code, especially with the immediate instructions: MVI, CLI, and so on. But don't use them. Define them in working storage, hopefully with a meaningful name. You will find this aids not only the coding but the testing and maintenance of the code. Literals cannot be found in the cross-reference listing, the data names can. The literal cross-reference listing will serve to identify the location of all equivalent literals, but a data name is still more understandable.

For example, consider Figure 19.1. You cannot tell which literal value 2 means record number and which means state code. Nor can you tell which state is referenced. Figure 19.2 shows the revised code. The metrics analyzer can count the number of occurrences of each literal and transform them into ALC source code files that could be changed to indicate the true data name and then included in the existing module. From the previous two examples, the analyzer could have produced:

```
CHAR2        DC         CL2'02'
```

1.3. Comments

Because of the cryptic nature of assembler language, using comments in-line and on the actual lines is a necessity. Without them, the maintenance programmer has to read the code and decipher what it is doing. Remember, use comments to explain what the code is doing that is not apparent from the program itself.

Don't, however, use comments to try to explain poorly written code. Rewrite the code for readability. Further, when maintaining ALC, make sure

```
        CLI   RECTYPE,=C"2"      IF RECORD TYPE = STATE
        BNE   LABEL1             THEN
        CLI   STATECD,=C"2"         IF ALASKA
        BNE   LABEL1                THEN
        .                               PROCESS RECORD
        .                         ELSE
        .                               NEXT SENTENCE
LABEL1  EQU   *                  ELSE
```

FIGURE 19.1.   Use of literals invites ambiguity.

```
        CLI   RECTYPE,STATEREC   IF RECORD TYPE = STATE
        BNE   LABEL1             THEN
        CLI   STATECD,ALASKA        IF ALASKA
        BNE   LABEL1                THEN
        .                               PROCESS RECORD
        .                         ELSE
        .                               NEXT SENTENCE
LABEL1  EQU   *                  ELSE
```

FIGURE 19.2.   Using data names for clarity and readability.

that the comments agree with what the code does; sometimes it won't. And if the comments leave something to be desired, change them to make them more clear.

2.   STRUCTURED PROGRAMMING CONSTRUCTS

Assembler language has only the following two constructs: IF and DO. It does not have an IF-THEN-ELSE, CASE, DOWHILE, or DOUNTIL. So you must unfortunately code them yourself, unless you have a macro guru to create them for you or you are willing to purchase them from IBM for $60. I strongly recommend the latter. The lack of structured programming constructs leads to an environment that works against the development of good, maintainable, cost-effective programs.

2.1.   IF-THEN-ELSE

The IF in ALC consists of a compare and a branch on condition statement. The compare and branch are often negative in form:

```
          CLC     STATENM,STATECD      IF STATE NAME = STATE CODE
          BNE     NEWSTATE             THEN
          statements                      PROCESS SAME STATE
          B       VALIDCITY
NEWSTATE EQU     *                     ELSE   NEW STATE CODE
          statements                      PROCESS NEW STATE
VALIDCITY EQU    *                     ENDIF
```

Using structured macros, this can be rewritten positively as:

```
          IF      (STATENM,EQ,STATECD),THEN
          statements                      PROCESS SAME STATE
          ELSE
          statements                      PROCESS NEW STATE
          ENDIF
```

Note that the introduction of the structured macros eliminates the use of CLC, BNE, and B. The macros expand to produce the same code, but they are much more readable. Should the program ever be rewritten into a higher-level language, it wouldn't take a very clever programmer to decipher the code.

Good ALC programmers will object to this sort of programming; they like to know exactly what is happening. Yet I know systems programmers who refuse to use anything else, simply because of what these macros buy them in terms of maintainability. Let's look at the other structured constructs.

The IF-THEN-ELSE can also represent the comparison of a range of values concisely:

```
          IF      (DAY,GE,DAYONE),AND,(DAY,LE,LASTDAY),THEN
             MVC     BILLDAY,DAY
          ELSE
             CALLX ERROR
          ENDIF
```

Two comparisons are easily represented by one IF statement. This reduces the Halstead metrics for the code.

2.2. CASE

The CASE macro does not come with the IBM structured macros. It can be created if you have an in-house macro guru, however. The case construct is used so often I recommend spending the time to develop it. A common use of the CASE construct involves checking fields for correct values. Checking the month field for the dates January–December or checking a field for record type are both examples that use the CASE construct. Figure 19.3 shows an example of checking a one-byte date field for valid values. Note how the comments should be used to give a pseudocode legibility to the code.

I have also seen programs that work with 40 different record structures, for example, the CASE construct effectively handles the processing of each record as it arrives (see Figure 19.4).

Once again, it wouldn't take a genius to read this code and possibly rewrite it into PL/I, using the SELECT verb. Mechanical analyzers should have a much easier time examining the code, and your maintenance staff should reach new peaks of productivity.

```
MONTHS    DS    0CL12
JAN       DC    XL1"01"
                  .
                  .
                  .
DEC       DC    XL1"12"

CHKMONTH  EQU   *                    SWITCH ON MONTHCD
          CLI   MONTHCD,JAN              CASE JANUARY:
          BNE   CHKFEB                      PROCESS JANUARY
                  .
                  .
          B     ENDMONTH                 LEAVE SWITCH
CHKFEB    EQU   *
          CLI   MONTHCD,FEB          CASE FEBRUARY
          BNE   CHKMAR                  PROCESS FEBRUARY
    .       .
    .       .
    .       .
          B     ENDMONTH                 LEAVE SWITCH
CHKDEC    EQU   *
          CLI   MONTHCD,DEC         CASE DECEMBER
          BNE   DEFAULT                PROCESS DECEMBER
                  .
                  .
          B     ENDMONTH                 LEAVE SWITCH
DEFAULT   EQU   *                    OTHERWISE
          CALL  ERROR                    REPORT ERROR
ENDMONTH  EQU   *                    END SWITCH
```

FIGURE 19.3. Using comments to document a CASE construct.

```
PROCESS    EQU  *                    SWITCH ON RECTYPE
           CLC  RECTYPE,REC01          CASE EQUIPMENT RECORD
           BNE  CHK02                    PROCESS EQUIPMENT
           CALL RECTYP01
           B    ENDREC                 LEAVE SWITCH
CHKFEB     EQU  *
           CLI  RECTYPE,REC02         CASE PARTS RECORD
           BNE  CHKMAR                  PROCESS PARTS
           CALL RECTYP02
           B    ENDREC                 LEAVE SWITCH
CHKDEC     EQU  *
           CLI  RECTYPE,REC03         CASE LEASE RECORD
           BNE  DEFAULT                 PROCESS LEASES
           CALL RECTYP03
           B    ENDREC                 LEAVE SWITCH
DEFAULT    EQU  *                    OTHERWISE
           CALL ERROR                    REPORT ERROR
ENDREC     EQU  *                    END SWITCH
```

. FIGURE 19.4. Using comments to document record processing.

2.3. DOWHILE and DOUNTIL

The DOWHILE and DOUNTIL implement the repetitive structures of a program. They often reduce the complexity of the program by eliminating redundant code. They further speed the program by reducing the paging that occurs. The only difference between the two is that the DOUNTIL will perform its function at least once; the DOWHILE checks its conditions first before doing anything.

Consider the examples shown in Figure 19.5. The first uses standard ALC verbs; the second uses structured macros. The latter is clear and concise. Comments would be redundant. Comments are necessary in the first example.

3. FUNCTIONS AND MACROS

Macros serve as ways to represent larger amounts of code in a single clear concise statement. The absence of macros tells of an inexperienced programmer. Each macro acts as a small function.

Usually, a function in ALC is referenced by a BAL or BCT instruction. When the function completes, control returns to the next statement after the BAL instruction. This is similar to the PERFORM in COBOL.

```
        DOWHILE                              DOUNTIL

LABEL1     EQU   *              LABEL1     EQU   *
           CLC   STATECD,ARIZONA           process once
           BNE   LABEL2                    read record
           process record                 CLC   STATECD, ARIZONA
           read record                     BE    LABEL1
           B     LABEL1
LABEL2     EQU   *
```

```
        DOWHILE (STATECD,EQ,ARIZONA)        DOUNTIL (STATECD,NE,ARIZONA)
        process record                      process record
        read record                         read record
        ENDDO                               ENDDO
```

FIGURE 19.5.   Using structured macros to improve readability.

Beware of the ALC GO TO, the branch statement (B and BR). The older programs have branches to existing functions that then branch not to the next statement, but to some other part of the program. In this case, the branch statement looks like it is going off to perform a function, but control never returns.

The branch may also be used to jump into the middle of a function. Any change in the function may change the external branch into its center. This is similar to the COBOL PERFORM THRU, a piece of code harmlessly stuck in between the performed paragraphs changes the entire complexion of the program.

The NOP (no operation) instruction is just a thinly veiled GO TO statement. It can be modified during program execution to branch to anywhere in the program. Similarly, branch instructions can be modified during execution to fall through to the next statement. A programmer reading the code will have a treacherous time following the program logic. Structured macros offer a way to avoid many of these potential structure violations.

Structured macros also have ways of creating internal functions using CALLM, BMOD, and EMOD. CALLM calls an internal module just like a BAL instruction, but also allows the passing of data via registers 0 and 1. This formalizes the interface between the calling point in the module and the submodule. BMOD is the beginning of the called module, setting up the data passed via the registers. EMOD returns control to the statement after the CALLM via a branch register (BR) instruction. Any data returns via register 0 or 1.

4. COMPLEXITY

ALC complexity measurement depends on the number of ELOC, cyclomatic complexity, and software science. Because ALC requires more statements, in most cases, to provide the same function as a single COBOL or PL/I statement, an ALC module should require more lines of code than an equivalent COBOL or PL/I module. The maximum boundaries for ELOC, $V(G)$, and effort (E) should be increased accordingly. I would propose ELOC < 300, $V(G) < 50$, and $E < 30,000$. Larger modules begin to use up the available base registers and become increasingly difficult to understand.

Another factor in ALC complexity is the statements themselves. Statements like translate and test (TRT), shift left double logical (SLDL), and test under mask (TM) are much more complex than a move (MVC) or subtract register (SR). Similarly, *or* instructions (OR, O, OI, and OC) may have a complexity somewhere between these two extremes. Although it has not been done, weighting the different operators from one to four and summing the weights gives a better indication of complexity than ELOC. The weights, when used with the software science metrics in place of unique and total operators, may provide a more exacting metric of complexity.

5. CORRECTNESS

Correctness consists of completeness, consistency, and traceability. ALC completeness involves a minimal use of the hard branch (B), use of comments on every line to describe the processing, and the use of data names in place of literals. Consistency requires that structured and local macros be used throughout a module in a consistent fashion. The use of MVC and MVI or CLC and CLI instructions should also be consistent. The use of branch on condition operators (BE, BNE, BNH, etc.) should also be consistent. Traceability requires a way to determine the origin of the code in the definition and design. Comments help provide traceability. Large numbers of hard branches (B) do not.

6. EFFICIENCY

You are already coding in assembler language, why worry about efficiency? You shouldn't be coding in assembler language unless you know the efficient ways to represent data and your application demands exacting efficiency.

7. FLEXIBILITY, MAINTAINABILITY, AND PORTABILITY

The use of ALC assumes a complete disregard for the future maintenance of the software or its potential uses in other hardware environments. Modules written with extensive use of structured macros, however, tend to be more maintainable and flexible than their more primitive counterparts. ALC modules that are kept to a size no greater than the extent of one base register also tend to stay maintainable and flexible.

The use of locally developed macros also increases flexibility. Macros are concise representations of the functions being performed. Concision is one of the submetrics of both flexibility and maintainability.

Modularity is determined from the ELOC, cyclomatic complexity, and software science metrics. Modular ALC programs benefit from having functional strength and data coupling, although they lose a small amount of efficiency when calling subordinant modules and passing data. The use of ad-cons and v-cons (address constants) in ALC code allows programmers to connect modules via the worst form of module coupling—content coupling. Using these little demons, an ALC programmer can directly address and change data inside of another module of the program.

Portability of ALC programs is restricted to machines using the same instruction set. Most ALC programs are not portable.

8. INTEGRITY

Integrity depends on auditability, instrumentation, and security. ALC programs can use system software packages like RACF and IMS to provide much of their auditability and security. Instrumentation can also be coded into each program, but the expense may be greater than the integrity gained.

9. INTEROPERABILITY

ALC programs and systems tend to operate well with other ALC systems. They speak the same language. ALC also allows for flexible interfaces to COBOL and PL/I programs. Common modules that need to be highly efficient and reliable, such as date conversions, can be written in ALC and coupled easily to whatever language needs the function. Even some fourth-generation products allow assembler language exits.

10. RELIABILITY

ALC reliability depends on accuracy, complexity, consistency, error tolerance, and modularity, and simplicity. In ALC, accuracy is left to the programmer.

In this aspect, ALC fails as a language. ALC is also more complex, because of the number of operators, and less simplistic than either COBOL or PL/I. ALC leaves error tolerance to the program, whereas both COBOL and PL/I provide a variety of preprogrammed means for implementing error-tolerant software. Small, well-designed and coded ALC modules can be highly reliable, but no more so than their COBOL or PL/I counterparts. ALC modules, if they require any maintenance at all, tend to cost more to maintain. Modules like date conversion routines rarely change. ALC programs can be as reliable as management wants as long as they are willing to invest the effort in making the software resilient. Otherwise, ALC can be as error-prone as COBOL or PL/I.

11. REUSABILITY

Small common modules, that are used extensively throughout an organization, may provide benefits when coded in ALC. They are more efficient and rarely change. They are not, however, portable and reusable on other hardware and software systems. The inability to port ALC code to other machines severely limits the benefits of reusable ALC modules.

12. TESTABILITY

ALC testability depends on auditability, complexity, instrumentation, modularity, self-documentation, and simplicity. As previously stated, ALC code can exhibit all of these traits, for better or worse. The number of paths through the code can be determined with the cyclomatic complexity metric. Small modules can be unit tested, integration tested, and finally system tested easily. Testability depends on modularity and low complexity. ALC is not the most self-documenting of all languages. It does, however, allow the programmer to use both full line comments and comments on each statement in the program. A program's ability to document itself depends largely on the programmer.

13. SUMMARY

ALC should not be chosen as a language to provide flexibility, maintainability, portability, or testability. ALC depends on the programmer to code correctness, integrity, interoperability, reliability, and reusability into the code.

An ALC programmer deals with the DNA of the system, while a COBOL or PL/I programmer uses whole cells or organisms to do his or her work. There is a certain pleasure in this detail work, which neither COBOL or PL/I ever satisfies. But the expense of programming and maintaining ALC far outweighs the pleasures of tinkering with the inner workings of the machine.

ALC lends itself to applications that require a high degree of efficiency. It lends itself to reusable modules that the entire department will use repetitively. It does not provide the kind of productivity and quality improvement goals that are needed to sustain an IS organization, however. It should be used when required, not for fun.

CHAPTER TWENTY

COBOL METRICS

COBOL was the first business-oriented language. It has not changed significantly in the last 10 years, completely missing the structured programming
revolution. Since the new standard has not been accepted or implemented
at the time of this publication, this chapter addresses the 1974 COBOL
standard.

COBOL lacked the preciseness of ALC and had lots of trouble with
hexadecimal data as well as bits. This presented a variety of problems when
interfacing new COBOL programs with old ALC programs. How do you test a
bit in COBOL that was set in a ALC module? PL/I was developed to meet the
needs that COBOL couldn't satisfy. Some designers feel that PL/I incorporated too much capability. Poorly written PL/I is almost as illegible as ALC.

With all its faults, COBOL is still the dominant business language. With
the time and money invested in training their personnel, management is
unlikely to swing magically to a new language. New languages cause problems, reduce productivity, and generally confuse the development effort
rather than aid it. I expect COBOL to be around forever, in one form or
another. So COBOL will always be with us, making the need for high-quality
programs essential.

1. BASICS

COBOL was designed to emulate English. Based on later evaluations, some of
its wordiness is counterproductive, making programs harder to read and

maintain. Other features, such as 32-character data names, are often under-used, leaving cryptic if not indecipherable names for future system maintainers. The basic rule in writing any code, especially COBOL, is *code for change*. Your program will undergo continuous changes, so anticipate them and program to minimize the impact of those changes. The following few rules will help meet the requirements of "coding for change."

1. Never use the ALTER verb. Altering the path of the program during execution is a sure way to confuse future maintainers and make the program impossible to maintain.

2. Restrict the use of the GO TO statement. Never use it in any situation other than with the DEPENDING ON option, to implement the CASE construct. And even then, consider using the IF-ELSEIF-ELSE form of the CASE construct. Believe it or not, Dijkstra (1976) has proven that a program can be written without the use of the GO TO.

3. Always use meaningful data names. Keep them in a data dictionary to minimize the impact of changes.

4. Always indent nested code under an IF-THEN-ELSE statement to make the code more readable.

5. Always use loops to eliminate redundant code.

6. Always limit modules to single functions. Don't try and cram the whole program into one module. You will make it hard to maintain, enhance, and reuse.

7. Always use SKIP and EJECT statements to clarify the code. EJECTS should be used before new paragraphs and SKIPs before IF and PERFORM statements to identify blocks of code just as this book uses labels and paragraphs to improve its readability.

8. Use comments to *clarify* what the code is doing, never to restate what is already obvious. Too many comments can obscure the executable code, making maintenance difficult.

2.   STRUCTURED CONSTRUCTS

Looking at COBOL, you discover that the basic building blocks of all structured constructs—Sequential, IF-THEN-ELSE, CASE, DOWHILE, and DOUNTIL—are available in one form or another. By excluding the ALTER and GO TO verbs, you have the makings of correct structured code. Excluding the THRU option of the PERFORM verb eliminates the need for the EXIT verb and helps prevent structure violations. But more on that in a minute.

Figure 20.1 shows the recommended way to code each of the five structured programming constructs. Sequential statements are always blocked, left justified, and indented under IF-THEN-ELSE statements. The IF and ELSE are always aligned to display how they correspond to the logic flow. Nested IF-THEN-ELSE statements are also indented under the previous IF or ELSE. CASE constructs are formed of IF, ELSE IF, ELSE statements that are left aligned to indicate that they are a CASE, not a nested IF-THEN-ELSE. DOWHILE is represented by the PERFORM-UNTIL; while a DOUNTIL consists of two PERFORMs; only the second has the UNTIL clause. Unfortunately COBOL checks the UNTIL condition before executing the PERFORMed code so the PERFORM UNTIL is actually a DO WHILE statement.

```
SEQUENTIAL

        MOVE A TO B.
        PERFORM GET-TRANSACTION-RECORD
            VARYING INDEX FROM ONE BY ON
            UNTIL INDEX > TABLE-MAXIMUM.

IF-THEN-ELSE

        IF ( A = B )
            statements
        ELSE
            statements

CASE

        IF ( VARIABLE = CASE-1 )
            statements
        ELSE IF ( VARIABLE = CASE-2 )
            statements
        ELSE IF ( VARIABLE = CASE-3 )
            statements
        ELSE
            statements.

DOWHILE

        PERFORM PARAGRAPH-NAME
            UNTIL EXIT-CONDITION.

DOUNTIL

        PERFORM PARAGRAPH-NAME.
        PERFORM PARAGRAPH-NAME
            UNTIL EXIT-CONDITION.
```

FIGURE 20.1.   The five COBOL structured coding constructs.

Note that there is only one verb per line and each qualifier of the PER-FORM is indented under the statement for clarity. Another tip involves decisions with more than one condition: Put the AND or OR connector on the line with the decision and put the condition on the next line (see Figure 20.2). This forces the reader to notice that there are more conditions on the next line. It is a mental stimulant to ensure that they read the next line. Without the connector, the maintainer might miss the additional condition, causing many wasted hours.

3. COMPLEXITY

COBOL complexity is based on four metrics: ELOC, decisions, cyclomatic complexity, and Halstead's software science metrics.

3.1. ELOC

The complexity of COBOL increases with each executable line of code. So much so, in fact, that I have seen programmers avoid entering a module that is 25–100 pages or 1000 to 5000 ELOC in length. No program can grow this large without some redundant code. The trick is to find it and remove the duplications. Figure 20.3 shows a simple example of multiple CALL statements reduced to a single call, which not only removed one line of code, but also reduced the number of interfaces to other modules. In the actual program, there were eight of these calls for a total reduction of seven ELOC and seven external interfaces. The programmers mentioned that most of their early problems with the module were during interface changes when not all of the CALL statements were changed to include the right data names.

Similarly, in larger modules you will find whole paragraphs repeated, often several times. When the time comes for module maintenance, one or two of the functions will be changed, but not all, causing a variety of program errors that often go undetected. When the programmer finds the first paragraph, he or she will often make the necessary changes, assuming incorrectly that there is only one such function. After several tests, the programmer will have found

```
IF ( condition1 AND
     condition2 )
   statements
ELSE
   statements.
```
FIGURE 20.2.   Indenting nested conditions for clarity.

```
     Old Code                         New Code

MOVE 'A' TO TYPE.                  MOVE ADDRESS TO TYPE.
CALL 'UPDATE' USING TYPE,          PERFORM CALL-PROCESS.
                  NAME1,           MOVE FISCAL TO TYPE.
                  NAME2,           PERFORM CALL-PROCESS.
                  NAME3,
                  RET-CODE.    PERFORM-PROCESS.
IF RET-CODE = ERROR                CALL 'UPDATE' USING TYPE,
   CALL 'ERROR' USING TYPE,                           NAME1,
                     RET-CODE.                         NAME2,
MOVE 'F' TO TYPE.                                      NAME3,
CALL 'UPDATE' USING TYPE,                              RET-CODE.
                  NAME1,          IF RET-CODE = ERROR
                  NAME2,             CALL 'ERROR' USING TYPE,
                  NAME3,                               RET-CODE.
                  RET-CODE.
IF RET-CODE = ERROR
   CALL 'ERROR' USING TYPE,
                     RET-CODE.
```

FIGURE 20.3.   Reducing complexity by removing redundant code.

most of the redundant functions, but rarely will they take the time to remove the duplicate code and rectify all references to each copy.

These redundant functions exist because previous programmers were asked to add a function to the module, and not knowing that one already existed, they went ahead and added a duplicate function. In other situations, they clone a paragraph or function, changing only one statement in the module, as shown in Figure 20.3.

In my own experience, this sort of analysis requires a minimum amount of effort and can reduce the ELOC in an existing module by 5–20%. A programmer who can demonstrate measurably that he or she has reduced the ELOC by this large a percentage has truly provided the company with a great benefit; the future maintenance costs of this module will decline. Of this reduction in ELOC, a small portion consists of decisions.

3.2.   Decisions and Decision Density

Decisions add to the complexity of the logic. Often the number of decisions can be reduced by simple transformation as shown in Figure 20.4. The number of decisions is reduced by two and two MOVE statements are removed for a total ELOC reduction of four.

The decision density of this module originally might have been 10%, or one decision for every 10 ELOC. After the suggested revision, the density could drop to 8%, a significant reduction. Since decision density runs as high as

```
IF ( B = '1' )
     MOVE C TO A
ELSE IF ( B = '2' )
     MOVE D TO A
ELSE IF ( B = '3' )
     MOVE D TO A
ELSE IF ( B = '4' )
     MOVE C TO A
ELSE
     MOVE D TO A.

     V(G) = 5
```

becomes

```
IF ( B = '1' OR
     B = '4' )
     MOVE C TO A
ELSE
     MOVE D TO A.

     V(G) = 3
```

FIGURE 20.4.   Reducing decision nesting complexity by combining comparisons.

30% in some modules, any reduction in the number of decisions would be welcome.

The next refinement of decision complexity involves the cyclomatic complexity $V(G)$.

3.3.   Cyclomatic Complexity

$V(G)$ represents the number of structural test paths in the module and consists of the number of decisions, ANDs, ORs, and NOTs in the executable code. Having covered the reduction of decisions, let's take a look at how to reduce the number of ANDs, ORs, and NOTs.

Figure 20.5 shows how the previous example could be rewritten to exclude the ORs. The new $V(G)$ is 2; the old $V(G)$ was 5. The programmer has made another significant contribution to the maintainability of the code.

COBOL's 88 levels are extremely useful for reducing the cyclomatic complexity of a module, especially one that contains a large number of alphabetic literals and IS EQUAL TO (=) statements. The example shown in Figure 20.6 reduces the number of literals (which is an excellent way to reduce complexity) while also reducing the number of ORs. The resulting $V(G)$ is again 2, instead of 5—another significant reduction in complexity.

ANDs are a tough nut to crack; 88 levels won't work on them.

NOT clauses are best rewritten, reversing the order of the logic to state the logic in a positive way. If something is not black, it is not necessarily white.

```
05  B              PIC X.
    88  B-IS-VALID  VALUES ARE '1', '4'.

IF B-IS-VALID
      MOVE C TO A
ELSE
      MOVE D TO A.

    V(G) = 2
```

FIGURE 20.5. Using 88 levels to reduce complexity.

Example 1	Example 2
```IF A = 'B' OR` `A = 'C' OR` `A = 'D' OR` `A = 'E'` `NEXT SENTENCE` `ELSE` `CALL 'ERROR' USING A.`  `V(G) = 5```	```05 A PIC X.` `88 A-IS-VALID` `VALUES ARE 'B','C','D','E'.`  `IF A-IS-VALID` `NEXT SENTENCE` `ELSE` `CALL 'ERROR' USING A.`  `V(G) = 2```

FIGURE 20.6. Using 88 levels to replace literals and reduce complexity.

But programmers have a way of thinking in binary, 0 and 1, black and white, so they often miss the ambiguity of a NOT clause. One of the most obvious reasons for NOT clauses is the systems analyst's concern with what might go wrong, rather than right, in a module. Consider the following example:

```
IF A NOT > B              IF A > B
      CALL 'ERROR'.             NEXT SENTENCE
                          ELSE
                                CALL 'ERROR'.

V(G) = 3                  V(G) = 2
```

Since A NOT > B translates into A < B OR A = B, the cyclomatic complexity is 1 (IF) + 1 (OR) + 1 = 3. So by eliminating the NOT clause, $V(G)$ is also reduced. This example also displays one of the fundamental principles of readability and efficiency:

Put the most frequently exercised path first.

Error handling for invalid data items is often quite extensive, causing the programmer to read it all, only to discover that the code is of no importance when making enhancements or changes.

3.4. Software Science

Halstead's equations for software science are based on the number of operators and operands. By reducing the total number of operators (ELOC) as previously shown the difficulty and effort metrics will decline. Similarly, reducing the ELOC also reduces the total number of operands, which further reduces these metrics. Using 88 levels, as shown in the cyclomatic complexity examples, will also cut down the number of total operands. If any of the unique operators and operands can also be removed, so much the better. The next few sections will examine the five structured programming constructs (Sequential, IF-THEN-ELSE, CASE, DOWHILE, and DOUNTIL) and show how software science can demonstrate differences in programming style.

Sequential

Figure 20.7 shows two groups of MOVE statements: one showing a MOVE to each variable name and the other showing one MOVE for all data names. How would the software science metrics grade these two coding styles?

	MOVEs	Single MOVE
Vocabulary	6.0	6.0
Length	12.0	6.0
Estimated length	11.6	11.6
Volume	31.0	15.5
Difficulty	0.8	0.5
Language level	48.46	62.0
Information content	38.8	31.0
Effort	24.8	7.8

The *effort* has been reduced to one third of the expanded example. Difficulty is also lower.

IF-THEN-ELSE

Perhaps the prime examples of removing unique operators involves the GO TO and the PERFORM THRU statements. The GO TO is the only mecha-

```
MOVE ZERO TO A.                    MOVE ZERO TO A,
MOVE ZERO TO B.                                  B,
MOVE ZERO TO C.                                  C,
MOVE ZERO TO D.                                  D.
```

FIGURE 20.7.   Reducing ELOC metrics.

nism that allows structure violations in source code; its elimination not only reduces the number of unique operators, but also the potential for structure and logic errors. Figure 20.8 shows two ways of coding an IF-THEN-ELSE. The example using GO TOs was coded by an ALC coder recently retrained in COBOL who was familiar with creating the IF-THEN-ELSE with branch statements. The other example uses the elegant features of COBOL to simplify the expression. The unique and total operators and operands in the GO TO example are:

Unique operands = A, B, C, D, E   = 5
Unique operators = IF, GO TO, MOVE, EXIT   = 4
Total operands   = A, B, D, E, C, D   = 6
Total operators = IF, GO, MOVE, GO, MOVE, EXIT = 6

The simple example has the same number of unique and total operands, but the operators have changed as follows:

Unique operators = IF, MOVE   = 2
Total operators = IF, MOVE, MOVE   = 3

Comparing the two:

	GO TOs	Without GO TOs
Vocabulary	9.0	7.0
Length	12.0	9.0
Estimated length	19.6	13.6
Volume	38.0	25.3
Difficulty	2.4	1.2
Language level	6.6	17.5
Information content	15.8	21.1
Effort	91.3	30.3

Example 1	Example 2

```
    IF A = B                          IF A = B
        GO TO LABEL1.                     MOVE C TO D
    MOVE D TO E.     .                ELSE
    GO TO PARAGRAPH-EXIT.                 MOVE D TO E.
LABEL1.
    MOVE C TO D.
PARAGRAPH-EXIT.
    EXIT.
```

FIGURE 20.8. Comparison of GO TO and simple COBOL IF-THEN-ELSE.

This simple transformation (there are old programs with this stuff in them) cut the difficulty in half and reduced the effort to a third of the original example. Remembering that the effort metric has been shown to reflect the actual work required to write or maintain a piece of code, the programmer can show that change improved the maintainability and reduced the complexity of the code.

Another way of looking at programming style is to look at how the programmer used the features of the language. In this case, the language level metric increased significantly, showing that the second example uses the more powerful features of COBOL. An increase in this metric usually implies an increase in concision.

Figure 20.6 showed how 88 levels could help reduce $V(G)$, but how do they affect the software science metrics? The following table shows the calculated metrics.

	Literals	88 Levels
Vocabulary	7.0	3.0
Length	10.0	3.0
Estimated length	13.6	2.0
Volume	28.1	4.8
Difficulty	1.6	1.0
Language level	11.0	4.8
Information content	17.5	4.8
Effort	44.9	4.8

The difficulty declined slightly, but the effort metric shows a 10:1 reduction in effort. Due to the low value for difficulty, the meanings of language level and information content break down, but the case for using 88 levels should be cemented with this example.

CASE

Figure 20.9 shows two alternate ways of writing a CASE statement in COBOL: the first uses GO TOs; the second does not. How much of a burden are those GO TOs? Perhaps the key item to note is that the use of the GO TO obscures the fact that there needs to be a default path (MOVE F TO A). The maintenance programmer would overlook this possibility if the default action was nonexistent. The GO TOs could be removed, but the potential problems from falling through the other decisions would be frightening.

	GO TOs	Without GO TOs
Vocabulary	10.0	8.0
Length	25.0	21.0
Estimated length	23.5	17.5
Volume	83.0	63.0
Difficulty	4.6	2.3
Language level	3.8	11.6
Information content	17.8	27.0
Effort	387.3	147.0

The difficulty of the GO TO example is twice that of the one without GO TOs. The effort metric is 2.5 times higher, implying twice as much effort to read, comprehend, and change the GO TO version of the CASE construct. Also note that the language level is higher for the GOTO-less example; the programmer was using the more powerful features of COBOL. The same sort of

```
      Example 1                          Example 2

   IF A = B                           IF A = B
      MOVE C TO A                         MOVE C TO A
       GO TO PARAGRAPH-EXIT.           ELSE IF A = C
   IF A = C                               MOVE D TO A
      MOVE D TO A                      ELSE IF A = D
      GO TO PARAGRAPH-EXIT.               MOVE E TO A
   IF A = D                           ELSE
      MOVE E TO A                         MOVE F TO A.
      GO TO PARAGRAPH-EXIT.
      MOVE F TO A.
PARAGRAPH-EXIT.
      EXIT.
```

FIGURE 20.9.   Comparison of GO TO and IF-ELSEIF-ELSE CASE constructs.

results hold true for the GO TO DEPENDING ON version of the CASE construct. (See Figure 20.10.)

The COBOL IF-ELSEIF-ELSEIF-ELSE CASE statement should be coded and indented as shown to differentiate it from the common IF-THEN-ELSE. The maintenance programmer can then easily recognize the CASE constructs no matter how many cases exist. In many designs, each case is not as simple as the ones shown here; they may encompass 10 to 100 ELOC. Programmers, analysts, and managers should minimize the scope of a CASE statement to a single page by the proper use of PERFORMs and CALLs to handle each case, making it easier for the maintainer to grasp the total control flow at a glance.

DOWHILE

Figure 20.11 shows an example of a hand-coded loop to initialize a table compared to a PERFORM VARYING loop. The results:

	Loop	PERFORM VARYING
Vocabulary	9.0	7.0
Length	14.0	10.0
Estimated length	19.6	13.6
Volume	44.4	28.1
Difficulty	3.6	1.6
Language level	3.4	11.0
Information content	12.3	17.5
Effort	159.8	44.9

Again, the difficulty is reduced and the effort metric reduced by a factor of 4. The language level is higher for the PERFORM example.

DOUNTIL

Figure 20.12 shows a common problem encountered in COBOL: the need to read a record and then process it. Because the programmer waits until entering the loop to read the first record, he or she then has to check for end of file before processing. But this check is already done by the calling PER-FORM. Since the processing code is extensive, the programmer also has to code an EXIT and GO TO when at end of file. In this example, to avoid repeating the end of file test in the READ routine, the programmer moved

```
GO TO PARAGRAPH-A,
        PARAGRAPH-B,
        PARAGRAPH-C,
        PARAGRAPH-D
      DEPENDING ON A.
    GO TO PARAGRAPH-EXIT.
PARAGRAPH-A.
    MOVE B TO A.
    GO TO PARAGRAPH-EXIT.
PARAGRAPH-B.
    MOVE C TO A.
    GO TO PARAGRAPH-EXIT.
PARAGRAPH-C.
    MOVE D TO A.
    GO TO PARAGRAPH-EXIT.
PARAGRAPH-D.
    MOVE E TO A.
    GO TO PARAGRAPH-EXIT.
PARAGRAPH-EXIT.
    EXIT.
```

FIGURE 20.10.   GO TO DEPENDING ON version of a CASE construct.

Example 1	Example 2

`SET INDEX TO ONE>`
`LOOP-START.`
`    IF INDEX < A-MAX OR`
`       INDEX = A-MAX`
`        MOVE ZERO TO A ( INDEX )`
`        SET INDEX UP BY ONE`
`        GO TO LOOP-START.`
	`PERFORM LOOP`
	`    VARYING INDEX`
	`        FROM ONE BY ONE`
	`        UNTIL INDEX > A-MAX.`
	`LOOP.`
	`    MOVE ZERO TO A ( INDEX ).`

FIGURE 20.11.   Comparison of a hand-coded and PERFORM DOWHILE construct.

the record counting logic into the processing paragraph. The future maintainers, when it comes time to PERFORM the READ from another location in the program, will have to repeat not only the PERFORM but also the end-of-file test.

All of this convoluted logic could have been avoided by priming the pump—reading a record before entering the loop. Then, to let the controlling PERFORM handle the end-of-file condition, we move the statement PERFORM READ-RECORD to the end of the processing paragraph, making it possible to eliminate a decision (IF), a GO TO, and an EXIT while adding a PERFORM (function statement) and a SUBTRACT (simple sequential).

Example 1	Example 2
| ```
PERFORM READ-PROCESS
    THRU READ-PROCESS-EXIT
    UNTIL EOF-INPUT-FILE.

READ-PROCESS.
    PERFORM READ-RECORD.
    IF EOF-INPUT-FILE
        GO TO READ-PROCESS-EXIT.
    ADD ONE TO INPUT-RECORD-COUNT.
    (process record)
READ-PROCESS-EXIT.
    EXIT.

READ-RECORD.
    READ MASTERIN
        INTO MASTER-RECORD
    AT END
        MOVE HIGH-VALUES TO
            MASTER-RECORD.
``` | ```
PERFORM READ-RECORD.
PERFORM PROCESS-RECORD
    UNTIL EOF-INPUT-FILE

PROCESS-RECORD.
    (process record)
    PERFORM READ-RECORD.


READ-RECORD.
    READ MASTERIN
        INTO MASTER-RECORD
    AT END
        MOVE HIGH-VALUES TO
            MASTER-RECORD
        SUBTRACT ONE FROM
            INPUT-RECORD-COUNT.
    ADD ONE TO INPUT-RECORD-COUNT.
``` |

FIGURE 20.12.   Comparison of code to read and process records.

	GOTO	PERFORM
Vocabulary	12.0	10.0
Length	14.0	14.0
Estimated length	31.3	23.2
Volume	50.2	46.5
Difficulty	4.2	3.5
Language level	2.8	3.8
Information content	11.9	13.3
Effort	210.8	162.8

In this example, the difficulty declined marginally, as did the effort metric, but because of the precision of these metrics the second example is preferable.

Implications

What I have demonstrated, hopefully, is that software science metrics can be used to evaluate different programming styles. Each of the examples focused on decisions—the major contributors to complexity. There should be one or perhaps two best ways to code a specific Structured Programming construct or any function that consists of them. Software Science metrics can be applied to new modules all the way through their development, allowing the programmers and analysts to evaluate and eliminate poor coding practices and to meet their quality improvement goals. Software Science metrics can also be used to examine a module before and after maintenance, again allowing inspection and correction before testing and release. Combined with a maintenance history of difficult programs, these metrics can be used to justify a preventive maintenance team to revise and improve existing modules and programs.

3.5. Complexity Summary

Each of the complexity metrics—ELOC, decisions, cyclomatic complexity, and software science—provide a yardstick for examining newly developed and existing code to verify the programming style. Programming style—using the best features of the language and using them wisely—is the cornerstone of reducing maintenance costs and elevating the image of the IS organization. Without these measurement tools and their application to improve code quality, IS is doomed to an endless cycle of rewriting existing systems that have become unmaintainable.

4. CORRECTNESS

Does the program do what the users want? And does it do so correctly? There are limited ways to establish the correctness of a program without actually testing it and examining the output, but let's look at possible ways of determining completeness, consistency, and traceability from the source code.

4.1. Completeness

For a program or module to be complete, it must provide a full implementation of the functions required. There are ways of examining each line of code to determine if the fullness of COBOL has been used to maximum potential. Such attention to detail at the code level will often reflect the attention given to the module or program over all. Consider the DATA and PROCEDURE DIVISIONs.

DATA DIVISION

Completeness may be determined from the occurrence of the key words PICTURE, COMP-3, COMP, SYNC, VALUE, OCCURS, INDEXED BY, and so on. One of the prime offenders that contributes to program failures year after year is the uninitialized data item. By comparing the number of PIC-TURE clauses to the number of VALUE clauses, you can arrive at a preliminary estimate of completeness. Similarly, numeric data that is properly defined as PIC S9(?) COMP-3 or COMP SYNC will provide further proof of completeness and attention to efficiency. A program that has a large number of arithmetic statements with few efficient data elements lacks an element of completeness. A module that uses COPY statements to include record structures and other common data definitions rather than redefining the code in several different modules will help ensure completeness. In a similar fashion, tables defined with the OCCURS clause should also be INDEXED BY one or more internal indexes. Compiler-generated indexes are not only more efficient, but also require the use of the SET statement—a perfect clue that the programmer is dealing with an index and not some ordinary data item.

PROCEDURE DIVISION

COBOL provides a number of ways to ensure the completeness of arithmetic, data manipulation, input/output, subprogram linkage, and table handling logic statements. Each of the key words ON SIZE ERROR, ON OVER-FLOW, AT END, INVALID KEY, and so on, indicates the programmer's concern with completeness.

Arithmetic statements are a common cause of errors. Either they replace a number that another part of the program needs, or they manipulate bad data and the program terminates. The statement:

ADD A TO B

adds A to B and replaces B. A more complete expression would be:

ADD A TO B GIVING C

The value of B is unchanged and can be used in further calculations without error. Similarly, the expression:

MULTIPLY A BY B GIVING C ROUNDED

provides a fuller implementation of the MULTIPLY verb, rounding the calculated value off to the proper level. A fraction of a cent, multiplied by millions of transactions can equate to a substantial loss of revenue. Rounding helps eliminate such loss. The same holds true for division:

DIVIDE A BY B GIVING C REMAINDER D

The ROUNDED or REMAINDER clause also provide a more complete implementation of the DIVIDE statement.

Because COBOL, with its varying numeric data sizes, can cause problems that are hard to detect, the ON SIZE ERROR clause provides for extended error handling when the ADD, COMPUTE, DIVIDE, MULTIPLY, or SUBTRACT statement encounters bad data. The use of this clause for error detection and correction provides a further measure of completeness and correctness.

In the data manipulation statements STRING and UNSTRING, the programmer can provide for exceeding the originating or receiving fields by use of the ON OVERFLOW clause. Similarly, in the CALL statement, the ON OVERFLOW provides for differences in parameter sizes and formats.

In the input/output statements DELETE, READ, RECEIVE, RETURN, REWRITE, START, and WRITE, the use of the AT END and INVALID KEY clauses provide a more correct and complete implementation of the record-handling process. READ INTO and WRITE FROM also provide more complete implementations of the code. Working in I/O buffers has proven to be dangerous.

The SEARCH statement should also have a matching AT END clause to handle situations where a table lookup failed to find a matching value. Without an AT END, the logic usually follows a path based on the previous match often causing a difficult program errors.

4.2. Consistency

Consistency depends on coding standards and style. A uniform style of indenting IF-THEN-ELSE and CASE constructs can provide maintenance benefits. Software exists to restructure existing code into a common format. I suggest you acquire or build one of these for you and your fellow programmers.

Consistency also requires that every IF have a matching ELSE and every SEARCH have an AT END, and so on. Because so many programmers affect code during its life span, it is important to keep the style constant throughout; otherwise, maintenance becomes more difficult.

Another metric, comment density, speaks to the programmer's consistency when documenting code. A 10−20% comment density should be appropriate. Similarly, the number of ELOC, the decision density, and the function density should be held to specific tolerances except in rare exceptions. The ELOC should be held to around 100. The decision density should be 0−15%. And the function density can vary from 0 to 50% depending on the module: Driver modules measure 25−50% while worker modules measure 0−25%. The software science effort metric should remain close to 10,000, and the cylcomatic complexity should stay in the range 0−20 except when implementing large CASE constructs or editing input records with many fields.

The absence of GO TOs and EXIT statements further explains the consistency of the module as does a high density of either of the two statements. Modules without the GOTO command are typically structured, although they may be complex, while modules with a high density of GO TOs were probably written before structured programming and are likely candidates for revision.

4.3. Traceability

The last submetric of correctness is traceability—the ability to work your way from the user's definition to the code and back again. One way to accomplish this goal is through the use of data dictionaries. Each of the data names in a program should have a common source—the data dictionary, providing the basis of a link from the requirements to the code. Since the metric code analyzers already extract the data names, data definitions, and their scope in the program, it is possible to put this data out to another file for review and comparison with the data dictionary. In cases where no design or dictionary exists, it is an inexpensive way to extract the information and populate the dictionary. From this, the data administrator can begin to locate and evaluate all the synonyms in the system and potential sources of error.

4.4. Correctness Summary

The COBOL language contains a wealth of information that can indicate the analyst's and programmer's concern with correctness, completeness, consistency, and traceability. Little work has been done in this area because complexity promised far greater rewards. But correctness is one of the keys to satisfying the user, and that is the ultimate goal. The measurement of correctness may one day provide IS with the tools to quantify their contribution to the client.

5. EFFICIENCY

There are three parts to efficiency: programmer effectiveness, data efficiencies, and procedural efficiencies. Programmer effectiveness has to do with efficiency/maintainability trade-offs that are often necessary when designing a system that humans must maintain. Procedural efficiency and maintainability make poor bedfellows, but there is no reason that they cannot coexist. Modules coded to maximize efficiency are difficult to maintain; modules coded to maximize maintainability rarely achieve optimum efficiency.

Program performance or efficiency depends on four observable and measurable factors:

1. Execution time.
2. I/O utilization.
3. Memory usage.
4. Program readability and maintanability.

Only 10—20% of the programs, modules, or code typically cause 30—80% of the run costs. Pareto analysis dictates that you find and repair only these prime offenders; the others simply are not worth the effort required to gain a marginal benefit. But a program that runs for 10 hours without a check point or a transaction processing system that cannot meet the user's response time needs are both candidates for examination and revision.

Because of the strides made in computer cost performance, efficiency no longer enjoys the raging importance it did five or ten years ago. But there is no excuse for poor program performance caused by lack of knowledge or poor programming practices. Many things can be accomplished in the DATA and PROCEDURE DIVISIONS to improve efficiency without sacrificing the flexibility or maintainability of the code.

5.1. DATA DIVISION

The prime efficiency problems in a COBOL program often stem from arithmetic (ADD, COMPUTE, DIVIDE, MULTIPLY, and SUBTRACT) statements and from table-handling problems. Inefficient definitions of the data and indexes involved in these calculations often consume a vast amount of CPU time unnecessarily.

In an IBM environment, the numeric data items have a significant impact on execution time. Data items defined as COMP (binary) are twice as efficient as COMP-3 (packed decimal) in most cases. And COMP-3 items are twice as efficient as DISPLAY numeric items. Signed data items (PIC S9) are more efficient than unsigned. COMP-3 items are more efficient than COMP when the length of the number exceeds nine places [PIC S9(10) COMP-3]. COMP-3 items are more efficient when handling an odd number of digits [PIC S9(1,3,5,7,9,11,13,15,17)].

Oddly enough, a sophisticated metrics analyzer can determine all these items and print a suggested change alongside the actual code or print a summary of each different metric for the programmer to use as a basis for revision.

Another example involves the use of tables. For every table that OCCURS some number of times, there should be a matching INDEXED BY clause so that the compiler will generate the most efficient index possible. Compiler indexes are more efficient than programmer-defined subscripts, because the programmer often does not know the proper way to define one [01 INDEX PIC S9(9) COMP VALUE 0]. But even then, the compiler index is more efficient. Figure 20.13 shows an example of a programmer-defined subscript that is not only inefficient, but may also cause an error when the subscript exceeds 99. This subscript was used in virtually all of the statements in the program. Using an index reduced the module's run time by 80%.

The positioning of data within a record or a system can also impact the run-time efficiency, especially in an IBM environment. Figure 20.14 shows the type of data alignment required by each type of data to provide maximum efficiency. Often a simple resequencing of the data items in a record can provide run-time reductions.

Programmers concerned with optimizing CPU usage should concern themselves with the way data is declared and the usage of COBOL statements other than input and output, predominantly the arithmetic statements. Programmers concerned with optimizing I/O usage should concentrate on file definitions and ways to reduce the number of I/O statements.

Proper file definitions should be the realm of the data administrator. For example, a data item defined as PIC S9(3) COMP-3 requires only two bytes of data instead of three for DISPLAY numeric data. Multiplied by millions and millions of records, the efficiency gained can be quite impressive. Another possibility involves eliminating data that is merely passed from program to program; place it in a file that other programs can use as they need it. Another

```
77  TABLE-INDEX                          PIC 99 VALUE ZERO.
    .
    .
    .
01 TABLE.
    05  DATA-NAME-1        OCCURS 200    PIC X.


    PERFORM INITIALIZE-TABLE 200 TIMES.
        VARYING TABLE-INDEX FROM 1 BY 1
        UNTIL TABLE-INDEX > 200.

INITIALIZE-TABLE.
    DATA-NAME-1 ( TABLE-INDEX ) = 'F'.
```

FIGURE 20.13. Example of how hand-coded indexes cause reliability and efficiency problems.

PICTURE (A,X) FIELDS

Field Length	Alignment
1	None
2	Half word
3–4	Full word
5–8	Double word
>9	None

PICTURE (9) Fields

Field Length	DISPLAY Alignment	COMP-3 Alignment	COMP Alignment
1	None	None	Half
2	Half	Half	Half
3	Full	Half	Half
4	Full	Full	Half
5	Double	Full	Full
6	Double	Full	Full
7	Double	Full	Full
8	Double	Double	Full
9	Double	Double	Full
10	Double	Double	Double
11	Double	Double	Double
12	Double	Double	Double
13	Double	Double	Double
14	Double	Double	Double
15	Double	Double	Double
16	Double	Double	Double
17	Double	Double	Double
18	Double	Double	Double

FIGURE 20.14.   Field alignments to maximize efficiency in IBM COBOL.

possibility requires reading or creating the file in core so that it can be accessed directly rather than through some intermediate file, trading I/O efficiency for memory usage.

5.2.   PROCEDURE DIVISION

Once the data is properly defined and aligned, the PROCEDURE DIVISION becomes the point of focus for efficiency improvements. The key ingredients of procedural efficiency are concision, execution efficiency, and operability.

Concision

There are module- and statement-level metrics to measure concision. At the module level, a low ELOC (ELOC < 100), a low decision density (DD < 15%), and a high function density (FD > 25%) all suggest that the module is concise and easily processed. At a code statement level, certain COBOL statements, such as the SEARCH ALL, make assertions about the efficiency.

Figure 20.15 shows an example of a hand coded table search and the same function coded as a COBOL SEARCH ALL. Although the hand-coded loop is slightly more efficient than the SEARCH ALL verb, the latter is much more readable and programmer efficient. The software science metrics for the two examples show a difference in difficulty and effort of almost 4:1.

The COBOL COMPUTE statement is more efficient than the same combination of the ADD, DIVIDE, MULTIPLY, and SUBTRACT verbs. It even allows exponentiation. The COMPUTE is also more concise, often stating a complicated equation in one line rather than several.

```
Example 1 - Hand-Coded Search


        MOVE FALSE TO RECORD-FOUND.
        MOVE 1 TO MINIMUM-TABLE-SIZE.
        MOVE TABLE-MAXIMUM TO MAXIMUM-TABLE-SIZE.

        PERFORM SEARCH-TABLE
            UNTIL MATCHING-TABLE-ENTRY-FOUND OR
                  SEARCH-GAP < 1.

    SEARCH-TABLE.
        COMPUTE SEARCH-GAP =
            ((MAXIMUM-TABLE-SIZE - MINIMUM-TABLE-SIZE) / 2).
        ADD SEARCH-GAP, MINIMUM-TABLE-SIZE GIVING TABLE-INDEX.
        IF STATE-CODE ( TABLE-INDEX ) < MASTER-STATE-CODE
            ADD TABLE-INDEX, 1 GIVING MINIMUM-TABLE-SIZE
        ELSE IF STATE-CODE ( TABLE-INDEX ) > MASTER-STATE-CODE
            ADD TABLE-INDEX, 1 GIVING MAXIMUM-TABLE-SIZE
        ELSE
            MOVE TRUE TO RECORD-FOUND.


    Example 2 - SEARCH ALL

        SEARCH ALL STATE-TABLE
            AT END
                PERFORM NO-MATCH-ERROR
            WHEN STATE-CODE ( TABLE-INDEX ) = MASTER-STATE-CODE
                PERFORM STATE-CALCULATIONS.
```

FIGURE 20.15.   Comparison of hand-coded search with the COBOL SEARCH ALL verb.

Execution Efficiency

Arithmetic statements are a primary source of efficiency improvement. Once the data has been defined efficiently, the statements can be examined to reduce the six types of code impurities described in Chapter 3: complimentary operation, ambiguous operands, synonymous operands, common subexpressions, unnecessary assignment, and unfactored expressions. Then long expressions, made up of ADD, DIVIDE, MULTIPLY, and SUBTRACT statements, can be converted into COMPUTE statements for further execution and programmer efficiencies.

The absence of GO TOs usually ensures that the code is well structured and that the flow of logic provides the optimal efficiency. The presence of GO TOs, however, leaves the door open to redundant code and all manner of inefficient algorithms for processing the data.

The use of PERFORM-VARYING-UNTIL indicates the presence of loops in the program. The loop-nesting metric indicates how deeply these loops intertwine. Each loop causes multiple executions of its underlying code. Each loop within a loop executes several times for itself and more times for the outside loop. The second loop of Figure 20.16 will be executed 100 times, compared to the calling loop's 10. Inner loops should be the first focus point for efficiency improvements.

These inner loops often have code that could be removed to the outer loop, thereby reducing the number of executions of that code. Code that initializes data to some constant or code that could be rewritten to process once for all iterations of the inner loop are both examples of efficiency improvements that stem from moving statements out of inner loops.

Programmers will also code loops to process all iterations rather than terminating the loop when it has completed its task. The example in Figure 20.17 shows a matching algorithm that continues looking even after it finds a match. This would be useful if you needed to find the last match in the table, but in this case, it is unnecessary. If the table had thousands of entries and it

```
  ┌──▶PERFORM LOOP-1
  │       VARING INDEX-1 FROM 1 BY 1
  │       UNTIL INDEX-1 > 10.
  │
  │   LOOP-1.
  │       PERFORM LOOP-2
  │           VARING INDEX-2 FROM 1 BY 1
  │           UNTIL INDEX-2 > 10.
  │
  │   LOOP-2.
  └────── MOVE 3.14159265 TO PI.
          COMPUTE AREA = PI * RADIUS ** 2.
```

FIGURE 20.16. Example of optimizing loops for efficiency.

```
       PERFORM SEARCH-TABLE
             VARYING TABLE-INDEX FROM 1 BY 1
             UNTIL TABLE-INDEX > TABLE-MAXIMUM.

    SEARCH-TABLE.
        IF STATE-CODE ( TABLE-INDEX ) = MASTER-STATE-CODE
           PERFORM STATE-PROCESSING.
```

FIGURE 20.17.   Hand-coded search with potential efficiency problems.

found a match on the first item, it would still look through the remaining thousands. Once the code is set up to terminate on a match, the program can be optimized by loading the table with the most frequent matching items first; the least frequent, last. In some instances, because of the frequency of matching the same item over and over, it is worthwhile to check for a previous match before invoking the SEARCH.

The IF statement combined with multiple conditions provides another chance for efficiency improvement. For example, the statement:

IF COND1 OR COND2 OR COND3 THEN

could be made more efficient if we knew which condition occurs most often. If, for example, COND2 is true 80% of the time; COND1, 25%; and COND3, 5%, then it would be more efficient to code COND2 as the first comparison since it is true most often, followed by COND1 and COND3. If the three conditions were ANDed together, we would want the least likely condition first so that all of the conditions would not be needed to pass to the ELSE part of the decision.

Another possible way to improve efficiency requires removal of redundant conditions. For example:

IF (A=B AND C=D) OR (A=B AND E=F)

becomes

IF A=B AND (C=D OR E=F)

The IF-ELSEIF-ELSE CASE statement provides other opportunities for efficiency. Figure 20.18 shows an example of a CASE statement to handle every different type of input record; the order shown is the order expected. In reality, the data records occur many times whereas the header and trailer records occur only once. The original statement can be reordered to using this knowledge to reduce the number of decisions made.

Executions

```
IF RECORD-TYPE = HEADER-RECORD            1000   ***

        PERFORM HEADER-RECORD-PROCESS        1

ELSE IF RECORD-TYPE = MASTER-RECORD       1000

        PERFORM MASTER-RECORD-PROCESS      999

ELSE IF RECORD-TYPE = TRAILER-RECORD         1

        PERFORM TRAILER-RECORD-PROCESS       1

ELSE

        PERFORM RECORD-TYPE-ERROR.            0
```

FIGURE 20.18.   Reordering CASE constructs for efficiencies.

In virtual memory computer systems, paging of program parts can kill efficiency. There are a number of ways to resolve these problems. First, group the infrequently executed paragraphs together. Then, group paragraphs that execute together or one after another. Usually they will remain in core for the duration of the run.

The example in Figure 20.3 shows a CALL that has been repeated several times throughout the program. Changing the code to have only one CALL will help keep the code resident on the system, reducing time to access the submodule.

One of the best ways to achieve efficiency is to use an optimizing compiler such as the CAPEX Optimizer III™. The object code produced is reduced 25–50% and the compiler has other features that make it a helpful tool for efficiency measurement and correction. The analyzer feature allows the programmer to compile and run his or her programs while providing statistics of which modules and statements used the most time while counting the number of executions of each statement. This helps identify which statements are executed 10, 100, 1000, or more times. The programmer can use this information to tune the code's loops and to determine the amount of time spent in arithmetic or I/O statements. It can also be used to eliminate redundant test data, thereby optimizing the programmer's time as well.

Operability

Operability relies on the programmer to anticipate how the program will run and what messages the personnel need to run it. For example, a program that opens four tape files and then reads them one at a time over the period of an hour is wasting precious computer center resources. It should open and close the files one at a time as it needs them, reducing the consumption of tape drives.

Using IBM, the programmer can specify BLOCK CONTAINS 0 REC-ORDS in the file description (FD) statement so that Operations can change the I/O block size at will. This simple change gives Operations a mechanism to optimize the I/O efficiency of the program by matching the blocksize to the type of storage media they are using.

5.3. Efficiency Measure

It is possible to have the program calculate and track its own efficiency. This metric is called the efficiency ratio:

$$\text{efficiency ratio (ER)} = \frac{\text{number of items processed}}{\text{amount of resources used}}$$

Since the COBOL program already knows (or should know) how many records, transactions, or whatever it processed, and it should be able to get the actual CPU seconds used by the system, the COBOL program can calculate and report ER for each run. The programming staff and Operations can use this as a method to track the change in efficiency over time. A system test organization could review ER in relation to their existing test data, verifying that the modified program would not unnecessarily impact operations.

5.4. Efficiency Summary

Efficiency can be determined directly from COBOL code by examining the numeric data items, arithmetic statements, and I/O statements, which are the three prime contributors to efficiency. Only by careful analysis of factors such as the Efficiency Ratio can IS managers make decisions to invest in efficiency tuning. Once properly tuned, software metrics can help identify the efficient coding techniques that reduced operational costs.

6. FLEXIBILITY AND MAINTAINABILITY

Flexibility and maintainability are almost synonymous. Flexibility examines the programmer's ability to enhance a module or program, while maintainability studies the ability to repair a module or program. Both depend on measurements of concision, consistency, modularity, self-documentation, and simplicity. Flexibility goes beyond these metrics to look at expandability and generality. The ability to enhance or repair a module also depends extensively on the complexity of the code, but this has already been covered in Section 3.

6.1. Concision

Concision, in COBOL programs, is represented by language statements that implement a function in a minimum amount of code. The prime contributors are listed in Figure 20.19. These are the function statements that are used to derive the function density, a metric of overall concision.

As function density represents concision at a statement level, ELOC represents concision at a module level. As the number of ELOC exceeds 100, the module's clarity and ease of understanding drop dramatically; the code no longer represents a single, concise function, but will often represent several intertwined functions. The resulting chaos ultimately reduces flexibility and maintainability.

Concision is also a function of the language used. COBOL is more concise than ALC, but less concise than PL/I. COBOL and PL/I both allow 32-character data names, with qualifiers, while FORTRAN and ALC allow only 8 characters. Although the latter are more concise, the problems with shortened data names can be cataclysmic, more often decreasing maintainability and flexibility rather than improving them.

6.2. Consistency

Consistency relies on design and coding standards to ensure common readability among all programmers. At the design level, walk-throughs and mechanized analysis of automated designs can provide the necessary levels of auditing. At the code level, mechanized formatting programs can indent, align, and generally straighten up rat-nest code, putting one statement per line and so on. Figure 20.20 contains an example.

Next, the metrics analyzer can ensure that all of the data names are verified in the data dictionary, providing data-naming consistency. I once had the misfortune to stumble over two modules of the same program that used the names "pseudo" and "sooto" (the Japanese pronunciation) to identify the same

CALL	INSPECT	SEARCH	TRANSFORM
COMPUTE	MERGE	SORT	UNSTRING
GENERATE	PERFORM	STRING	

FIGURE 20.19. List of COBOL functions.

```
IF A = B THEN MOVE C TO D ELSE MOVE E TO F.

becomes

IF A = B THEN
      MOVE C TO D
ELSE
      MOVE E TO F.
```

FIGURE 20.20.   Indenting code for readability.

data item. It was not funny when we found the error after 13 hours of nonstop debugging. The computer's screen editor corrected all of the misspellings in about a second.

The use of the COPY statement to retrieve data structures helps reduce errors and ensures consistency throughout the programs that use the COPYed code. The use of generic design and code skeletons also helps ensure that the programmer is using the best designs and programs possible.

Finally, the use of a standard commenting conventions also helps ensure consistency. The comment density provides a metric of the number of comments per 100 ELOC. Programmers who undercomment will have a measurement of 0–5%. Programmers who overcomment may find that 30–80% of their code is comments, which tends to obscure rather than document the code.

6.3.   Expandability

Data expansion depends on the use of a data dictionary, data base management system (DBMS), and COPY statements. Without the data dictionary, changing the size of a data item will be haphazard, causing numerous programs to blow up from invalid data. Similarly, using the COPY statement for including DATA DIVISION code helps ensure that the code need only be changed in one place and then recompiled into every module that uses it. If a record description appears in 100 places in the system, then COPY statements are the only way to make sure that the code is changed correctly in all places.

Mechanized code analyzers can identify the number of unique and total operands (data names and literals) used in the DATA and PROCEDURE DIVISIONS. As these numbers increase, the complexity of the DATA DIVISION also increases, causing expandability to decline. Analyzers can also extract, summarize, and report on each data name or literal used in the PROCEDURE DIVISION. Unreferenced data names can be deleted from the DATA DIVISION, while the literals can be used to provide machine-readable declarations of literals, which can be included in the program in place of the existing literals.

Literals can impact the expansion of a program. For example, the literal "1" could stand for one, TRUE, Alabama (the first state in an alphabetical list), and so on. The two statements:

SET INDEX UP BY 1.
SET INDEX TO 1.   (ALABAMA)

have completely different meanings. Coding a meaningful data name, like ALABAMA, in every situation where "1" is used provides for further expansion of the program. For example, if Puerto Rico became the fifty-first state, then all of the other states would have to be shifted to allow insertion of Puerto Rico between Pennsylvania and Rhode Island in the state tables. This would be simple if each literal had a data name; the programmer could change the VALUE clause for RHODE-ISLAND through WYOMING rather than changing all occurrences of 39−50 to 40−51.

In the PROCEDURE DIVISION, the complexity metrics ELOC, $V(G)$, effort, and function density play an important part in predicting expandability. As the ELOC, $V(G)$, and programming effort increase, it becomes more difficult to determine where to insert new functions and capabilities. If the existing metrics of a module are over the 100 ELOC, $V(G) >= 10$, and effort $> 10,000$, the programmer should consider adding the new capabilities as separate modules, rather than as inserted code. This is one of the problems with COBOL: It is always easier to insert new paragraphs than to create a new module. Programmers under pressure will always follow the easiest route unless quality measurements force them to do it right the first time.

Function density also provides an indicator of the module's expandability. Modules with a high function density are usually straightforward, making it easier to move functions around or to insert new functions in the appropriate place. Modules with a function density under 10%, are the worker modules of the program. Programmers will find it more difficult to insert new functionality into these modules unless the changes are trivial. An example of this kind of module might be one that edits a certain file and passes the valid information back to its superior. If the module needs to be enhanced to validate not one, but two different files, and merge the validated output of each, then the expansion will be difficult.

A driver module, that controls modules that edit, update, and report on certain data, will have little problem adding a new report or additional edit. The structure chart to add another input file would change as shown in Figure 20.21. The expansion requires adding two modules: one that validates the

second file and passes the data, and another module that merges the two
validated inputs. The expansion of the driver module involves changing only
the statement that calls the validation routine.

6.4. Generality

Once again, modules with a high complexity are probably not generic, but
ones with a high function density probably are. On the other hand, a module
with a low complexity and a low function density may also be general in
nature. Such modules might validate date fields, Social Security numbers, or
print report headings.

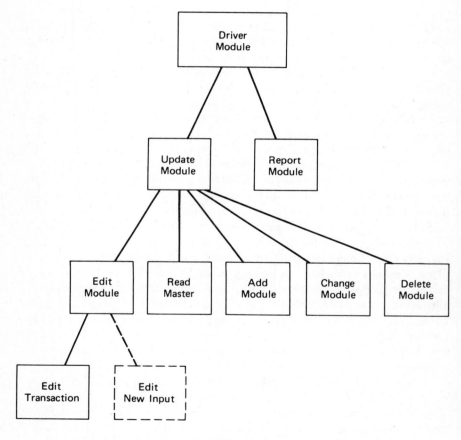

FIGURE 20.21. Example of how modularity allows flexibility.

Generic program designs and code are general in nature. The presence of these generic skeletons should be detectable through some common knowledge of the code analyzers and the code. Modules and programs built from these code skeletons will be easier to understand, enhance, and modify because of their generality.

Commonly used modules, such as date edits, should be carefully built by the programmer support staff and included (via CALL) in programs that require these generic functions. The presence of CALLs to these modules can be detected easily by the code analyzers and usually represent a programmer's interest in using and building programs that are general in nature.

6.5. Modularity

The preliminary metrics of modularity are again the ELOC, cyclomatic complexity, and programming effort. As these metrics exceed the limits previously stated, the modules tend to lose their single-function orientation and their modularity. When enhancing a program or module, the manager, analyst, and programmer should be aware of radical changes in these metrics. Ask the question: Are we enhancing the existing function or adding a new one? The way to answer this question is through examination of the module strength and coupling as described in Chapter 3.

Module Strength

To examine module strength in a COBOL program the programmer should look first at the number of ENTRYs and exits (GOBACK, STOP RUN, or EXIT PROGRAM statements) in the module. If there is more than one entry point, then the programmer can be assured that the module strength is one of the following: information strength, communication strength, logical strength, or coincidental strength. Modules with information strength operate on the same data, like a table load and table lookup. Modules with communication strength often perform many functions related by their use of data, like field and cross-field validation modules. Logical strength modules contain many common functions that are executed one at a time, for example, modules that handle all of the input and output for a program. And modules with coincidental strength contain many functions that are unrelated by their use of data or logic—just sort of a junk drawer for extra pieces of the program.

Modules with a single entry point but multiple exit points usually possess communicational, logical, or coincidental strength. The calling module normally passes a parameter to the module to tell it what to do rather than calling each function separately. Then, as each function completes, it exits from the current point.

Modules with a single entry and exit point usually possess functional, procedural, or classical strength. Functional strength is the best; the module does only one function and then exits. Modules with procedural strength execute many functions in their logical sequence instead of having a driver module and the many subfunctions. Modules with classical strength execute many related functions, but in no logical order. Such a module might set up report headings for three different reports; it does not matter in which order they are done.

The same sort of analysis can be performed on COBOL paragraphs. Using the PERFORM THRU, a programmer may invoke several paragraphs that have communication, procedural, or classical strength. Similarly, the use of the PERFORM without the THRU option indicates a paragraph of functional, procedural, or classical strength. The use of a PERFORM THRU implies a paragraph grouping with multiple entry points (you can branch to any paragraph name) and possibly multiple exit points.

Each paragraph may be analyzed for multiple exits in the form of GO TOs, GOBACK, STOP RUN, and so on. Each of these exit points reduces the flexibility and maintainability of the module. Remember that McCabe found that a module's complexity could be reduced if there were few, if any, structure violations. His reduction metric, essential complexity (ev), is a function of the cyclomatic complexity $V(G)$ and the number of reducible subgraphs. Every subgraph (or COBOL paragraph) is reducible if there is only a single exit point. If the analyzer measures $V(G)$—number of paragraphs without multiple exits. In a well-structured program, essential complexity will go to zero. By definition, a module with a single exit and no GO TOs will have an essential complexity of zero; it can be reduced to improve flexibility and maintainability.

Module Coupling

The next area of modularity depends on the data passed between modules and paragraphs; the data passed between modules should have the same attributes. In other words, you should never pass alphabetic data into numeric fields nor should you pass binary data into packed decimal. The fields should be of the same length in both the calling and subordinate modules, and so on. Each of these comparisons can be automated by a code analyzer.

There are five different kinds of module coupling described in Chapter 3: data, stamp, external, common, and content. With COBOL, it is possible to determine the presence of each of these forms of coupling. For example, data coupling implies that only data elements are passed via the parameter list. Using an analyzer, it is possible to retain and evaluate the parameters. Parameters with a PICTURE clause are data elements; parameters without are data structures. If all the parameters have PICTURE clauses, then the module is usually data coupled. If some or all of the parameters are data structures, then the module is stamp coupled.

External and common coupling are both within the province of the COBOL paragraphs. Paragraphs that refer to the same data item are external coupled. Paragraphs that refer to a common data structure are common coupled. Both external and common coupling are less desirable than data or stamp coupling, which is why large single-module programs are discouraged: The degree of coupling makes maintenance more difficult. Content coupling, on the other hand, is virtually impossible; one module cannot access data contained in another module directly. This alone gives COBOL an advantage over ALC.

Further analysis reveals that a mechanized analyzer could look at each paragraph, determining which data names are used as input and which are used as output. This information could be used to develop documentation of the program if none existed or to determine which paragraphs read and modify data produced in other paragraphs and the relative dependence of each paragraph on the other.

The analyzer could also detect words like FLAG or SWITCH in the data name which indicates that the controlling module tells its subordinates what to do and how to do it rather than passing the data and letting the subordinate choose the correct course of action.

6.6. Self-Documentation

Self-documentation depends on the use of comments and meaningful data names. As previously discussed, a mechanized count of the comment lines and their density in COBOL source code can tell much about the module's self-documentation. A comment density of 10−20% is often representative of well documented code.

The mechanized analyzer, since it already identifies and stores each data name, can be used to determine the length of data names. For example, the seven-character EOFFLAG is less readable than the equivalent MASTER-FILE-AT-EOF; EOFFLAG provides less documentation. Further, the use of the OF and IN reserved words to qualify data names often implies better documentation. For example:

MOVE SOCIAL-SECURITY-NUMBER OF TRANSACTION-RECORD TO
    SOCIAL-SECURITY-NUMBER OF MASTER-RECORD

provides better documentation than:

MOVE TRAN-SSN TO MAST-SSN.

Similarly, using many MOVE statements instead of the MOVE CORRE-SPONDING option is usually better documentation of what is really happening. The CORRESPONDING option leaves the program open to errors from future maintenance changes.

6.7. Simplicity

Simplicity is really the opposite of complexity, so you can measure a module's simplicity from the ELOC, $V(G)$, and effort metrics. If these metrics all fall within the bounds you have established, then the module has simplicity. If not, the maintainability and flexibility will usually suffer.

7.   INTEGRITY

Software integrity is composed of auditability, instrumentation, and security. Auditability is the domain of operating, data-base management, and configuration management systems. In COBOL, the presence of DBMS calls often implies that the system will be more auditable and also secure.

The auditability and security of the source code depends on the capabilities of the source code control and configuration management systems. So this is not easily measured.

The major opportunity for measuring software integrity in COBOL programs comes from examination of a module's or program's instrumentation. Calls to run control or standard message modules may indicate a degree of instrumentation. The use of generic code skeletons that contain record counting and reporting logic or calls to audit modules will also indicate a concern for integrity. Each of these items is installation dependent, so they will have to be built into the metrics analyzer.

The absence of integrity-enhancing commands does not necessarily mean that the code is in error. Management decisions can be made to exclude the costs of this excess development because of the low risk presented by the data processed. But as on-line systems with microcomputer terminals expand their current bounds, the need for system integrity—auditability, instrumentation, and security—will increase dramatically. Measurement is the only way to ensure the presence of integrity-enhancing code in a system's modules and programs.

8.   INTEROPERABILITY

Interoperability depends on the submetrics: communications commonality, data commonality, generality, and modularity. Systems have an inherent need to get their data from other systems that already exist. For example, a personnel system may drive aspects of the payroll system, which may in turn drive part of the accounting system. The ability of these systems to operate together is known as interoperability.

On-line systems that need to interact will require the same communications interface. This can be determined manually. Two systems that need to share data will require Data Commonality, which normally is provided via the use of data dictionaries and the COBOL COPY statement. The presence of data commonality can be detected by use of the data dictionary (Do these programs both use the same data items names or data-base structures?) or the use of common data structures COPYed into both programs.

Generality implies that the code or module may be used interchangeably among programs. Common modules that handle file I/O or data-base access, updates, or reports will provide a generic interface to the system's data. Coupling these modules with other modular systems will make interoperability possible. Generality is measured by the use of common generic logic modules and the reuse of other logic modules.

Modularity makes changes to a program simpler and less costly, making it possible to add the interface to another program or system with less effort. Coupled with general interface modules that are possibly already available, a modular program can be enhanced in short order to improve interoperability. Modularity is measured by ELOC, $V(G)$, and programming effort.

9. PORTABILITY

Portability depends on generality, modularity, self-documentation, hardware, and software independence. With the boundaries between micros, minis, and mainframes disappearing, software suppliers are looking for ways to easily port their products from any one of these environments to another. A large number of them code their products in portable languages like "C" or PASCAL. Next, they focus on general programs that will be of value in all environments, thereby maximizing their potential marketplace.

Generality usually is determined from the design. If the design and code are extracted from some generic library of routines, then the module will be general in nature. Spread sheets, data-base management systems, and word processing packages are all examples of software that have uses in a variety of markets and hardware.

Modularity is also a sign of portability. Modules with sufficiently small metrics of ELOC, $V(G)$, and programming effort, will be easier to examine, modify, and transport to other hardware. Since porting software is simply enhancing the existing software to run under a different operating system on other hardware, ELOC, $V(G)$, and programming effort provide an excellent measure of the effort required to modify the existing code.

Self-documentation, or the comment density as it is measured in COBOL, provides another clue to portability. Well-documented code will be easier to understand and modify. Comment density, data-name consistency, and the presence or absence of literals will help identify the level of self-documentation.

Hardware independence is rarely a problem in COBOL. Assembler languages are completely hardware dependent; COBOL rarely depends on the hardware. The only exception might be the use of BLOCK CONTAINS in the file description section: record and block sizes are a function of the media being read or written. In the IBM environment, BLOCK CONTAINS 0 RECORDS implies hardware independence; block sizes are chosen by use of the JCL rather than by programmer choice.

Software Independence affects portability in a variety of ways. First, the use of IBM or other vendors extensions to the basic language will affect the code's portability. A quick check of the language reference manual will usually pinpoint the reserved words that are extensions to the standard language. The metrics analyzer should collect statistics on these words and their frequency in the code.

Second, with the increase in the number of systems that depend on a data-base management system or telecommunications interface, COBOL becomes more deeply connected to software that may only run on one brand of hardware. The software metrics analyzer should collect statistics on the calls to IMS or any of the various DBMS and telecommunication software packages that provide for connections to COBOL programs. Because of the design of these external I/O packages, COBOL programs often are designed around their interfaces, making it difficult to port the program without re-designing or rewriting the code.

Portability is the ultimate aim of most application software developers. System software developers are not as concerned, but as their software must interface with software running in microcomputers and the like, their concern will grow. Measurement is one of the few ways of identifying the extent of the problem and the direction to take in making the software portable.

10. RELIABILITY

Another concern of virtually all software developers is reliability. Any kind of software failure, whether it results in erroneous data or program termination, increases costs and reduces productivity. Software reliability depends on accuracy, consistency, complexity, simplicity, error tolerance, and modularity, each of which can be determined from analysis of the code.

Accuracy, in COBOL, depends on the data definition and the use of GIVING, ROUNDED, REMAINDER, and ON OVERFLOW clauses. Metrics analyzers should determine the size of sending and receiving fields in COBOL statements like MOVE or ADD, and indicate possible problems when the receiving field is smaller than the sending field or the receiving field has fewer decimal places, or whatever. This information comes from examination of the data definitions for each data item.

The use of GIVING, ROUNDED, REMAINDER, and ON OVERFLOW clauses all help identify the programmer's concern with accuracy and reliability. The GIVING option ensures that neither of the two original data fields are changed; only the receiving field is changed. The ROUNDED and REMAINDER clauses help ensure that something logical is done with the fractional leftovers from MULTIPLY, DIVIDE, and COMPUTE statements.

Consistency plays a strong role in reliability. Edits of numeric data, boundary tests on loops and indexes, and so on should be performed uniformly throughout a system. Sections 4.2 and 6.2 give specific examples.

Complexity often indicates that a program may be unreliable, but is not a totally reliable predictor. Highly complex mathematical software may be very reliable. Simple report programs, on the other hand, may be unreliable. The complexity metrics described in Section 3 are useful predictors of reliability. The ELOC, cyclomatic complexity, and software science metrics indicate that the codes processing is either simple or complex. They also indicate degrees of complexity, giving us a ruler to compare different programs or modules. These programs often have many paths [measured by $V(G)$] and some of those paths may not be exercised during testing. Or they are executed in ways not previously envisioned by the designers. The software science metrics rely on the ELOC and the number of operands to determine complexity. It is intuitively logical that as you add more executable statements, with additional data names and literals, that the chance for failure goes up.

Error tolerance is another key feature of reliable systems. What happens when the data isn't numeric and the statement is performing a numeric operation on it? What happens when the code reads past end of file? A module or program that can handle these problems is error tolerant. It has enough intelligence to handle the usual types of program bugs.

One of the more difficult errors revolves around missing logic paths. In COBOL, every IF should have an ELSE, every SEARCH or READ should have an AT END, and so on. This is one of the rules of programming style: State actions explicitly instead of implicitly, it forces programmers to think about the default logic path. When the time comes to change the default path, the new logic can be inserted easily. There are many cases when the default path needs to be replaced by a call to an error routine; the program detects errors and tries to handle them in an intelligent fashion. Programs that abort on any error are not error tolerant.

A module that examines data before processing them is more likely to avoid errors over a lifetime than one that blindly expects its neighbor to pass it good data. At the minimum, this involves testing numeric data before using it to ADD, DIVIDE, MULTIPLY, SUBTRACT, or COMPUTE. Then, the use of the OVERFLOW option of these statements provides for the data to expand beyond the present limits and for the program to take some intelligent action.

Modularity affects reliability. Modularity tends to restrict complexity, data problems, and so on. In doing so, it restricts the possibilities of other pieces of code affecting it adversely. With a well-defined interface, edits of incoming data, and good internal error handling logic, these modules can become highly reliable—virtually indestructible. Measurements of modularity are described in Section 6.5.

11. REUSABILITY

Reusability depends on the measurements of generality, hardware independence, software independence, modularity, and self-documentation. Reusable code reduces development and maintenance costs. These savings allow you to invest in making these modules have high quality and reliability. This in turn will provide savings from high reliability, maintainability, and so on.

For a module to be reusable, it must be general in nature. More than one program must have some use for it. Date edits, Social Security number edits, report headings, update logic, table handling logic, and data selection modules are just a few examples of modules that exhibit generality. The metrics of generality are further described in Section 6.4.

Unless a module is only going to be used in one hardware and software environment, reusable modules must possess hardware and software independence. They cannot depend on special extensions to the language, software systems that only run on one kind of hardware, or one operating system. In the microcomputer marketplace, the presence of reusable code can be determined by how fast a manufacturer can upgrade their software to run under CP/M, MS-DOS, XENIX, POS, or go from 8- to 16- to 32-bit machines.

Modularity also affects reusability. Modularity implies that the module performs only one function; as such, there is a greater likelihood that the code can be used in another program that needs a similar function. With diligent application of the module strength and coupling metrics in Section 6.5, programmers will find that fewer modules need to be written for each new program. Increasingly, new programs can be constructed using existing modules. This is the key to productivity.

Self-documentation is a lessor contributor to reusability, but a contributor none the less. Comments help the developer ensure that the existing code will provide the function required or help them determine if it can be changed to meet their needs. The measures of self-documentation are described in Section 6.6.

12. STRUCTURE

Program and module structure are functions of data commonality, expandability, and modularity. The ability to examine structure mechanically, using graphic and static analyzers, enhances the analyst's and programmer's chances of spotting potential weaknesses that can be corrected before the program is released.

Data structures, for records and data bases, often change. The user wants to add some new information or delete some from the existing system. Or an enhancement that requires the addition of some fields is needed. In either case, the data structure must change. In a data-base environment, dozens or hundreds of programs may access the same data. The reliability of these programs depends on common data definitions and structures. Data dictionaries are the starting point for identifying data commonality. The use of COPY statements or their equivalent, in COBOL, shows a definite concern for data commonality and the potential for improved reliability. When one structure is changed, all modules can be recompiled and relinked, minimizing the chance of reliability problems.

Data structures are not the only things that change. Modules and programs need to be repaired and enhanced. Enhancements often require the addition of functions to the program. The simplicity or difficulty involved in making these changes depends on the measurement of expandability, which is described in Section 6.3. Modularity affects, or is an outgrowth, of structure. Single-function modules will tend to have a simple, easily understood, reliable structure. Programs built of these modules will be more easily understood and reliable. Modularity is described in Section 6.5.

13. TESTABILITY

Your ability to test a module, program, or system depends on the measurements of auditability, complexity, simplicity, instrumentation, modularity, and self-documentation. Some estimates testing process indicate that 40–60% of the development (and probably the maintenance) process are consumed by testing. It would be handy to know before hand how much effort it will take to test a given module, program, or system.

The same tools that auditors use to study programs and systems are ideally suited to testing programs. In most cases, however, auditability depends on the operating system accounting logs, data-base logs, and teleprocessing logs. The programs that do audit their own processing, by use of record and process counting, can be examined mechanically to determine auditability. Usually, auditability will have to be determined from the existing software environment rather than from the code.

Complexity and simplicity are the smiling and frowning faces of the jester. A person testing a module or program can use the cyclomatic complexity $V(G)$ to determine the minimum number of paths that must be tested. $V(G)$ does not indicate the total number of paths in the module, only the number of structural paths. $V(G)$ should provide a reasonable estimate of the effort a testing person will spend developing test data and cases for the module. Of course, they must have some desire to test all of the structural paths, which does not ensure that all of the possible paths will be tested. COBOL complexity metrics are described in Section 3.

The program's instrumentation, which provides the statistics of the program's execution, affects testability. Suppose the tester inputs 2000 records and the execution report only shows 1999 records read? What if there were 1000 valid adds, 800 valid changes, and 200 deletes and the report only shows 199 deletes? Doesn't this information facilitate the job of testing, helping to pinpoint the potential source of the errors?

Modularity affects testability. A function module can be tested independently to examine its internal workings. Then its interfaces can be tested separately. Finally, the entire program can be tested as an integrated whole. This breaks the testing process into manageable pieces. A large, multifunction module cannot be tested easily, however. Isolating problems becomes more difficult as each function is added to the existing module. Eventually, it is too difficult to fully test the module and some errors slip out into production. At this point, the module becomes unreliable. Modularity can greatly affect error detection and correction by isolating tests to small, easily managed components. Modularity metrics are described more fully in Section 6.5.

Self-documentation affects testability too. If the testing organization has access to the sourcecode, which it must in order to build meaningful test cases, then the analysts will appreciate any and all documentation. Comments help to explain the code that they did not write and do not maintain. Self-documentation metrics are described in Section 6.6.

14. SUMMARY

Measuring all aspects of code quality in COBOL programs is neither impossible nor overly difficult. The application of mechanized analyzers and the use of their output can help programmers, analysts, and managers determine the quality of the code. And the results can provide them with statistics to identify problems early and effect solutions before the code goes into testing or production.

Poor quality is a cancer that can eat into a program or system. Software measurement is a method of early detection and correction. COBOL code can be changed easily to reduce the cancer in increments as the programmers have time. With practice, they will avoid the very things that bring about the decline of quality. When this happens, you will no longer need measurement tools.

CHAPTER TWENTY-ONE

PL/I METRICS

1. BASICS

PL/I was designed to overcome some of the shortfallings of COBOL. Based on later evaluations, some of its power can be counterproductive, making code harder to read and maintain. Other features, such as 31-character data names, are often underused, leaving cryptic if not indecipherable names for future system maintainers. The basic rule of writing any code, but especially PL/I, is *code for change*. Your program will undergo continuous changes, so anticipate them and program to minimize the impact of those changes. The following few rules will help meet the requirements of this basic rule.

1.   Never use the LABEL declaration. The LABEL is the PL/I equivalent of the ALTER. Altering the path of the program during execution is a sure way to confuse future maintainers and make the program impossible to maintain.

2.   Restrict the use of the GO TO statement. Restructure the code to show the true logic path. Believe it or not, Dijkstra has proven that a program can be written without the use of the GO TO (Dijkstra, 1976).

3.   Always use meaningful data names. Keep them in a data dictionary to minimize the. impact of changes. Use one level of qualification to further clarify the code.

4.   Always indent nested code under an IF-THEN-ELSE statement to make the code more readable.

5.   Use the SELECT verb to implement case constructs rather than using the IF-ELSEIF-ELSE form of the case construct.

6.   Always use loops to eliminate redundant code.

7.   Always limit modules to single functions. Don't try to cram the whole program into one module. You will make it hard to maintain, enhance, and reuse, while reducing efficiency (optimizing compilers cannot work well on large modules).

8.   Always use format statements—%SKIP, %PAGE, or $(-+0)$ in column one—to clarify the code. Eject page before new subroutines or functions, and skip lines before IF, SELECT, CALL, DO WHILE, and DO UNTIL statements to identify blocks of code, just as this book uses labels and paragraphs to improve its readability.

9.   Use comments to *clarify* what the code is doing, never to restate what is already obvious. Too many comments can obscure the executable code, making maintenance difficult. Use comments to describe each procedure's processing, the function of each declared variable, and so on.

2.   STRUCTURED CONSTRUCTS

Looking at PL/I, you discover that the basic building blocks of all structured constructs—Sequential, IF-THEN-ELSE, CASE, DOWHILE, and DOUNTIL—are available in one form or another. By excluding the LABEL declarations and GO TO verbs, you have the makings of correct structured code.

Figure 21.1 shows the recommended way to code each of the five structured programming constructs. Sequential statements are always blocked, left justified, and indented under IF-THEN-ELSE statements. The IF and ELSE are always aligned to display how they correspond to the logic flow. Nested IF-THEN-ELSE statements are also indented under the previous IF or ELSE. CASE constructs are formed of SELECT, WHEN, OTHERWISE statements. The DOWHILE and DOUNTIL are represented as shown.

Note that there is only one verb or qualifier per line. The qualifiers— WHEN, OTHERWISE, and so on—are indented under the statement for clarity. Another tip involves decisions with more than one condition: Put the AND or OR connector on the line with the decision and put the condition on the next line (see Figure 21.2). This forces the reader to notice that there are more conditions on the next line. It is a mental stimulant to ensure that they read the next line. Without the connector, the maintainer might miss the additional condition, causing many wasted hours.

3.   COMPLEXITY

PL/I complexity is based on four metrics: ELOC, decisions, cyclomatic complexity, and Halstead's software science metrics.

```
SEQUENTIAL

     A = SQRT(X);
     CALL GET_TRANSACTION_RECORD;

IF-THEN-ELSE

     IF ( A = B ) THEN
        DO;
             statements
        END;
     ELSE
        DO;
             statements
        END;

CASE

     SELECT ( CASE_VARIABLE );
        WHEN ( CASE_1 )
           DO;
                statements
           END;
        WHEN ( CASE_2 )
           DO;
                statements
           END;
        OTHERWISE
           DO;
                statements
           END;
     END; /* END SELECT */

DOWHILE

     DO WHILE ( condition );
        statements;
     END; /* END WHILE */

DOUNTIL

     DO UNTIL ( condition );
        statements
     END; /* END WHILE */
```

FIGURE 21.1. The five PL/I structured coding constructs.

3.1. ELOC

The complexity of PL/I increases with each executable line of code. No procedure can grow to several hundred or thousand ELOC without having some redundant code. The trick is to find it and remove the duplications. In large modules, you will find whole functions repeated, often several times.

```
IF ( condition1 &
     condition2 ) THEN
    DO;
        statements
    END;
ELSE
    DO;
        statements
    END;                        FIGURE 21.2.  Indenting nested conditions for clarity.
```

When the procedure is modified, one or two of the functions will be changed, but not all, causing a variety of program errors that often go undetected. When the programmer finds the first function, he or she will often make the necessary changes, assuming incorrectly that there is only one such function. After several tests, the programmer will have found most of the redundant functions, but programmers rarely take the time to remove the duplicate code and rectify all references to each copy.

These redundant functions exist because previous maintainers were asked to add a function to the module, and not knowing that one already exists, they went ahead and added a duplicate function. In other situations, they would copy an existing subroutine or function, changing only one or two statements.

In my own experience, analyzing the code and removing redundancy requires a minimum amount of effort and can reduce the ELOC in an existing module by 5–20%. A programmer who can measurably demonstrate that he or she has successfully reduced the ELOC by this large a percentage truly has provided the company with a great benefit; the future maintenance costs of this module will decline. Of this reduction in ELOC, a small portion consists of decisions.

3.2. Decisions and Decision Density

Decisions add to the complexity of the logic. Often the number of decisions can be reduced by simple transformation, as shown in Figure 21.3. Although this does not reduce the cyclomatic complexity $V(G)$, the number of decisions is reduced by two, and we also removed two assignment statements for a total ELOC reduction of four.

The decision density of this module originally might have been 10%, or one decision for every 10 ELOC. After the suggested revision, the density could drop to 8%, a significant reduction. Since decision density runs as high as 30% in some modules, any reduction in the number of decisions would be welcome. The next refinement of decision complexity involves the cyclomatic complexity $V(G)$.

```
IF ( B = '1' ) THEN
    A = C;
ELSE
    IF ( B = '2' ) THEN
        A = D;
    ELSE
        IF ( B = '3' ) THEN
            A = C;
        ELSE
            IF ( B = '4') THEN
                A = D;
            ELSE
                A = E;
```

becomes

```
IF ( B = '1' |
     B = '3' ) THEN
    A = C;
ELSE IF ( B = '2' |
          B = '4' ) THEN
    A = D;
ELSE
    A = E;
```

FIGURE 21.3. Reducing complexity by removing redundant code.

3.3. Cyclomatic Complexity

$V(G)$ represents the number of structural test paths in the module and consists of the number of decisions, ANDs (&), ORs (|), and NOTs (¬) in the executable code. Having covered the reduction of decisions, lets take a look at how to reduce the number of ANDs, ORs, and NOTs.

Figure 21.4 shows how the previous example could be rewritten to exclude the ORs. The new $V(G)$ is 3; compared to the old $V(G)$ of 5, the programmer has made another significant contribution to the maintainability of the code.

NOT clauses are best rewritten, reversing the order of the logic to state the logic in a positive way. If something is not black, it is not necessarily white. But programmers have a way of thinking in binary, 0 and 1, black and white, so they often miss the ambiguity of a NOT clause. One of the most obvious reasons for NOT clauses is the systems analyst's concern with what might go wrong, rather than right, in a module. Consider the following example:

```
IF A ¬> B THEN              IF A > B THEN;
    CALL ERROR;                 /* A SHOULD BE > THAN B*/
                            ELSE
                                CALL ERROR;

V(G) = 3                        V(G) = 2
```

```
IF ( VERIFY( B, '13') = 0 ) THEN
    A = C;
ELSE IF ( VERIFY ( B, '24') = 0 ) THEN
    A = D;
ELSE
    A = E;
```

FIGURE 21.4.   Reducing complexity with built-in functions.

Since A $\neg>$ B translates into A $<$ B OR A $=$ B, the cyclomatic complexity is 1 (IF) + 1 (OR) + 1 = 3. So by eliminating the NOT clause, $V(G)$ is also reduced. This example also displays one of the fundamental principles of readability and efficiency:

Put the most frequently exercised path first.

Often quite extensive, error handling for invalid data items is quite extensive, causing the programmer to read it all, only to discover that the code is of no importance when making enhancements or changes.

3.4.   Software Science

Halstead's equations for software science are based on the number of operators and operands. By reducing the total number of operators (ELOC), as previously shown, the difficulty and effort metrics will decline. Similarly, reducing the ELOC also reduces the total number of operands, which further reduces these metrics. If any of the unique operators and operands can be removed also, so much the better. The next few sections will examine the structured programming constructs (IF-THEN-ELSE, CASE, DOWHILE, and DOUNTIL) and show how software science can demonstrate differences in programming style.

IF-THEN-ELSE

Perhaps the prime examples of removing unique operators involves the GO TO and CALLed functions. The GO TO is the only mechanism that allows structure violations in source code; its elimination not only reduces the number of unique operators, but also the potential for structure and logic errors. Figure 21.5 shows two ways of coding an IF-THEN-ELSE. The example using GO TOs was coded by an ALC coder recently retrained in PL/I who was used to creating the IF-THEN-ELSE using branch statements. The

Example 1	Example 2

```
    IF A = B THEN              IF A = B THEN
       DO;                        C = D;
          C = D;               ELSE
          GOTO LABEL1;            D = E;
       END;
    D = E;
LABEL1:
```

FIGURE 21.5.   Comparison of GO TO and simple PL/I IF-THEN-ELSE.

simple example uses the elegant features of PL/I to simplify the expression. The unique and total operators and operands in the GO TO example are:

Unique operands = A, B, C, D, E   = 5
Unique operators = IF, GOTO, "="   = 3
Total operands   = A, B, D, E, C, D   = 6
Total operators = IF, "=", GOTO, "="   = 4

The simple example has the same number of unique and total operands, but the operators have changed as follows:

Unique operators = IF, "="   = 2
Total operators = IF, "=", "=" = 3

Comparing the two:

	GO TOs	Without GO TOs
Vocabulary	8.0	7.0
Length	10.0	9.0
Estimated length	16.4	13.6
Volume	30.0	25.3
Difficulty	1.8	1.2
Language level	9.3	17.5
Information content	16.7	21.1
Effort	54.0	30.3

This simple transformation (there are old programs with this stuff in them) cut the difficulty by a third and reduced the effort to a half of the original example.

Remembering that the effort metric has been shown to reflect the actual work required to write or maintain a piece of code, the programmer can show that change improved the maintainability and reduced the complexity of the code.

Another way of looking at programming style is to look at how the programmer used the features of the language. In this case, the language level metric increased significantly showing that the second example uses the more powerful features of PL/I. An increase in this metric usually implies an increase in concision. The information content also increased slightly, but this has relatively little meaning.

CASE

Figure 21.6 shows three alternate ways of writing a CASE statement in PL/I: the first uses GO TOs; the second, IF-THEN-ELSE statements; the third, the IBM SELECT verb. How much of a burden are those GO TOs? Perhaps the key item to note is that the use of the GO TO obscures the fact that there needs to be a default path (F = A;). The maintenance programmer overlooks this possibility when the default action is nonexistent. In such a case, the GO TOs could be removed, but the potential problems from falling through the other decisions would be frightening.

```
    Example 1                  Example 2                  Example 3
IF A = B THEN              IF A = B THEN          SELECT ( A );
    DO;                        DO;                    WHEN (B)
        statements                 statements         DO;
        GOTO LABEL_EXIT;       END;                       statements
    END;                   ELSE IF A = C THEN        END;
IF A = C THEN                  DO;                  WHEN (C)
    DO;                            statements        DO;
        statements             END;                     statements
        GOTO LABEL_EXIT;   ELSE IF A = D THEN        END;
    END;                       DO;                  WHEN (D)
IF A = D THEN                      statements        DO;
    DO;                        END;                     statements
        statements         ELSE                      END;
        GOTO LABEL_EXIT;       DO;                  OTHERWISE
    END;                           statements        DO;
LABEL_EXIT:                    END;      .              statements
                                                    END;
                                       END; /* SELECT */
```

FIGURE 21.6.   Comparison of GO TO, IF-ELSEIF-ELSE, and SELECT CASE constructs.

	GO TOs	IF-THEN-ELSE	SELECT
Vocabulary	7.0	6.0	6.0
Length	15.0	13.0	9.0
Estimated length	12.7	10.0	10.0
Volume	42.1	33.6	23.3
Difficulty	2.3	1.5	1.0
Language level	8.3	14.9	23.3
Information content	18.7	22.4	23.3
Effort	94.7	50.4	23.3

The difficulty of the GO TO example is twice the IF-THEN-ELSE example. The effort metric is 2.5 times higher, implying twice as much effort to read, comprehend, and change the GO TO version of the CASE construct. Also note that the language level is higher for the IF-THEN-ELSE example; the programmer was using the more powerful features of PL/I.

Using the IF-ELSEIF-ELSE construct or the SELECT verb, the maintenance programmer can easily recognize the CASE constructs no matter how many cases exist. In many designs, each case is not as simple as the ones shown here; it may encompass 10 to 100 ELOC. Programmers, analysts, and managers should minimize the scope of a CASE statement to a single page by the proper use of CALLs to handle each case, making it easier for the maintainer to grasp the total control flow at a glance.

DO WHILE

Figure 21.7 shows an example of a hand-coded loop to initialize a table compared to a DO WHILE loop. The results:

	Loop	DO WHILE	DO INDEX
Vocabulary	8.0	7.0	7.0
Length	15.0	14.0	9.0
Estimated length	16.4	13.6	13.6
Volume	45.0	39.3	25.3
Difficulty	3.0	2.0	1.4
Language level	5.0	9.8	12.9
Information content	15.0	19.6	18.6
Effort	135.0	78.6	35.4

| Example 1 | Example 2 |

```
        INDEX = ONE;                  |  INDEX = ONE;
LOOP_START:                           |  DO WHILE ( INDEX <= A_MAX );
        IF ( INDEX <= A_MAX ) THEN    |      A ( INDEX ) = ZERO;
            DO;                       |      INDEX = INDEX + ONE;
                A ( INDEX ) = ZERO;   |  END; /* DO WHILE */
                INDEX = INDEX + ONE;  |
                GOTO LOOP_START;      |
            END;                      |
```

| Example 3 |

```
DO INDEX = ONE BY ONE TO A_MAX;
    A ( INDEX ) = ZERO;
END'
```

FIGURE 21.7.   Comparison of a hand-coded loop and DOWHILE construct.

Again, the difficulty is reduced and the effort metric reduced by a factor of 4. The language level is higher for the DO WHILE example. The DO INDEX is superior to either.

DO UNTIL

Figure 21.8 shows a common problem encountered in PL/I: the need to read a record and then process it. Because the programmer waits until entering the loop to read the first record, he or she then has to check for end of file before processing. But this check is already done by the DO UNTIL. Since the processing code is extensive, the programmer also has to code a label and GO TO it when at end of file. In this example, to avoid repeating the end of file test in the READ routine, the programmer moved the record-counting logic into the processing function. The future maintainers, when it comes time to CALL the READ from another location in the program, will have to repeat not only the CALL but also the end-of-file test.

All of this convoluted logic could have been avoided by priming the pump—reading a record before entering the loop. Then to let the controlling DO UNTIL handle the end-of-file condition, we move the statement CALL READ-RECORD to the end of the processing paragraph, making it possible to eliminate a decision (IF), a GO TO, and a label while adding a CALL (function statement) and an assignment (simple sequential).

```
            Example 1                    |          Example 2
─────────────────────────────────────────────────────────────────────────
  ON ENDFILE ( MASTERIN);               |     ON ENDFILE ( MASTERIN);
     BEGIN;                             |        BEGIN;
          EOF_MASTER = TRUE;            |          EOF_MASTER = TRUE;
     END;                               |        END;
                                        |
  READ (MASTERIN)                       |     READ (MASTERIN)
      INTO MASTER_RECORD;               |         INTO MASTER_RECORD;
PROCESS_LOOP:                           |     DO UNTIL (EOF_MASTERIN);
  process the record                    |        process the record
  READ (MASTERIN)                       |        READ (MASTERIN)
      INTO MASTER_RECORD;               |            INTO MASTER_RECORD;
  IF ( ¬EOF_MASTERIN ) THEN             |     END; /* DO UNTIL */
      GOTO PROCESS_LOOP;                |
```

FIGURE 21.8.   Comparison of a hand-coded loop with DOUNTIL construct.

	GOTO	DO UNTIL
Vocabulary	9.0	8.0
Length	14.0	13.0
Estimated length	19.6	16.0
Volume	44.0	39.3
Difficulty	5.0	4.0
Language level	1.8	2.4
Information content	18.9	9.7
Effort	221.0	156.0

In this example, the difficulty declined marginally, while the effort metric was cut in half. The second example is preferable.

Implications

What I have demonstrated, hopefully, is that software science metrics can be used to evaluate different programming styles. Each of the examples focused on decisions—the major contributors to complexity. There should be one or perhaps two best ways to code a specific structured programming construct or any function that consists of them. Software science metrics can be applied to new modules all the way through their development, allowing the programmers and analysts to evaluate and eliminate poor coding practices and to meet their quality improvement goals. Software science metrics also can be used to examine a module before and after maintenance, again allowing inspection and correction before testing and release. Combined with a maintenance history of difficult programs, these metrics can be used to justify a preventive maintenance team to revise and improve existing modules and programs.

3.5. Complexity Summary

Each of the complexity metrics—ELOC, decisions, cyclomatic complexity, and software science—provide a yardstick for examining newly developed and existing code to verify the programming style. Programming style—using the best features of the language and using them wisely—is the cornerstone of reducing maintenance costs and elevating the image of the IS organization. Without these measurement tools and their application to improve code quality, IS is doomed to an endless cycle of rewriting existing systems that have become unmaintainable.

4. CORRECTNESS

Does the program do what the users want? And does it do so correctly? There are limited ways to establish the correctness of a program without actually testing it and examining the output, but let's look at possible ways of determining completeness, consistency, and traceability from the source code.

4.1. Completeness

For a program or module to be complete, it must provide a full implementation of the functions required. There are ways of examining each line of code to determine if the fullness of PL/I has been used to maximum potential. Such attention to detail at the code level will often reflect the attention given to the module or program over all.

Data Declarations

Completeness may be determined from the occurrence of the key words CHAR, BIT, BIN, DECIMAL, FIXED, INIT, and so on. Uninitialized data items are a constant source of program errors. By comparing the number of CHAR, BIT, and BIN clauses to the number of INIT clauses, you can arrive at an estimate of completeness; a high percentage of INIT clauses to data items indicates a high degree of completeness when defining data. Similarly, numeric data that is properly defined as FIXED (DECIMAL or BIN) will provide further proof of completeness and attention to detail. The precision of each numeric data name should be specified explicitly: FIXED DEC (7,2). A program that has a large number of arithmetic statements with few efficient data structures lacks an element of completeness. A module that uses %INCLUDE statements to include record structures and other common data definitions rather than redefining the code in several different modules will help ensure completeness.

PROCEDURE Statements

PL/I provides a number of ways to ensure the completeness of arithmetic, data manipulation, I/O, subprogram linkage, and table-handling logic statements.

Arithmetic statements are a common cause of errors. Either they replace a number that another part of the program needs, or they manipulate bad data and the program terminates. The statement:

    B = A + B;

adds A to B and replaces B. A more complete expression would be:

    C = A + B;

The value of B is unchanged and can be used in further calculations without error.

Each of the key words ON CONDITION, ON ERROR, and so on, indicates the programmer's concern with completeness. ON conditions are used to detect and correct errors as they occur. ON conditions provide a more complete implementation of any function. Because PL/I, with its varying data, can cause hard to find problems, the ON CONVERSION, FIXED-OVERFLOW, OVERFLOW, SIZE, STRINGRANGE, STRINGSIZE, SUB-SCRIPTRANGE, UNDERFLOW, and ZERODIVIDE clauses provide for extended error handling when data manipulation statements encounter bad data. The use of this clause for error detection and correction provides a further measure of completeness and correctness.

In the input/output statements, the use of the ON ENDFILE, ENDPAGE, KEY, NAME, PENDING, RECORD, TRANSMIT, and UNDEFINED-FILE clauses provide a more correct and complete implementation of the record-handling process. Reading records into and writing records from specific record structures also provide more complete implementations of the code. Working in I/O buffers has proven to be dangerous.

The use of data names in place of literals also demonstrates a concern for completeness. The PL/I programmer can code:

    %DCL ALABAMA CHAR;
    %ALABAMA = '''01'''

and the PL/I preprocessor will substitute '01' for every occurrence of ALA-BAMA. Or, he or she could have coded:

DCL ALABAMA CHAR (2) INIT('01');

Every reference to ALABAMA can use the data name or preprocessor name instead of an ambiguous literal ('01'). Using data names in place of literals also affects consistency.

4.2. Consistency

Consistency depends on coding standards and style. A uniform style of indenting IF-THEN-ELSE, CASE, DO WHILE, and DO UNTIL constructs (as shown in Figure 21.1) can provide maintenance benefits. Software exists to restructure existing code into a common format. I suggest you acquire or build one of these for you and your fellow programmers.

Consistency also requires that every IF have an ELSE and every SELECT have an OTHERWISE and so on (see Figure 21.9). Because so many programmers affect code during its life span, it is important to keep the style constant throughout; otherwise, maintenance becomes more difficult.

Another metric, comment density, speaks to the programmer's consistency when providing self-documenting code. A 10−20% comment density should be appropriate. Similarly, the number of ELOC, the decision density, and function density should be held to specific tolerances except in rare exceptions. The ELOC should be held to around 100. The decision density should be 0−15%, and the function density can vary from 0−50% depending on the module: Driver modules measure 25−50% while worker modules measure 0−25%. The software science effort metric should remain close to

```
IF ( condition1 ) THEN
     statements
ELSE;      /* DO NOTHING IF CONDITION FAILS */


SELECT (CASE_VARIABLE);
     WHEN (condition1)
          .
          .
          .
     OTHERWISE
          PUT LIST ('BUT ... BUT THIS CAN NEVER HAPPEN');
END; /* END SELECT */
```

FIGURE 21.9. Consistent use of ELSE and OTHERWISE to improve reliability.

10,000 and the cyclomatic complexity should stay in the range 0−20 except when implementing large CASE constructs.

The absence of GO TOs further explains the consistency of the module; GOTO-less modules are typically well structured. Modules with a high density of GOTOs probably were written before structured programming and are likely candidates for revision.

4.3. Traceability

The last submetric of correctness is traceability—the ability to work your way from the user's definition to the code and back again. One way to accomplish this goal is through the use of data dictionaries. Each of the data names in a program should have a common source—the data dictionary, providing the basis of a link from the requirements to the code. Since the metrics code analyzers already extract the data names, data definitions, and their scope in the program, it is possible to put this data out to another file for review and comparison with the data dictionary. In cases where no design or dictionary exists, it is an inexpensive way to extract the information and populate the dictionary. From this, the data administrator can begin to locate and evaluate all of the synonyms in the system and potential sources of error.

4.4. Correctness Summary

The PL/I language contains a wealth of information that can indicate the analyst's and programmer's concern with correctness, completeness, consistency, and traceability. Little work has been done in this area because complexity promised far greater rewards. But correctness is one of the keys to satisfying the user and that is the ultimate goal. The measurement of correctness may one day provide IS with the tools to quantify their contribution to the client.

5.   EFFICIENCY

There are three parts to efficiency: programmer effectiveness, data efficiencies, and procedural efficiencies. Programmer effectiveness has to do with efficiency/maintainability trade-offs that are often necessary when designing a system that humans must maintain. Programmer effectiveness depends on flexibility and maintainability.

Program performance or efficiency depends on four observable and measurable factors:

1. Execution time.
2. Input/Output utilization.

3. Memory usage.

4. Program readability and maintainability.

Only 10−20% of the programs, modules, or code typically generate 30−80% of the costs. Pareto analysis dictates that you find and repair only these prime offenders; the others simply are not worth the effort required to gain a marginal benefit. But a program that runs for 10 hours without a checkpoint or a transaction-processing system that cannot meet the user's response time needs are both candidates for examination and revision.

Because of the strides made in computer cost performance, efficiency no longer enjoys the raging importance it did five or ten years ago. But there is no excuse for poor program performance caused by lack of knowledge or poor programming practices. Many things can be accomplished in the data declaration and procedural code to improve efficiency without sacrificing the flexibility or maintainability of the code.

5.1. Data Declarations

The prime efficiency problems in a PL/I program often stem from arithmetic and table-handling code. Inefficient definitions of the data and indexes involved in these calculations often consume a vast amount of unnecessary CPU time.

In an IBM environment, the numeric data items have a significant impact on execution time. Data items defined as FIXED BIN (binary) are twice as efficient as FIXED DECIMAL (packed decimal) in most cases. And FIXED DECIMAL items are twice as efficient as PICTURE numeric items. FIXED DECIMAL items are more efficient when handling an odd number of digits (FIXED DEC([1,3,5,7,9,11,13,15,17],0)).

Oddly enough, a sophisticated metrics analyzer can determine all of these things and print a suggested change alongside the actual code, or print a summary of each different metric for the programmer to use as a basis for revision.

Another example involves the use of tables. For every table, there should be a matching binary index so that the compiler will generate the most efficient code possible.

Programmers concerned with optimizing CPU usage should concern themselves with the way data is declared and the usage of PL/I statements other than input and output, predominantly the arithmetic statements. Programmers concerned with optimizing I/O usage should concentrate on file definitions and ways to reduce the number of I/O statements.

Proper file definitions should be the realm of the data administrator. For example, a data item defined as FIXED DEC (3,0) requires only two bytes of data instead of three for PICTURE numeric data. Multiplied by millions and millions of records, the efficiency gained can be quite impressive. Another possibility involves eliminating data that is merely passed from program to program; place it in a file that other programs can use as they need it. Another possibility requires reading or creating the file in core so that it can be accessed directly rather than through some intermediate file, trading I/O efficiency for memory usage.

5.2. Procedural Code

Once the data is properly defined and aligned, the procedural code becomes the focal point for efficiency improvements. The key ingredients of procedural efficiency are concision, execution efficiency, and operability.

Concision

When it comes time to measure concision, there are module and statement level metrics. At the module level, a low ELOC (ELOC < 100), a low decision density (DD < 20%), and a high function density (FD > 25%) all suggest that the module is concise and can be processed easily. At the statement level, the use of built-in functions, ON conditions, and multi-function sequential statements implies the presence of concision. (see Figure 21.10)

Execution Efficiency

PL/I optimizing compilers depend on small modular components to allow optimization. The PL/I optimizing compiler issues diagnostics about the number of variables or flow units in a single block inhibiting automatic optimization. If the compiler issues either message, restructure the code (if possible) to reduce the module's size. Module size can be measured using either ELOC or software science metrics.

Arithmetic statements are a primary source of efficiency improvement. Once the data has been efficiently defined, the statements can be examined to

Example 1	Example 2

```
E = A + B;                        |    Z = SQRT( (A+B)**2 / (C+D)**2);
F = C + D;                        |
G = E * E;                        |
H = F * F;                        |
I = G / H;                        |
Z = SQRT(I);                      |
```

FIGURE 21.10.   Reducing complexity by using concise representations of algorithms.

reduce the six types of code impurities described in Chapter Three: complimentary operation, ambiguous operands, synonymous operands, common subexpressions, unnecessary assignment, and unfactored expressions.

The absence of GO TOs usually ensures that the code is well structured and that the flow of logic provides the optimal efficiency. The presence of GO TOs, however, leaves the door open to redundant code and all manner of inefficient algorithms for processing the data.

The use of DO WHILE and DO UNTIL statements indicates the presence of loops in the program. The loop-nesting metric indicates how deeply these loops intertwine. Each loop causes multiple executions of its underlying code. Each loop within a loop executes multiple times for itself and more times for the outside loop. The second loop of Figure 21.11 will be executed 100 times, compared to the calling loop's 10. Inner loops should be inspected for possible efficiency improvements. These inner loops often have code that could be removed to the outer loop, thereby reducing the number of executions of that code. Code that initializes data to some constant or code that could be rewritten to process once for all iterations of the inner loop are examples of possible efficiency improvements.

Programmers will also code loops to process all iterations rather than terminating the loop when it has completed its task. The example in Figure 21.12 shows a matching algorithm that continues looking even after it finds a match. This would be useful if you needed to find the last match in the table, but in this case, it is unnecessary. If the table had thousands of entries and it found a match on the first item, it would still look through the remaining thousands. Once the code is set up to terminate on a match, the program can be optimized by loading the table with the most frequent matching items first; the least frequent, last. In some instances, because of the frequency of matching the same item over and over, it is worthwhile to check for a previous match before invoking the matching algorithm.

The IF statement combined with multiple conditions provides another chance for efficiency improvement. For example, the statement:

IF COND1 | COND2 | COND3 THEN

could be made more efficient if we knew which condition occurs most often. If, for example, COND2 is true 80% of the time; COND1, 25%; and COND3,

```
DO I = 1 TO 10 BY 1;
    DO J = 1 TO 10 BY 1;
        PI = 3.1417;
        AREA = PI * J**2;
    END;
END;
```

FIGURE 21.11. Improving efficiencies by examining nested loops.

```
DO I = 1 TO TABLE_MAXIMUM BY 1;
    IF ( TABLE_ENTRY(I) = MATCHING_DATANAME) THEN
        J = I;
END;

I = 0;
DO WHILE ( TABLE_ENTRY(I) ¬= MATCHING_DATANAME);
    I = I + 1;
END;
J = I;
```

FIGURE 21.12.   Terminating loops to improve efficiency.

5%, then it would be more efficient to code COND2 as the first comparison since it is true most often, followed by COND1 and COND3. If the three conditions were ANDed together, we would want the least likely condition first so that all of the conditions would not be needed to pass to the ELSE part of the decision.

Another possible way to improve efficiency requires removal of redundant conditions. For example:

IF ((A=B & C=D) | (A=B & E=F)) THEN

becomes

IF (A=B & (C=D | E=F)) THEN

The CASE statement provides other opportunities for efficiency. Figure 21.13 shows an example of a CASE statement to handle every different type of input record; the order shown is the order expected. In reality, the data records occur many times, whereas the header and trailer records occur only once. The original statement can be reordered using this knowledge to reduce the number of decisions made.

One of the best ways to achieve efficiency is to use an optimizing compiler. The object code is often reduced 15–25%.

Operability

Operability relies on the programmer to anticipate how the program will run and what messages the personnel need to run it. For example, a program that opens four tape files and then reads them one at a time over the period of an hour is wasting precious computer center resources. It should open and close the files one at a time as it needs them, reducing the consumption of tape drives.

```
SELECT (RECORD_TYPE);
    WHEN (HEADER)
        CALL HEADER_PROCESSING;
    WHEN (TYPE_01)
        CALL TYPE_01_PROCESSING;
    WHEN (TYPE_02)
        CALL TYPE_02_PROCESSING;
    WHEN (TYPE_03)
        CALL TYPE_03_PROCESSING;
    WHEN (TRAILER)
        CALL TRAILER_PROCESSING;
    OTHERWISE
        CALL ERROR(RECORD_TYPE);
END; /* END SELECT */
```

FIGURE 21.13. Ordering CASE constructs to improve efficiency.

5.3. Efficiency Ratio

It is possible to have the program calculate and track its own efficiency. This metric is called the ER:

$$ER = \frac{\text{number of items processed}}{\text{amount of resources used}}$$

Since the PL/I program already knows (or should know) how many records, transactions, or whatever it processed, and it should be able to call an assembler language subroutine to get the actual CPU seconds used by the system, the PL/I program can calculate and report ER for each run. The programming staff and operations personnel can use this as a method to track the change in efficiency over time. A system test organization could review ER in relation to their existing test data, verifying that the program won't impact operations unnecessarily.

5.4. Efficiency Summary

Efficiency can be determined directly from PL/I code by examining the numeric data items, arithmetic statements, and I/O statements, which are the three prime contributors to efficiency. Only by careful analysis with metrics like the ER can IS managers make decisions to invest in efficiency tuning. Once properly tuned, software metrics can assist in identifying the changes made to reduce operational costs.

6. FLEXIBILITY AND MAINTAINABILITY

Flexibility and maintainability are almost synonymous. So examining them
one at a time would be redundant. Flexibility examines the programmer's
ability to enhance a module or program while maintainability studies the
ability to repair a module or program. Both depend on measurements of
concision, consistency, modularity, self-documentation, and simplicity. Flexibility goes beyond these metrics to look at expandability and generality.

6.1. Concision

Concision in PL/I programs is represented by language statements that
implement a function in a minimum amount of code. The prime contributors
to concision, the built-in functions, are listed in Figure 21.14. Built-in functions are used to derive the function density, a metric of overall concision.

As function density represents concision at a statement level, ELOC
represents concision at a module level. As the number of ELOC exceeds 100,
the module's clarity and ease of understanding drop dramatically; often the

ABS	DELAY	POINTER
ACOS	DIM	POLY
ADD	DIVIDE	PRECISION
ADDR	ERF	PRIORITY
ALL	ERFC	PROD
ALLOC	EXP	REAL
ANY	FIXED	REPEAT
ASIN	FLOAT	ROUND
ATAN	FLOOR	SIGN
ATAND	HBOUND	SIN
ATANH	HIGH	SIND
BIN	IMAG	SINH
BIT	INDEX	SQRT
BOLL	LBOUND	STATUS
CEIL	LENGTH	STRING
CHAR	LINENO	SUBSTR
COMPLETION	LOG	SUM
COMPLEX	LOG2	TAN
CONJG	LOG10	TAND
COS	LOW	TANH
COSD	MAX	TRANSLATE
COSH	MIN	TRUNC
COUNT	MOD	UNSPEC
DATE	MULTIPLY	VERIFY
DECIMAL	OFFSET	

FIGURE 21.14.   PL/I builtin functions that contribute to the function density metric.

code no longer represents a single, concise function, but several intertwined functions. The resulting chaos ultimately reduces flexibility and maintainability.

Concision is also a function of the language used. PL/I is more concise than either ALC or COBOL.

6.2. Consistency

Consistency relies on design and coding standards to ensure common readability among all programmers. At the design level, walk-throughs and mechanized analysis of automated designs can provide the necessary levels of auditing. At the code level, mechanized formatting programs can indent, align, and generally straighten up rat-nest code, putting one statement per line and so on. Figure 21.15 contains an example.

Next, the metrics analyzer can ensure that all of the data names are verified in the data dictionary, providing data-naming consistency.

The use of common designs and code also indicate consistency. The use of %INCLUDE statements to retrieve data structures helps reduce errors and ensures consistency throughout the programs. The use of common, generic design and code skeletons also helps ensure that the programmer is using the best designs and programs possible.

Finally, the use of a standard commenting convention also helps ensure consistency. The comment density provides a metric of the number of comments per 100 ELOC. Programmers who undercomment will have a measurement of 0–5%. Programmers who overcomment may find that 30–80% of their code is comments, which tends to obscure rather than document the code.

6.3. Expandability

Data expansion depends on the use of a data dictionary, DBMS and %INCLUDE statements. Without the data dictionary, changing the size of a data item will be haphazard, causing numerous programs to blow up from invalid

```
IF A = B THEN C = D; ELSE C = E;


IF A = B THEN
        C = D;
ELSE
        C = E;
```

FIGURE 21.15. Indenting code to improve readability.

data. Similarly, using the %INCLUDE statement for including data declarations helps ensure that the code need only be changed in one place and then recompiled into every module that uses it. If a record description appears in 100 places in the system, then %INCLUDE statements are the only way to make sure that the code is changed correctly in all places.

Mechanized code analyzers can also identify the number of unique and total operands (data names) used in the program. As these numbers increase, the complexity of the module also increases, causing expandability to decline. Analyzers can also extract, summarize, and report on each data name or literal used in the program. These can be used to verify that the data names correspond to the data dictionary and to provide automatic declarations of literals that could be included in the program in place of the existing literals.

Literals can impact the expansion of a program. For example, the literal '1' could stand for one, TRUE, Alabama (the state alphabetically first), and so on. The two statements:

TABLE_INDEX = TABLE_INDEX + 1;
TABLE_INDEX = 1;   (ALABAMA)

have completely different meanings. Coding a meaningful data name, like ALABAMA, in every situation where '1' is used provides for further expansion of the program.

The complexity metrics ELOC, $V(G)$, effort, and function density, play an important part in predicting expandability. As the ELOC, $V(G)$, and programming effort increase, it becomes more difficult to determine where to insert new functions and capabilities. If the existing metrics of a module are over the 100 ELOC, $V(G) <= 10$, and effort $> 10,000$, then the programmer should consider adding the new capabilities as separate modules rather than as inserted code.

Function density also provides an indicator about the module's expandability. Modules with a high function density usually are straightforward, making it easier to move functions around or to insert new functions in the appropriate place. Modules with a function density under 10% are the worker modules of the programs. Programmers will find it more difficult to insert new functionality into these modules unless the changes are trivial. An example of this kind of module might be one that edits a certain file and passes the valid information back to its superior. If the module needs to be enhanced to validate not one, but two different files, and merge the validated output of each, then the expansion will be difficult. Another way to look at function density is that it increases a module's generality.

6.4. Generality

Once again, modules with a high complexity probably are not generic, but ones with a high function density probably are. On the other hand, a module with a low complexity and a low function density may also be general in nature; such modules might validate date fields, Social Security numbers, or print report headings.

Generic program designs and code are general in nature. The presence of these generic skeletons should be detectable through some common knowledge of the code analyzers and the code. Modules and programs built from these code skeletons will be easier to understand, enhance, and modify because of their generality.

Commonly used modules, such as date edits, should be carefully built by the programmer support staff and included (via CALL) in programs that require these generic functions. The presence of CALLs to these modules can be detected easily using the code analyzers and usually represent a programmer's interest in using and building programs that are general.

6.5. Modularity

The primary metrics of modularity are again the ELOC, cyclomatic complexity, and programming effort. As these metrics exceed the limits previously stated, the modules tend to lose their single-function orientation and their modularity. When enhancing a program or module, the manager, analyst, and programmer should be aware of radical changes in these metrics. Ask the question: Are we enhancing the existing function or adding a new one? The way to answer these questions is through examination of the module strength and coupling, as described in Chapter 4.

Module Strength

To examine module strength in a PL/I program, the programmer should look first at the number of entries and exits in the module. If there is more than one entry point, then the programmer can be assured that the module strength is one of the following: information strength, communication strength, logical strength, or coincidental strength. Modules with information strength operate on the same data, for example, a table load and table lookup. Modules with communication strength often perform many functions related by their use of data such as field and cross-field validation modules. Logical strength modules, for example, the modules that handle all of the input and output for a program, contain many common function that are executed one at a time. And modules with coincidental strength contain many functions that are unrelated by their use of data or logic, rather like a junk pile of program logic.

Modules with a single entry point but multiple exit points are usually communication, logical, or coincidental strength. The calling module normally passes a parameter to the module to tell it what to do rather than calling each function separately. Then, as each function completes, it exits from the current point.

Modules with a single entry and exit point usually possess functional, procedural, or classical strength. Functional strength is the best; the module does only one function and then exits. Modules with procedural strength execute many functions in their logical sequence instead of having a driver module and many subfunctions (each of which would have functional strength). Modules with classical strength execute many related functions, but in no logical order. Such a module might set up report headings for three different reports; it does not matter in which order they are done.

Module Coupling

The next area of modularity depends on the data passed between modules and paragraphs. The data passed between modules should have the same attributes. In other words, you should never pass alphabetic data into numeric fields nor should you pass binary data into packed decimal. The fields should be of the same length in both the calling and subordinate modules. The data fields should have the same names in the calling and subordinate modules. The %INCLUDE statement allows this common naming convention. Each of these comparisons can be automated by a code analyzer.

Five different kinds of module coupling are described in Chapter 3: data, stamp, external, common, and content. With PL/I, it is possible to determine the presence of each of these forms of coupling. For example, data coupling implies that only data elements are passed via the parameter list. Using an analyzer, it is possible to retain and evaluate the parameters. Using an analyzer, it is possible to retain and evaluate the parameters. Parameters with a BIT, BIN, CHAR, or DEC clause are data elements; parameters without such clauses are data structures. If all of the parameters are data elements, then the module is usually data coupled. If some or all of the parameters are data structures, then the module is stamp coupled.

External and common coupling are both the province of the PL/I data declaration. The use of EXTERNAL with a data item implies external coupling. The use of EXTERNAL with a data structure means common coupling. Both external and common coupling are less desirable than data or stamp coupling, which is why large single-module programs are discouraged: The degree of coupling makes maintenance more difficult. Content coupling, on the other hand, is virtually impossible; one module cannot directly access and change another module. Further analysis reveals that a mechanized analyzer could look at each procedure, determining which data names are used as input and which are used as output. This information could be used to develop documentation of the program if none existed or to determine which procedures read and modify data produced in other procedures, to determine the scope of a data item or structure, and the relative dependence of each procedure on the other.

The analyzer also detects words such as FLAG or SWITCH in the data name which indicate that the controlling module tells its subordinates what to do and how to do it rather than passing the data and letting the subordinate choose the correct course of action.

6.6. Self-Documentation

Self-documentation depends on the use of comments and meaningful data-names. As discussed earlier, a mechanized count of the comment lines and their density in PL/I source code can tell much about the module's self-documentation. A comment density of 10−20% is often representative of well documented code.

The mechanized analyzer, since it already identifies and stores each data name, can be used to determine the length of data names. For example, the seven-character EOFFLAG is less readable than the equivalent MASTER_FILE_AT_EOF; EOFFLAG provides less documentation. Further, the use of qualified data names often implies better documentation. For example:

MASTER_RECORD.SOCIAL_SECURITY_NUMBER =
      TRANSACTION_RECORD.SOCIAL_SECURITY_NUMBER;

provides better documentation than:

MAST_SSN = TRAN_SSN;

6.7. Simplicity

Simplicity is really the opposite of complexity, so you can measure a module's simplicity from the ELOC, $V(G)$, and effort metrics. If these metrics all fall within the bounds you have established, then the module has simplicity. If not, the maintainability and flexibility will suffer.

7. INTEGRITY

Software integrity is composed of auditability, instrumentation, and security. Auditability is the domain of operating, data-base management, and configuration management systems. In PL/I, the use of DBMS calls often implies that the system will be more auditable and secure.

The auditability and security of PL/I code depends on the capabilities of the source code control and configuration management systems. So this is not easily measured.

The major opportunity for measuring software integrity in PL/I programs comes from examination of a module's or program's instrumentation. Calls to run control or standard message modules may indicate a degree of instrumentation. The use of generic code skeletons that contain record counting and reporting logic or calls to audit modules will also indicate a concern for integrity. Each of these items is installation dependent, so they will have to be built into the metrics analyzer.

The absence of integrity-enhancing comments does not necessarily mean that the code is in error. Management decisions can be made to exclude the costs of this excess development because of the low risk presented by the data processed. But as on-line systems with microcomputer terminals expand their current bounds, the need for system integrity—auditability, instrumentation, and security—will increase dramatically. Measurement is the only way to ensure the presence of integrity-enhancing code in a system's modules and programs.

8. INTEROPERABILITY

Interoperability depends on the submetrics: communications commonality, data commonality, generality, and modularity. Systems need to get their data from other systems that already exist. For example, a personnel system may drive aspects of the payroll system which may in turn drive part of the accounting system. The ability of these systems to operate together is known as interoperability.

Two systems that need to share data will require data commonality, which is normally provided via the use of data dictionaries and the PL/I %INCLUDE statement. The presence of data commonality can be detected by use of the data dictionary (Do these programs both use the same data item names or data-base structures?) or the use of common data structures IN-CLUDED in both programs.

Generality implies that the code or module may be used interchangeably among programs. Common modules that handle file I/O, data-base access, updates, or reports will provide a generic interface to the system's data. Coupling these modules with other modular systems will make interoperability possible. Generality is measured by the use of common generic logic modules and the reuse of other logic modules.

Modularity makes program changes simpler and less costly, making it possible to add new interfaces to existing program or system with less effort. Coupled with general interface modules that may be available already, a modular program can be enhanced in short order to improve interoperability. Modularity is measured by ELOC, $V(G)$, and programming effort.

9. PORTABILITY

Portability depends on generality, modularity, self-documentation, hardware, and software independence. With the boundaries between micros, minis, and mainframes disappearing, software suppliers are looking for ways to easily port their products from any one of these environments to another.

Generality is determined from the design. If the design and code are extracted from some generic library of routines, then the module will be general in nature. Spreadsheets, data-base management systems, and word processing packages are all examples of software that have uses in a variety of markets and hardware.

Modularity is also a sign of portability. Modules with sufficiently small metrics of ELOC, $V(G)$, and programming effort, will be easier to examine, modify, and transport to other hardware. Since porting software is simply enhancing the existing software to run under a different operating system on other hardware, ELOC, $V(G)$, programming effort, and function point metrics provide an excellent measure of the effort required to modify the existing code.

Self-documentation, or the comment density as it is measured in PL/I, provides another clue to portability. Well-documented code will be easier to understand and modify. Comment density, data-name consistency, and the presence or absence of literals will help identify the level of self-documentation.

Hardware independence is rarely a problem in PL/I. The only exception might be the use of BLKSIZE: Record and block sizes are a function of the media being read or written.

Software independence affects portability in a variety of ways. First, the use of IBM or other vendors extensions to the basic language will affect the code's portability. A quick check of the language reference manual usually will pinpoint the reserved words that are extensions to the standard language. The metrics analyzer should collect statistics on these words and their frequency in the code.

Second, with the increase in the number of systems that depend on a data-base management system or telecommunications interface, PL/I becomes more deeply connected to software that may only run on one brand of hardware. The software metrics analyzer should collect statistics on the calls to IMS or any of the various DBMS and telecommunication software packages that provide for connections to PL/I programs. Because of the design of these external I/O packages, PL/I programs often are designed around their interfaces, making it difficult to port the program without redesigning or rewriting the code.

Portability is the ultimate aim of most application software developers. System software developers are not as concerned, but as their software comes into contact with software running in microcomputers and the like, their concern will grow. Measurement is one of the few ways of identifying the extent of the problem and the direction to take in making the software portable.

10. RELIABILITY

Another concern of virtually all software developers is reliability. Any kind of software failure, whether it results in erroneous data or program termination, increases costs and reduces productivity. Software reliability depends on accuracy, consistency, complexity, simplicity, error tolerance, and modularity, each of which can be determined from analysis of the code.

Accuracy, in PL/I, depends on the data declarations and the use of built-in functions. Metrics analyzers should determine the size of sending and receiving fields in PL/I statements, and indicate possible problems when the receiving field is smaller than the sending field or the receiving field has fewer decimal places, or whatever. This information comes from examination of the data definitions for each data item. The use of built-in functions such as ROUND( ) help identify the programmer's concern with accuracy and reliability.

Consistency plays a strong role in reliability. Edits of numeric data, boundary tests on loops and indexes, and so on should be performed uniformly throughout a system.

Complexity often indicates that a program may be unreliable, but is not a totally reliable predictor. Highly complex mathematical software may be very reliable. Simple report programs, on the other hand, may be unreliable. The complexity metrics described in Section 3 are useful predictors of reliability.

The ELOC, cyclomatic complexity, and software science metrics indicate that the code's processing is either simple or complex. They also indicate degrees of complexity, giving us a ruler to compare different programs or modules. Application programs often have many paths [measured by $V(G)$] and some of those paths may not be exercised during testing. Or they are executed in ways not previously envisioned by the designers. The software science metrics rely on the ELOC and the number of operands to determine complexity. Logically, as you add more executable statements, with additional data names and literals, the chance for failure increases. Research (Basili, 1983) supports this intuition.

Error tolerance is another key feature of reliable systems. What happens when the data isn't numeric and the statement is performing a numeric operation on it? What happens when the code reads past end of file? A module or program that can handle these problems is error tolerant; it has enough intelligence to handle the usual types of program bugs. PL/I, with its extensive error-handling facilities, is especially suited to fault detection and correction.

One of the more difficult programming errors revolves around missing logic paths (Glass, 1981). In PL/I, every IF should have an ELSE, every SELECT should have an OTHERWISE, and so on. This is one of the rules of programming style: State actions explicitly instead of implicitly, it forces programmers to think about the default logic path. When the time comes to change the default path, the new logic can be easily inserted. There are many cases when the default path needs to be replaced by a call to an error routine; the program detects errors and handles them in an intelligent fashion. Programs that abort on any error are not error tolerant.

A module that examines incoming data before processing it is more likely to avoid errors over a lifetime than a module that blindly expects its neighbor to pass it good data. At the minimum, this involves the use of ON conditions when working on numeric data to allow the program to take some intelligent action when an error occurs.

Modularity affects reliability. Modularity tends to restrict complexity, data problems, and so on. In doing so, it restricts the possibilities of one module affecting another adversely. With a well-defined interface, edits of incoming data, and good internal error-handling logic, these modules can become highly reliable—virtually indestructible. Measurements of modularity are described in Section 6.5.

11. REUSABILITY

Reusability depends on the measurements of generality, hardware independence, software independence, modularity, and self-documentation. Reusable code reduces development and maintenance costs. Because of these savings, it allows you to invest in the quality of these modules, which in turn provides savings from high reliability, maintainability, and so on.

For a module to be reusable, it must be general in nature. More than one program must have some use for it. Date edits, Social Security number edits, report headings, update logic, table-handling logic, and data selection modules are just a few examples of modules that exhibit generality. The metrics of generality are described further in Section 6.4.

Unless a module is used in only one hardware and software environment, reusable modules must possess hardware and software independence. They cannot depend on special extensions to the language, software systems that only run on one kind of hardware, or one operating system. In the microcomputer marketplace, the presence of reusable code affects how fast a manufacturer can upgrade their software to run under CP/M, MS-DOS, XENIX, POS, or migrate from 8- to 16- to 32-bit machines.

Modularity also affects reusability. Modularity implies that the module performs only one function; as such, there is a greater likelihood that the code can be used in another program that needs a similar function. With diligent application of the module strength and coupling metrics in Section 6.5, programmers will find that fewer modules need to be written for each new program. Increasingly, new programs can be constructed from libraries of existing modules. This is the key to productivity.

Self-documentation is a lesser contributor to reusability, but a contributor none the less. Comments help the developer ensure that the existing code will provide the function required or help them determine if it can be changed to meet their needs. The measures of self-documentation are described in Section 6.6.

12. STRUCTURE

Program and module structure are functions of data commonality, expandability, and modularity. The ability to examine structure mechanically, using graphic and static analyzers, enhances the analyst's and programmer's chances of spotting potential weaknesses that can be corrected before the program is released.

Data structures, for records and data bases, often change. The user wants to add some new information or delete some from the existing system. Or they need an enhancement that requires the addition of some fields. In either case, the data structure must change. In a data-base environment, dozens or hundreds of programs may access the same data. The reliability of these programs depends on common data definitions and structures. Data dictionaries are the starting point for identifying data commonality. The use of %INCLUDE statements shows a definite concern for data commonality and the potential for improved reliability. When one structure is changed, all modules can be recompiled and relinked, minimizing the chance of reliability problems.

Data structures are not the only things that change. Modules and programs need to be repaired and enhanced. Enhancements often require the addition of functions to the program. The simplicity or difficulty involved in making these changes depends on the measurement of expandability, which is described in Section 6.3.

Modularity affects, or is an outgrowth, of structure. Single-function modules will tend to have a simple, easily understood, reliable structure. Programs built of these modules usually will be more easily understood and reliable. Modularity is described in Section 6.5.

13. TESTABILITY

Your ability to test a module, program, or systems depends on the measurements of auditability, complexity, simplicity, instrumentation, modularity, and self-documentation. Some estimates testing process indicate that 40—60% of the development (and probably the maintenance) process are consumed by testing. It would be handy to know beforehand how much effort it will take to test a given module, program, or system. Function point metrics, described in Chapter 2, give the programmer, analyst, and manager a starting point for estimating testability.

The same tools that auditors use to study programs and systems are ideally suited to testing programs. In most cases, however, auditability depends on the operating system accounting logs, data-base logs, and teleprocessing logs. The programs that do audit their own processing, by use of record and process counting, can be examined mechanically to determine auditability. Usually, auditability will have to be determined from the existing software environment rather than from the code.

Complexity and simplicity present two opposing faces of testability. A person testing a module or program can use the cyclomatic complexity, $V(G)$, to determine the minimum number of paths that must be tested. $V(G)$ does not indicate the total number of paths in the module, only the number of structural paths. $V(G)$ should provide a reasonable estimate of the effort a testing person will spend developing test data and cases for the module. Of course, he or she must have some desire to test all of the structural paths, which does not ensure that all of the possible paths will be tested.

The program's instrumentation, which provides the statistics of the program's execution, affects testability. Suppose the tester inputs 2000 records and the execution report only shows 1999 records read? What if there were 1000 valid adds, 800 valid changes, and 200 deletes and the report only shows 199 deletes? Doesn't this information facilitate the job of testing, helping to pinpoint the potential source of the errors? Instrumentation is measured by the presence of this kind of logic in the code.

Modularity affects testability. A module possessing functional strength and data coupling can be tested independently to examine its internal workings. Then its interfaces can be tested separately. Finally, the entire program can be tested as an integrated whole. This breaks unit, interface, program, and system testing into a manageable process.

On the other hand, a large, multifunction module cannot be unit tested easily. Isolating problems becomes impossible as each new function is added to the existing module. Eventually, it becomes too difficult to fully test the module and some errors slip into production. At this point, the module becomes unreliable as well as untestable. Modularity affects error detection and correction by isolating tests to small, easily managed components. Modularity metrics are described more fully in Section 6.5.

Self-documentation affects testability as well. If the testing organization has access to the source code, which they must if they intend to build meaningful test cases, then they will appreciate any and all documentation. Comments help to explain the code that they did not write and will not maintain. Self-documentation metrics are described in Section 6.6.

14. SUMMARY

Measuring all aspects of code quality in PL/I programs is neither impossible nor overly difficult. The application of mechanized analyzers and the use of their output can help programmers, analysts, and managers determine the quality of the code. And the results can provide them with statistics to identify problems early and effect solutions before the code goes into testing or production.

Poor quality is a cancer that can eat into a program or system. Software measurement is a method of early detection and correction. PL/I code can undergo surgery to remove the cancer in bits and pieces as the programmers have time. With practice, they will avoid the very things that bring about the decline of quality. When this happens, you will rarely need measurement tools.

CHAPTER TWENTY-TWO

IMPLEMENTING SOFTWARE MEASUREMENT

Measuring software quality and productivity is only a part of a larger project—creating a quality program that laces all of the available methodologies and technologies together to form a highly productive, cost-effective software development organization. There are excellent ways to test programs: component test, integration test, system test, and environmental test. There are methodologies to ensure definition and design quality: project management and structured design. Software metrics of code quality and productivity aim to fill the void that exists in software development and maintenance.

In Chapter One, you were introduced to the idea that measurements support the growth of quality and productivity. Measurements are not meant to be harmful. They allow us a more precise view of the world around us. They provide us with information that makes constructive change possible. Software metrics provide both productivity information for management and quality information for the analysts and programmers.

Software metrics gives IS managers productivity information to evaluate new technology and methodology. Chapter 2 discussed the various kinds of productivity information available. Productivity consists of many different and unique I/O ratios: cost per function, cost per line of code, person days per function, and so on. Productivity, as usual, is difficult, but not impossible to quantify. The measurement tools, however, are less than exact. The error involved in using just lines of code per person day has been shown to vary by as much as 6:1. But regardless of the variance in the measurement tool, it provides data that was previously unavailable in any form. The crude tools for measuring programmer productivity will be improved and refined as the data from existing tools gives us new insight into the measurement process. But the major benefit of software metrics comes from the use of the tool to improve quality.

Software metrics gives the analyst and programmer a tool to quickly identify emerging quality problems in new designs and code. They give maintenance programmers the information to support quality enhancements to existing unmaintainable programs. Chapters Three through Twenty-one address the various quality metrics—complexity, correctness, efficiency, flexibility, integrity, interoperability, maintainability, portability, reliability, reusability, structure, testability, and usability. The analyst must factor each of these metrics into the design. The programmer must use proven techniques to build these qualities into the code.

The complexity, maintainability, flexibility, and reliability metrics have been studied and applied in laboratory and industrial environments. They are more precise than their fellow quality metrics or the productivity metrics. They have been more rigorously examined and applied. An ongoing measurement program will constantly refine the measurement tools to reflect each new level of understanding; each metric will grow in precision and usefulness. The measurement of dimensions was fairly imprecise until someone invented the screw micrometer. The application of this tool led to a manufacturing methodology using interchangeable parts. The measurement of software quality and productivity is also fairly imprecise. Programmers and analysts are like craftsmen—hand tooling each module to fit its neighbor, never dreaming that proper measuring tools might allow interchangeable software modules. But programmers may not adapt any more quickly to assembly lines than their industrial revolution predecessors. The quality and productivity benefits derived from a measurement program, however, will quickly become obvious to most of the programmers and analysts. The necessary measurements can no longer be done by labor-intensive design and code inspections; it must be mechanized.

It should be obvious from the preceding chapters that any attempt to measure software productivity and quality without mechanization will require a large amount of manual effort at a prohibitive cost. The only alternative is to automate wherever possible. The major advances in manufacturing productivity and quality came through installation of new technology and ways to mechanize measurement and control of the production process. The same will be true of software engineering.

Because code is already maintained on computers, it readily lends itself to mechanized measurement. The majority of this chapter will address mechanized code analysis. Operational information is also machine readable, so it also play a part in automated analysis. Designs, definitions, and all documentation are largely unmechanized, making it difficult to extract the kind of detailed measurements that would be useful. Error tracking and change management has been automated by stand-alone systems that provide additional metrics.

All of these measurement systems can provide much needed information about productivity and quality. But they cannot be implemented simultaneously unless you have a large staff to dedicate to development, training, and installation. Figure 22.1 shows the measurement system as it should ultimately exist. Because of the rapidly changing nature of software measurements, these systems will need the quality characteristics of *flexibility* and *maintainability*. Because each of the subsystems must integrate with the other, they will require *interoperability*. The code analyzers will apply to many different languages; they will need *reusability* and *portability*.

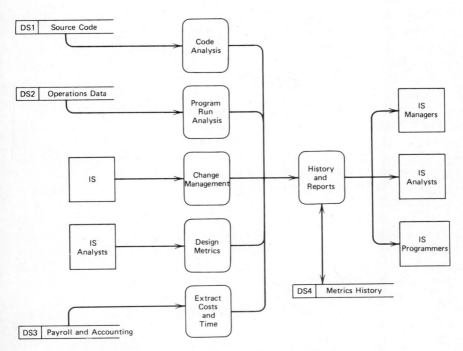

FIGURE 22.1.   System design of a software measurement system.

1. MEASUREMENT PROGRAM

The measurement program is an integral piece of an overall quality program. Just taking care of the quality problems in software development and maintenance often eliminates productivity problems. Using software metrics to improve code quality will generate significant productivity gains.

When attempting to automate quality and productivity measurements, you should concentrate on areas of maximum return of investment first, and the others later. Project management concentrated on requirements definition or specification. Structured design concentrated on system and program design. The most cost-effective point to apply software metrics is in the coding phase of development. The first phase of a measurement program should develop, use, and expand the use of code analyzers.

Next, the measurement program should seek to determine the efficiencies and inefficiencies in the development and maintenance process. Change management systems provide both the ability to control change in developing and existing systems and the ability to extract much needed information. These systems should be able to identify weaknesses throughout the definition, design, code, test, and production phases of a system's life cycle.

Next, operational data should be gathered and assembled to study the reliability of the system once it enters production. The operational metrics should pinpoint error-prone programs for preventive maintenance. Operational data should also identify programs that could stand efficiency improvements with the potential to delay the capital outlay for new machines and reduce the user's costs.

Once these high priority measurement tools are in place, the measurement program can turn to metrics of documentation readability, usability, and so on. Each system definition document must be interpreted by an analyst; every design document must be interpreted by a programmer. A concise, readable document will enable the reader to create a true representation of what the writer intended, not some system or program that will require endless enhancements to meet the user's needs.

The people in charge of the measurement program will need to exercise infinite care in the development, training, and application of the measurement tools. The insertion of new technology and methodology is often met with skepticism, reluctance, and even sabotage. But each of these problems can be countered, as you will see in the following sections.

2. AUTOMATED CODE ANALYSIS

Figure 22.2 shows a suggested structure for a code analyzer. The analyzer starts by getting a word (GETWORD). In the case of a COBOL program, the

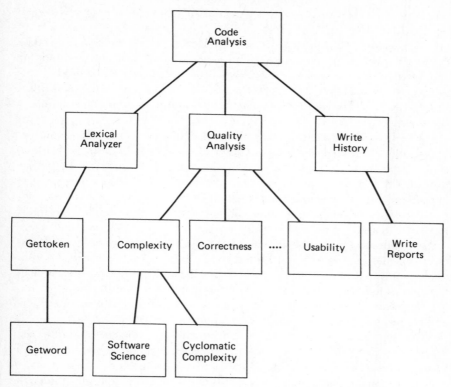

FIGURE 22.2.   Hierarchy chart of a software metrics code analyzer.

first word would most likely be IDENTIFICATION. The next word would be DIVISION, followed by a period.

The next routine (GETTOKEN) looks for words that have meaning together, such as IDENTIFICATION DIVISION, FILE SECTION, and so on. These two words together have a special meaning to the calling module (LEXICAL ANALYZER). The period also has a special meaning in COBOL: It terminates a sentence. The period terminates file descriptions (FDs), data definitions, IF-THEN-ELSE statements, and so on. It should be handled as a separate word and token unless it is embedded in a number like 999.99. GETWORD normally makes these determinations.

The lexical analyzer is the heart of the measurement device. It distinguishes data names from literals or keywords. It compares the tokens it gets from GETTOKEN with the language keywords to determine what measurements to take. The lexical analyzer accumulates the total occurrences of each ADA, ALC, COBOL, FORTRAN, or PL/I operator and counts the number of unique operators for the software science metrics. It should also count data names and literals to accumulate the number of unique and total operands for the software science metrics. In COBOL, the lexical analyzer should distinguish among the IDENTIFICATION, ENVIRONMENT, DATA, and PROCEDURE DIVISIONS. Tokens may have a different meaning in different divisions.

Aside from counting the occurrence of every keyword, data name, or literal, the lexical analyzer needs to determine complexity metrics like decision and loop nesting. How many nested decisions are there? How deeply are they nested? How deeply nested are the loops? Which modules present potential areas for efficiency investigation or restructuring to reduce cyclomatic complexity? These questions will aid the programmer in his or her quest for better quality.

Once the module has been analyzed and summarized by the lexical analyzer, the information should be fed to routines to calculate the different quality metrics described in Chapters 3−16. Because of the lack of research in the area, some of these quality subroutines may just be a stub. For example, future research will provide methods of measuring integrity or interoperability, but current measurements are almost nonexistent.

Once the detailed lexical analysis and quality analysis are complete, the software metrics program can report the findings. All of these raw and refined measurements should be written to a data base for further reporting.

A historical data base of measurements allows management to summarize and extract productivity and quality information as needed. The number of functions, modules, or ELOC can be compared to the person days worked, and so on. Flexibility is the key to reporting metrics information.

Appendices A−C have the keywords and tokens necessary for analyzing IBM ALC, COBOL, and PL/I. These measurements and analyses can be designed and coded in PL/I for flexibility and productivity. The designs for GETWORD, GETTOKEN, and the lexical analyzer can be found in *Software Tools*, by B. Kernighan and C. Plauger. Code analyzers can also be implemented in the UNIX™ language development tools—lex and C.

Code analyzers can be built for virtually any language. Code analyzers are essentially no different from the lexical analysis that occurs in language compilers, but no compiler suppliers have incorporated software metrics into their reports. But why wait on someone else? Development of basic code analyzers takes about a month. Many of the routines, such as GETWORD and GETTOKEN, are reusable. Code analyzers are the best tools for programmers in search of high quality.

3. CHANGE MANAGEMENT METRICS

Managing change is another key to productivity and quality. Knowing what, when, where, why, and who are developing or modifying a system gives managers the fundamental metrics of quality control. Tracking changes to software is best accomplished by a mechanized control system. The kinds of information that need to be tracked are shown in Figure 22.3.

The vast majority of IS work involves maintaining existing systems. There are three kinds of maintenance activities: corrective, perfective, and preventive. Tracking the reasons for these changes often gives insight into the cause of frequently recurring errors. These can subsequently be eliminated from existing programs to reduce maintenance costs.

Corrective maintenance fixes problems in the code. Figure 22.4 shows the usual reasons for these kinds of changes. Tracking this information should help management pinpoint loopholes in the development and maintenance process that allow recurring errors to slip into production systems. Perfective maintenance includes enhancements of all types. Figure 22.5 shows many of the typical reasons for perfective changes. Since perfective maintenance is probably 80–90% of your maintenance workload, it is especially important to track these changes.

1. Originator's name, phone, address, etc.

2. System name

3. Program name

4. Date problem occurred and date resolution required

5. Description of the change

6. Description of benefits

7. Urgency of change (the system is down, or we can wait)

8. Impact of change (other programs or data affected)

9. Person assigned to change

10. Description of problem resolution

11. List of modules, programs, or data changed

FIGURE 22.3.   Information required on a change request.

1. Requirement left out of specification

2. Incorrect requirements specification

3. Standards violation

4. Incomplete design specification

5. Incorrect design specification

6. Database design error

7. Logic error

8. Program or module interface error

9. Error due to previous change

10. Hardware failure

11. System software failure

12. Incorrect program run in operations

13. Incorrect program shipped to operations

14. Incorrect or inadequate documentation

15. Misinterpretation of definition, design, or documentation

FIGURE 22.4.   Reasons for corrective change.

1. Add new capability

2. Modify existing capability

3. Expand current capability

4. Delete existing capability

5. Support hardware change

6. Support system software change

7. Support standards change

8. Support external changes (Internal Revenue Service)

9. Improve efficiency or reduce costs

FIGURE 22.5.   Reasons for perfective change.

Finally, there is preventive maintenance: working on the code, even though nothing is defective or needs enhancement. Preventive maintenance focuses on improving the code to reduce maintenance and operation costs. Flexibility, maintainability, and reliability are the main reasons for preventive changes to the code. Tracking these changes and the resulting reduction in corrective and perfective maintenance costs should help justify continued quality improvement via preventive maintenance. Figure 22.6 shows the typical reasons for preventive maintenance.

Change management is also useful during development of new systems. Design and definition errors can be tracked. As these errors cause rework, project delays can be identified and action taken to correct course. A project overruns its schedule one day at a time. Change management is a method of measuring development problems and the resulting impacts, which gives timely feedback and allows management flexibility in dealing with problems. Figure 22.4 shows many of the typical reasons for development' delays. Problems related to the user are quite useful when they want to know why the system will not arrive on schedule. Hardware and software problems are useful when dealing with operations.

```
 1. Reduce Complexity

 2. Improve Correctness

 3. Improve Efficiency

 4. Improve Flexibility

 5. Improve Integrity and Security

 6. Improve Interoperability

 7. Improve Maintainability

 8. Improve Portability

 9. Improve Reliability

10. Improve Reusability

11. Improve Program Structure

12. Improve Testability

13. Improve Usability

14. Improve documentation quality and readability
```

FIGURE 22.6.   Reasons for preventive maintenance.

4. OPERATIONAL METRICS

The operations center has a great deal of information that deals with productivity and quality analysis in the IS department. Mechanizing this measurement with system accounting, data-base logs, and cost accounting information will help identify the quantities and costs of many of the inputs to the development and maintenance process. Productivity analysis depends on this kind of information. Reliability, efficiency, and maintainability analysis depend on system logs to identify programs, via Pareto analysis, for improvement. Once improved, the operational costs of these programs or systems will decline, improving the company's return on investment and IS's credibility.

Operational data can be used to provide metrics on both quality and productivity. Products exist to extract accounting and operational data from virtually any system log. Quality assurance personnel can use the data to determine:

1. Frequency of run by program.
2. Run time per program.
3. CPU time per program.
4. Frequency of premature or abnormal program termination (and MTBF for each program).
5. Time to repair and rerun the program (MTTR).
6. Type of program termination and frequency. In an IBM environment, a system OC7 may occur most frequently.
7. Connect hours per programmer.
8. CPU hours per programmer.
9. Jobs run per programmer.
10. Connect hours per systems analyst (word processing).
11. Commands executed per systems analyst.
12. Connect hours per manager (project management).
13. Commands executed per manager.
14. Data-base transaction volumes, types of access, etc.
15. Costs for machine operation, maintenance, etc.

These operational statistics form the groundwork for development of many quality and productivity metrics.

4.1. Quality Metrics

Frequency of execution, run time, and CPU time per program will help isolate programs that could benefit from efficiency analysis and maintenance.

Mean time between failures will help isolate programs that require reliability improvements. Mean time to repair will help select programs that need maintainability improvements.

Knowing the frequency of program termination and type of termination can help identify frequent errors and how to avoid them in future systems. The study may indicate that a certain program fails frequently because of invalid load cards or job card parameters. This program should be redesigned to handle parameters automatically, rather than manually. Other analysis may show that IBM system OC7 abend occur most frequently, often at significant cost for rework and rerunning the system. Quality assurance can trace the source of these erors and make sure the proper changes are made to the development process to avoid similar future errors. Quality assurance can also provide training to all programmers to alert them to the potential ways OC7 abends occur. The programmers, in turn, correct any occurrences that they find in programs undergoing maintenance. This process of identifying the most frequent source of program termination and correcting the development and maintenance process, is imperative to productivity and quality improvements.

Data-base transaction volumes and similar data-base information may serve to identify impending efficiency problems, potential security violations, and so on. With the continual growth of data-base systems, many quality metrics will depend on the organization and use of data bases. Operational data from the DBMS should anticipate or provide quality measurements.

4.2. Productivity Metrics

Productivity measurement consists of a network of input versus output ratios. Connect hours, CPU hours, and jobs or commands executed will provide metrics of the inputs to software development. Management may find that managers using office automation project management tools always bring their projects in on schedule, while managers who do not use these tools often incur significant delays. Programmers that use on-line testing tools are often more productive than their peers in terms of functions produced or whatever output measurement is used. Based on these I/O ratios, management may invest in training all IS personnel to use the new technology. They may also find that certain practices or machine uses actually degrade productivity or quality, in which case, they will want to restrict the use of those tools.

The costs for operating the development and maintenance computer system and any peripheral office automation or personal computer systems provide another input metric. Costs per input and costs per output are important productivity metrics. Costs are available from corporate accounting systems, while time worked should be available from payroll or human resource systems.

5. DOCUMENTATION METRICS

One of the key sources of productivity losses and quality problems is in the definition, design, training, and user documentation. Poorly written documentation causes reader confusion, misinterpretation, and all kinds of other problems. The solution is to measure readability and improve the documentation before it ever reaches its intended audience.

If your definition and design documentation is automated via word processors or personal computers the readability can be determined by spelling checkers, grammatical analyzers, and readability analyzers. Spelling and grammatical analyzers find errors that would otherwise derail the reader's concentration on the subject. Readability analyzers work much as the software science metrics to determine complexity and readability of each documents. Documents written in high-level jargon might require a college-level audience. Simple, well-written documents, however, might only require an eighth grade reading ability. Most newspapers, magazines, and the Bible are written at this level. At the time of this publication, the author knows of only one system that provides all of these mechanized analyzers: the UNIX system. A subsystem, called the Writer's Workbench, provides the readability and grammatical analysis. But other companies are working on similar projects, so they should be widely available soon.

Using these tools, the writer can examine their documents for spelling and grammatical errors, correcting each in their turn. Then the writer can tailor the readability of the document to meet the needs of his or her audience. Use of the measurement system will reinforce clear writing habits and discourage bad ones just as the software metrics aid the programmer to write high-quality code.

6. HUMAN AND POLITICAL FACTORS

Implementing a measurement program is not as simple as it might seem. First, someone in management has to approve it, and then the personnel have to accept it. Software technicians do not respond to changes in technology any more readily than anyone else in the corporation. They may, in fact, resist it strenuously. Any change in technology is accompanied by a change in the working society. It is this societal change that must be handled with infinite care to make the measurement program a success.

Social changes impact the habits, beliefs, attitudes, practices, traditions, and status of the people affected. Behavioral scientists state that every continuing society forms patterns of behavior called cultural patterns. New members of the society must accept and learn these traditions or be expelled: "You just don't fit in here." Cultural patterns are so important that the society resists any attempt to change them. This resistance can result in rejection of a metrics program because the "cost" in terms of habits, beliefs, attitudes, traditions, and so on is too great in the minds of the programmers, analysts, and managers.

Anticipating and dealing with cultural patterns forms the basis for generating acceptance for any new technological change, especially software measurement. As you understand the rules of the society, it becomes possible to use them to introduce a measurement program to management and the people who will ultimately use it.

First, secure the participation of the people affected by the change. Politically, management wants to know the benefits of such a plan. Anticipate their needs for dollars and cents benefits. Enlist "disciples" in the work groups that will first use measurement tools. Obtain their participation in the development and application of measurements.

Implement metrics in phases to allow the working society to adjust to each measurement tool. Code analyzers may help programmers the most. Once comfortable with this tool, the remaining tools and measurements will be easier to weave into the fabric of the society. Metrics must be seen as a tool to help each person.

You can reduce the impact of metrics by introducing it to new personnel (who are still open to innovation) or by letting it ride in on the back of some generally anticipated change, like moving to a new language, new hardware, or whatever. You can do this by putting yourself in the programmer's, analyst's, or manager's place. What are they thinking? How would you react to a similar change? Treat them with the respect they deserve.

Then, create a social climate that favors these changes. Make it easy for each person to change their point of view. Isolate the leaders of resistance, let society overwhelm them. Allow sufficient time for the changes to sink in, to be accepted. Start small and keep the measurement program growing. Prevent management from coming up with big surprises such as "We expect 1000 ELOC per programmer month from *everyone*."

In spite of all of the benefits to be derived from software metrics, the careful preparation to counter political forces and cultural patterns, and vast research into measurement, the measurement analyst may still find that the plan is not accepted. In which case, you can give up, fight like crazy, or become more subversive. The latter is often the best way to go.

Having made management aware of measurement and its potentials, wait for them to discover the wealth of articles that are published every year on software measurement. Send them some yourself. Wait for them to resurrect the idea or wait for newer, more receptive management.

Develop the metrics program as best you can and then implement it on a limited basis with one of your disciples. Let them work from within the society to bring about change. Let society overwhelm the resistance.

If in doubt, review your proposal and your thinking with the best politicians and technicians you know. Let them comment on your thinking. Can they find the flaw in your logic that prevents the acceptance of the proposal? Often, they will shed new light on measurement plan, giving it a brighter future, just as design walk-throughs affect program quality.

7. SUMMARY

To maximize the benefits from software metrics, you must mechanize the measurement data and tools wherever possible. The cost of manual analysis is typically prohibitive. Using Pareto analysis, it makes sense to mechanize the measurements of data that already exists on computers: source code, payroll, accounting, and operational data. The measurement of documentation can be automated if the documentation resides in word processors or personal computers.

Tracking all changes to a system's software also provides a means of acquiring measurement data. Change management has been automated via several vendor systems. I am familiar with the UNIX Change Measurement Tracking System, which has proven invaluable in providing quality measurement data.

Involving the programmers and analysts in the development and enhancement of the measurement program will encourage the acceptance of the tools and methodology in the IS culture. Attempts to misuse the measurement tools will generate distrust, lower quality, reduced productivity, and employee subversion. The acceptance of a software measurement program depends on the implementation and the people involved. The people who develop and install the metrics tool will benefit from an extended conversion period to integrate measurement into the fabric of software development and maintenance.

The development and application of software measurement tools is the best way to determine productivity and quality. Properly applied, they can reap great benefits for the corporation. Improperly used, however, they can destroy an IS organization. Without measurement tools, you can only justify the benefits of new technology and methodology with gut-level feelings. With metrics, however, you can begin to quantify those unknowns and to make real progress toward establishing your own software factory.

BIBLIOGRAPHY

Albrecht, A. J., "Measuring Application Development Productivity," IBM Corp, 1981.

Albrecht, A. J. and J. E. Gaffney, Jr., "Software Function, Source Lines of Code, and Development Effort Prediction: A Software Science Validation," *IEEE Trans. on Soft. Eng.*, 9(6), 639–647, November 1983.

Arnett, R., "Management perspectives on programs, programming, and productivity," *GUIDE*, 45, 1977.

Arthur, J. and Jayashree Ramanathan, "Design of analyzers for selective program analysis," *IEEE Trans. on Soft. Eng.*, 7(1), January 1981.

Baker, A. L. and Stuart Zweben, "A comparison of measures of control flow complexity," *IEEE Trans. on Soft. Eng.*, 6(6), November 1980.

Behrens, C. A., "Measuring the Productivity of Computer Systems Development Activities with Function Points," *IEEE Trans. on Soft. Eng.*, 9(6), 648–651, November 1983.

Boehm, B. W., J. R. Brown, and M. Lipow, "Quantitative Evaluation of Software Quality," *Proceedings of the Second International Conference on Software Engineering*, 592–605, IEEE, 1976.

Boehm, B. W., et al., *Characteristics of Software Quality*, North-Holland, New York, 1978.

Bowen, W., "Better prospects for our ailing productivity," *Fortune*, 68–86, December 3, 1979.

Brooks, F. P., Jr., *The Mythical Man-Month*, Addison-Wesley, Reading, MA, 1975.

Brown, G. D., *Advanced ANS COBOL with Structured Programming*, Wiley, New York, 1977.

Budney, J. C., "Improving the efficiency of applications programs," *ICP INTERFACE*, 13–14, Fall 1978.

Christensen, K., G. P. Fitsos, and C. P. Smith, "A perspective on software science," *IBM Syst. J.*, 20(4), 372–387, 1981.

Cooper, J. D. and M. J. Fisher, *Software Quality Management*, Petrocelli, New York, 1979.

Crossman, T. D., "Taking the measure of programmer productivity," *DATAMATION*, 142–147, May 1979.

Curtis, B. et al., "Measuring the psychological complexity of software maintenance tasks with the Halstead and McCabe metrics," *IEEE Trans. Soft. Eng.*, 5(2), 96–103, March 1979.

DATAPRO Research Corp., "Measuring program complexity in a COBOL environment," *Application Software*, DATAPRO, 1982.

DATAPRO Research Corp., "Maximizing the growth of software reliability," *Application Software*, DATAPRO, 1982.

DATAPRO Research Corp., "Guidelines to reliable software development," *Application Software*, DATAPRO, 1982.

Doebelin, E. O., *Measurement Systems*, McGraw-Hill, New York, 1975.

Dunn, R., and R. Ullman, *Quality Assurance for Computer Software*, McGraw-Hill, New York, 1982.

Elshoff, J. L., "An analysis of some commercial PL/I programs," *IEEE Trans. Soft. Eng.*, **2**(2), 113–120, June 1976.

Elshoff, J. L., "The influence of structured programming on PL/I program profiles," *IEEE Trans. Soft. Eng.*, **3**(5), 364–368, September 1977.

Fagan, M. E., "Design and code inspections to reduce errors in program development," *IBM Syst. J.*, **15**(3), 182–211, 1976.

Feuer, A. R., and F. B. Fowlkes, "Relating Computer Program Maintainability to Software Measures," *Proceedings of the 1979 National Computer Conference*, June 1979.

Fitsos, G. P., "Vocabulary Effects in Software Science," *COMPSAC 80*, 751–756, IEEE, 1980.

Fitzsimmons, A., and T. Love, "Review and evaluation of software science," *Computing Surveys*, 10–17, 10(1), March 1978.

Fox, J. (Ed.), *Proceedings of the Symposium on Computer Software Engineering*, Vol. XXIV, Polytechnic Press, New York, 1969.

Friedman, R. C., "Measuring those 'forgotten' factors," *Data Management*, 34–37, March 1981.

Gilb, T., *Software Metrics*, Winthrop, Cambridge, MA, 1977.

Gillin, Paul, "Ways to measure productivity still inadequate," *ComputerWorld*, **4**, January 17, 1983.

Glass, R. L., and R. A. Noiseux, *Software Maintenance Guidebook*, Prentice-Hall, Englewood Cliffs, 1981.

Glass, R. L., "Persistent Software Errors," *IEEE Trans. on Soft. Eng.*, **7**(2), 162–168, March 1981.

Gunning, R. *More Effective Writing in Business and Industry*, Cahners Books, Boston, 1963.

Halstead, M. H., *Elements of Software Science*, North-Holland, New York, 1977.

Harrison, W., et. al., "Applying software complexity metrics to program maintenance," *Computer*, 65–79, September 1982.

Hecht, H., "Mini-tutorial on software reliability," *COMPSAC 80*, 383–385, IEEE, 1980.

Henry, S., and D. Kafura, "Software structure metrics based on information flow," *IEEE Trans. Soft. Eng.*, **7**(5), 510–517, September 1981.

Howard, P. C., "Improving COBOL applications," *System Development*, **2**(9), 4–5, November, 1982.

IBM, *An Introduction to Structured Programming in COBOL*, IBM, 1975.

Jancura, E. G., and A. H. Berger, *Computers: Auditing and Control*, Auerbach, Philadelphia, 1973.

Johnson, J. R., "A working measure of productivity," *DATAMATION*, 106–110, February, 1977.

Johnson, S. C., and M. E. Lesk, "Language development tools," *Bell Syst. J.*, **57**(6) Part 2, 2155–2176, 1978.

Jones, T. C., "Measuring programming quality and productivity," *IBM Syst. J.*, **17**(1), 39–63, 1978.

Juran, J. M., *Quality Control Handbook*, McGraw-Hill, New York, 1974.

Kernighan, B., and P. J. Plauger, *The Elements of Programming Style*, McGraw-Hill, New York, 1974.

Kernighan, B., and P. J. Plauger, *Software Tools*, Addison-Wesley, Reading, MA, 1976.

Lipow, M., "Number of faults per line of code," *IEEE Trans. Soft. Eng.*, 8(4), 437–439, July, 1982.

Manz, J. M., "Measuring productivity in an ADF environment," *IBM Tech. Rep.*, September 11, 1981.

McCabe, T. J., "A complexity measure," *IEEE Trans. Soft. Eng.*, 2(4), 308–320, December 1976.

McCall, J. A., P. K. Richards, and G. F. Walters, "Factors in Software Quality," Rome Air Development Center, November 1977.

Meyer, P. J., "Reaching for higher productivity?" *Data Management*, 18–20, October 1980.

Myers, G. J., *Reliable Software through Composite Design*, Petrocelli, New York, 1975.

Myers, G. J., *Software Reliability*, Wiley, New York, 1976.

Myers, G. J., *The Art of Software Testing*, Wiley, New York, 1979.

Paige, M., "A metric for software test planning," *COMPSAC 80*, 499–504, IEEE, 1980.

Pascale, R. T., "Zen and the art of management," *Harvard Bus. Rev.*, 153–162, March–April 1978.

Patrick, R. L., "The productivity gap," *DATAMATION*, 131–132, December 1979.

Peercy, D. E., "A software maintainability evaluation methodology," *IEEE Trans. on Soft. Eng.*, 7(4), 343–351, July 1981.

Perlis, A., F. Sayward, M. Shaw, *Software Metrics*, MIT Press, Boston, MA, 1981.

Perry, W. E., "Modernized code extends dated program's life," *Info. Sys. News*, 21–22, June 27, 1983.

Peters, T. J., and R. H. Waterman, *In Search of Excellence*, Harper & Row, Cambridge, 1982.

SHARE, *The PL/I Project Programming Techniques Library*, SHARE, Chicago, 1979.

Shneiderman, B., *Software Psychology*, Winthrop, Cambridge, MA, 1980.

Stanford Research Institute, *System Auditability and Control*, Institute of Internal Auditors, Altamonte Springs, FL, 1977.

Tharrington, J. M., "A manager's guide to measuring programmer productivity," *Computerworld*, 57–66, September 1, 1981.

Thayer, T. A., *Software Reliability*, North-Holland, New York, 1978.

Vessey, I., and R. Weber, "Some factors affecting program repair maintenance: An empirical study," *Commun. ACM*, 26(2), 128–134, February 1983.

Weinberg, G. M., *The Psychology of Computer Programming*, Van Nostrand, New York, 1972.

Whitworth, M. H., and P. A. Szulewski, "The measurement of control and data flow complexity in software designs," *COMPSAC 80*, 735–742, IEEE, 1980.

Yourdon, E. N., *Techniques of Program Structure and Design*, Prentice-Hall, Englewood Cliffs, 1976.

Yourdon, E. N. (Ed.), *Classics in Software Engineering*, Yourdon Press, New York, 1979.

Zachmann, W. F., *Keys to Enhancing System Development Productivity*, AMACOM, New York, 1981.

Zelkowitz, M. V., "Perspectives in software engineering," *Computing Surv.*, 10(2), 197–216, June 1978.

APPENDIX A

ALC RESERVED WORDS

All IBM Assembler language statements are of the form:

    label   operator   operands   comments

Data definitions are of the forms:

```
DATANAME   DS    OCL50
DATANAME   DC    CL50
DATANAME   EQU   1
R1         EQU   1
```

Functions include any macros you use locally like CALL, IF-THEN-ELSE, and CASE, as well as the BAL (branch and link) instruction, which is similar to the COBOL PERFORM.

Decisions are based on the comparison operators (CLC, CLI, etc.) or the branch operators (BE, BH, etc.).

The hard branch (B) should be considered to be a GO TO.

The NOP (no operation) instruction is like the COBOL ALTER. Typically, some other operation modifies the NOP to branch to some location in the program. Programs should not modify themselves as they run.

Operators, other than the ones described earlier, are typically instructions to the compiler, like EJECT to break page and so on. These operators generally are ignored.

Operands may be either registers (0−15 or RO−R15), data names, literals (like X'FF'), or displacements based on registers. It is difficult to keep them all in core, but necessary to calculate the software science metrics.

IBM ALC operators are:

A	BNP	HDR	MC	SETA	STOSM
AD	BNPR	HDV	MD	SETB	STPT
ADR	BNZ	HER	MDR	SETC	STPX
AE	BNZR	HIO	ME	SH	SU
AER	BO	IC	MER	SIGP	SUR
AH	BOR	ICM	MH	SIO	SVC
AL	BP	IPK	MI	SIOF	SW
ALR	BPR	ISEQ	MP	SL	SWR
AP	BXH	ISK	MR	SLA	SXR
AR	BXLE	L	MVC	SLDA	TCH
AU	BZ	LA	MVCL	SLDL	TIO
UAR	BZR	LCDR	MVI	SLL	TM
AW	C	LCER	MVN	SLR	TR
AWR	CD	LCLA	MVO	SP	TRT
AXR	CDR	LCLB	MVZ	SPKA	TS
B	CDS	LCLC	MXD	SPM	UNPK
BAL	CE	LCR	MXDR	SPT	WRD
BALR	CER	LCTL	MXR	SPX	WTO
BC	CH	LD	N	SR	WXTRN
BCR	CL	LDR	NC	SRA	X
BCT	CLC	LE	NI	SRDA	XC
BCTR	CLI	LER	NOP	SRDL	XI
BE	CLM	LH	NR	SRL	XR
BER	CLRIO	LINK	O	SRP	ZAP
BH	CP	LM	OC	SSK	ZIC
BHR	CR	LNDR	OI	SSM	
BL	CS	LNER	OPSYN	ST	
BLR	CSECT	LNR	OR	STAP	
BM	CVB	LPDR	PACK	STC	
BMR	CVD	LPER	POP	STCK	
BNE	D	LPR	PTLB	STCLC	
BNER	DD	LPSW	RDB	STCM	
BNH	DDR	LR	RRD	STCTL	
BNHR	DE	LRA	S	STD	
BNL	DER	LRDR	SCK	STE	
BNLR	DP	LRER	SCKC	STH	
BNM	DR	LTDR	SD	STIDC	
BNMR	ED	LTER	SDR	STIDP	
BNO	EDMK	LTR	SE	STM	
BNOR	EX	M	SER	STNSM	

Comments may exist on the command line or as stand-alone comments of the form:

* COMMENT LINE . . . .

Both types of comments should be counted and summarized to indicate self-documentation.

APPENDIX B

COBOL RESERVED WORDS

COBOL data definitions are usually of the form:

    level_ number   dataname   PICTURE format VALUE whatever.

```
01  STRUCTURE-NAME.
    05  DATA-NAME-1          PIC X VALUE SPACE.
    88  COMPARE-1-TRUE           VALUE 'T'.
    05  DATA-NAME-2          PIC S9 VALUE ZERO COMP-3.
```

VALUE clauses signify that the data is initialized by the compiler before execution, helping to improve reliability.

COMP-3 and COMP define packed decimal and binary numbers, which are more efficient than display numeric data when used in arithmetic calculations.

Similarly, the use of INDEXED BY indicates the use of compiler subscripts for maximum efficiency.

A list of IBM COBOL operators appears on the following page.

IBM COBOL operators include the following:

ACCEPT	EXIT	PRINT-SWITCH	STRING
ADD	EXIT PROGRAM	READY TRACE	SUBTRACT
ALTER	GENERATE	RESET TRACE	TERMINATE
CALL	GO TO	RECEIVE	TRANSFORM
CANCEL	GOBACK	RELEASE	UNSTRING
CLOSE	IF	RETURN	WRITE
COMPUTE	INITIATE	REWRITE	=
DELETE	INSPECT	SEARCH [ALL]	+
DISABLE	MERGE	SEND	−
DISPLAY	MOVE	SET	*
DIVIDE	MULTIPLY	SORT	/
ENABLE	ON	START	**
ENTRY	OPEN	STOP	
EXHIBIT	PERFORM	STOP RUN	

Function operators are the CALL, COMPUTE, GENERATE, INSPECT, MERGE, PERFORM, SORT, SEARCH [ALL], STRING, and UNSTRING.

Decisions are the IF, UNTIL, ON, WHEN, and GO TO. Comparison keywords are AND, OR, and NOT.

Comments are indicated by a '*' or '/' in column seven.

APPENDIX C

PL/I RESERVED WORDS

PL/I data names are of the form:

    DCL DATA_NAME [CHAR, BIT, FIXED DEC, FIXED BIN](99)
    INIT(?);

Each of these data names is a unique operand for the software science metrics. Each occurrence in the procedural code increments the total number of operands.

A list of IBM PL/I operators appears on the following page.

IBM PL/I operators are:

ABS( )	DELAY( )	LOG2( )	ROUND( )
ACOS( )	DELETE	LOG10( )	SIGN( )
ADD( )	DIM( )	LOW( )	SIGNAL
ADDR( )	DISPLAY	MAX( )	SIN( )
ALL( )	DIVIDE( )	MIN( )	SIND( )
ALLOCATE	DO	MOD( )	SINH( )
ALLOC( )	EMPTY	MULTIPLY( )	SQRT( )
ANY( )	END	NULL	STATUS( )
ASIN( )	ENTRY	OFFSET( )	STOP
ATAN( )	ERF( )	ON	STRING( )
ATAND( )	ERFC( )	ONCHAR	SUBSTR( )
ATANH( )	EXIT	ONCODE	SUM( )
BEGIN	EXP( )	ONCOUNT	TAN( )
BIN( )	FIXED( )	ONFILE	TAND( )
BIT( )	FLOAT( )	ONKEY	TANH( )
BOOL( )	FLOOR( )	ONLOC	TIME
CALL	FORMAT	ONSOURCE	TRANSLATE( )
CEIL( )	FREE	OPEN	TRUNC( )
CHAR( )	GET	POINTER( )	UNLOCK
CLOSE	GOTO	POLY( )	UNSPEC( )
COMPLETION( )	HALT	PRECISION( )	VERIFY( )
COMPLEX( )	HBOUND( )	PRIORITY( )	WAIT
CONJG( )	HIGH( )	PROCEDURE	WRITE
COS( )	IF	PROD( )	=
COSD( )	IMAG( )	PUT	+
COSH( )	INDEX( )	READ	−
COUNT( )	LBOUND( )	REAL( )	*
DATAFIELD	LENGTH	REPEAT( )	/
DATE( )	LINENO( )	RETURN	**
DECIMAL( )	LOCATE	REVERT	
DEFAULT	LOG( )	REWRITE	

Functions include most of the keywords followed by "( )". Also included are the CALL, DO WHILE, and DO UNTIL.

Decisions include the IF, SELECT (an IBM extension), DO WHILE, and DO UNTIL.

Comments include all lines contained between the PL/I delimiters "/*" and "*/".

INDEX